Cognitive and Social Neuroscience of Aging

Cognitive and Social Neuroscience of Aging is an introduction to how aging affects the brain, intended for audiences with some knowledge of psychology, aging, or neuroscience. The book includes figures illustrating brain regions so that extensive familiarity with neuroanatomy is not a prerequisite. The depth of coverage also makes this book appropriate for those with considerable knowledge about aging. This book adopts an integrative perspective, including topics such as memory, cognition, cognitive training, emotion, and social processes. Topics include consideration of individual differences and the impact of disorders (e.g., Alzheimer's disease) on brain function with age. Although many declines occur with age, cognitive neuroscience research reveals plasticity and adaptation in the brain as a function of normal aging. This book is written with this perspective in mind, emphasizing the ways in which neuroscience methods have enriched and changed thinking about aging.

At Brandeis University, **Dr. Angela Gutchess** *is an Associate Professor of Psychology with appointments in Neuroscience and the Volen Center for Complex Systems. She received her Ph.D. in Psychology from the University of Michigan and her B.A./B.S. from Boston University. Her research investigates the influence of age and culture on memory and social cognition, using behavioral, neuroimaging (fMRI), electrophysiological (ERP), and patient (aMCI) methods. She has authored over sixty peer-reviewed papers on these topics. Her research has been funded by the National Institute on Aging, the National Science Foundation, the Alzheimer's Association, and the American Federation for Aging Research. As a Fulbright Scholar, she had the opportunity to spend a research semester in Istanbul, Turkey, at Boğaziçi University. Dr. Gutchess was elected to the Memory Disorders Research Society. She currently serves as an Associate Editor for the journals* Memory *and* Memory & Cognition, *is an incoming Associate Editor for the Journals* Cognition *and the* Journal of Gerontology: Psychological Sciences, *and serves as a Consulting Editor for the journals* Psychology and Aging *and* Culture and Brain.

Cambridge Fundamentals of Neuroscience in Psychology

Developed in response to a growing need to make neuroscience accessible to students and other non-specialist readers, the *Cambridge Fundamentals of Neuroscience in Psychology* series provides brief introductions to key areas of neuroscience research across major domains of psychology. Written by experts in cognitive, social, affective, developmental, clinical, and applied neuroscience, these books will serve as ideal primers for students and other readers seeking an entry point to the challenging world of neuroscience.

Books in the Series

Cognitive and Social Neuroscience of Aging

Angela Gutchess

Brandeis University, Massachusetts

CAMBRIDGE
UNIVERSITY PRESS

CAMBRIDGE
UNIVERSITY PRESS

University Printing House, Cambridge CB2 8BS, United Kingdom

One Liberty Plaza, 20th Floor, New York, NY 10006, USA

477 Williamstown Road, Port Melbourne, VIC 3207, Australia

314–321, 3rd Floor, Plot 3, Splendor Forum, Jasola District Centre,
New Delhi – 110025, India

79 Anson Road, #06–04/06, Singapore 079906

Cambridge University Press is part of the University of Cambridge.

It furthers the University's mission by disseminating knowledge in the pursuit of
education, learning, and research at the highest international levels of excellence.

www.cambridge.org
Information on this title: www.cambridge.org/9781107084643
DOI: 10.1017/9781316026885

© Angela Gutchess 2019

First published 2019

Printed in the United Kingdom by TJ International Ltd. Padstow Cornwall

A catalogue record for this publication is available from the British Library.

Library of Congress Cataloging-in-Publication Data
Names: Gutchess, Angela, author.
Title: Cognitive and social neuroscience of aging / Angela Gutchess.
Description: Cambridge ; New York, NY : Cambridge University Press, 2019. | Includes
    bibliographical references and index.
Identifiers: LCCN 2018023260 | ISBN 9781107084643 (hardback : alk. paper) |
    ISBN 9781107446557 (pbk. : alk. paper)
Subjects: | MESH: Cognitive Aging–physiology | Brain–physiology
Classification: LCC QP376 | NLM WT 145 | DDC 612.8/2–dc23
LC record available at https://lccn.loc.gov/2018023260

ISBN 978-1-107-08464-3 Hardback
ISBN 978-1-107-44655-7 Paperback

This book is dedicated to Jutta Wolf, friend and frequent "writing day" companion.

Contents

The plate section can be found between pages 144 and 145

Preface

This book is intended as an introduction to how the brain changes with age. It is intended for audiences with some knowledge of the fields of psychology, aging, or neuroscience who wish to learn more about the combination of these topics. The book does not assume intensive knowledge of neuroanatomy, as chapters include several figures illustrating the brain regions relevant to the processes affected by aging. The depth of coverage, however, also makes this book appropriate for those with considerable knowledge of the topic of aging, as it reviews primary literature across a wide variety of functions impacted by aging.

This book will introduce readers to the effects of aging on the brain, presenting research across several domains of psychological function, including memory, cognition and training of cognitive function, emotion, and social processes. Topics include consideration of individual differences and the impact of disorders (e.g., Alzheimer's disease or mental health) on brain function with age. Although behavioral methods typically identify declines with aging, particularly for cognitive abilities (e.g., perception, memory), cognitive neuroscience research reveals plasticity and adaptation in the brain as a function of normal aging. The book is written with this perspective in mind, emphasizing the ways in which neuroscience methods have enriched and changed our ways of thinking about aging, as well as an appreciation of the number of types of changes that can occur.

Advantages of this text include the following:

- Comprehensive review of the aging literature, with coverage of a wealth of topics
- An eye to social and emotional aging processes, which often are not treated in an integrated manner with cognitive processes
- A number of figures displaying effects, as well as an introduction to the methods, making the findings clearer to novices to the field
- Depth of coverage of the literature on different topics, making the text also appropriate for advanced students and scholars in the field.

The book is written for an advanced college-level audience, and could be adopted as a primary textbook for an advanced undergraduate or graduate course on the cognitive neuroscience of aging. It could be used as a supplementary text for a course on aging; it is written to be used in tandem with a textbook overviewing the field of aging. As such, the text could be employed in courses about aging and life-span development, drawing from disciplines such as psychology, neuroscience, gerontology, nursing, human services, and pre-health tracks.

Acknowledgments

As completing this book has been a long time in coming, I have many people to thank. First, the *Brandeis University* Aging, Culture, and Cognition lab members and the students who read early drafts and gave me suggestions. In particular, John Ksander generously created the colored brain figures that appear in many of the chapter boxes, using software created by Chris Madan. Eileen Rasmussen advised on coloring these figures. Laura Paige and Isabelle Moore assisted in organizing and formatting references; Laura also helped to request figure permissions. I am indebted to Matthew Bennett at Cambridge University Press for approaching me about this opportunity, allowing me to fulfill the "English major's dream" to write a book. I thank my colleagues Elizabeth Kensinger, who encouraged me to say yes and assured me that this was not such a bad idea at this stage of my career, and Ellen Wright, who swapped semesters teaching "Intro" with me. I am also appreciative of all of the teachers who encouraged me to write throughout school (even if this wasn't quite the type of writing we had in mind!), especially Ted Walsh, and the mentors who shaped me as a scientist, particularly Denise Park and Dan Schacter. Finally, I thank my friends who remained enthusiastic and supportive throughout the process, my family, who sent me flowers when I finally completed the first draft, and Dave Rocco, who had the good timing to come along the day after I submitted that draft.

Acknowledgements

CHAPTER ONE

Introduction to *Cognitive and Social Neuroscience of Aging*

Learning Objectives

- What are some of the theories that explain how cognition changes with age?
- How have cognitive neuroscience data led to new theories of cognitive aging?
- What are some of the overall ways in which the patterns of brain activity change with age?
- Which methods are employed to study the aging brain?
- What are some of the current trends in the study of aging?

1.1 Introduction

Studying the brain has dramatically altered how scientists think about aging. Initially, the study of aging presented a gloomy picture, with most behavioral research illustrating losses in cognitive ability. These included poorer vision and audition, poorer attentional control and ability to ignore distractions, and declines in the accuracy, amount, and quality of information in memory. Although there are some notable exceptions, such as suggestions that wisdom increases in old age (Baltes, 1993) and consideration of gains and optimization of function (Baltes & Linden-berger, 1997), most of the literature emphasized impairments and losses that occur with age. Cognitive neuroscience methods, however, have highlighted the reorganization and even compensatory gains that can occur with age. Early papers showed that older adults could engage the brain *more* than younger adults, with additional brain regions activated for tasks compared to younger adults. This was a surprising finding, indicating that older adults' brains are more active than those of their younger adult counterparts. There were many attempts to establish that these additional activations of the brain indicate **compensation** such that older adults boost task performance, or stave off further declines, by recruiting brain regions more flexibly than younger adults. Literature consistent with, and in opposition to, this interpretation will be reviewed throughout the book. At the very least, neuroscience methods opened up new ways of considering questions of how cognitive, social, and affective abilities change with age.

In this chapter, I will briefly review theories of cognitive aging. These are largely based on behavioral data accumulated over years of research; the rest of the book will allow the reader to explore ways in which neuroscience data converge with these theories, or have led to the development of new ways of thinking about the process of cognitive aging. The chapter will then present the cognitive neuroscience methods that are commonly employed to study brain activity with age, and discuss recent advances.

1.2 Theories of Cognitive Aging

Much research has been devoted to attempts to identify a single mechanism that explains cognitive changes with age. These approaches are reviewed briefly here; readers are urged to consult other edited volumes on the topic (Craik & Salthouse, 2007; Lemaire, 2016; D. C. Park & Schwarz, 2000; Perfect & Maylor, 2000).

Processing speed theory purports that aging is associated with slowing, possibly reflecting reduced neural transmission speed due to the demyelination, or loss of white matter, that occurs with age (Salthouse, 1996; Salthouse & Babcock, 1991). More than simply slowing down how long it takes to reach a solution for a problem or retrieve information from memory, speed of processing also could impact the *quality* of information processing. This also has implications for cognitive abilities that are not under time pressure. For example, information may be degraded to the point that it is no longer useful, or outcomes from earlier stages of processing may no longer be available by the time the later stages are complete.

Working memory research considers the amount of cognitive resources that are available to accomplish challenging tasks (Craik & Byrd, 1982; D. C. Park et al., 2002; D. C. Park et al., 1996). Classic models of working memory focus on the ways in which we store visuospatial or verbal information alongside a central executive system that coordinates processes and an episodic buffer that integrates and orders information (Baddeley, 2000; Baddeley & Hitch, 1974). For example, information must be taken in from the environment, comprehended, and transmitted to brain regions or other processes that allow one to formulate a goal or response, and then a response must be executed. Theories focused on working memory ability suggest that the amount of information one can keep in mind and coordinate at a time differs across individuals, and this resource accounts for differences across individuals in a number of different abilities such as long-term memory and reasoning. Because working memory capacity decreases with age, individuals become more limited in a variety of cognitive abilities. The fluid nature of working memory differs from world knowledge, which is accumulated over a lifetime and is intact, or even enhanced, with age.

Inhibition theory also emphasizes the importance of the ability to keep multiple pieces of information in mind simultaneously, but highlights the competition or interference that is in play (Hasher & Zacks, 1988; Zacks & Hasher, 1997). Being able to focus on target information, while ignoring irrelevant information, becomes more difficult with age, and this may underlie a host of cognitive declines that occur with age. Early research critiqued inhibition theory for not being distinct enough from working memory theory, but recent work with neural measures emphasizes the importance of **cognitive control** (the ability to control how one uses information, perhaps ignoring some information while focusing on other aspects), particularly with age.

Rather than focusing on specific cognitive abilities, such as speed, working memory, or inhibition, another theory purports that **sensory function** reflects the integrity of the brain and cognitive processes. Early data revealed striking relationships between how well one performs on acuity measures for vision and audition and performance on a variety of cognitive abilities, spanning from speed of processing to memory to world knowledge (Lindenberger & Baltes, 1994). These connections led Baltes and Lindenberger (1997) to propose the **common cause hypothesis** of aging. This theory suggests that aging has a widespread and consistent impact on the brain, which may be detected by measures of these sensory abilities.

Although each of the reviewed approaches highlights a single ability, many of the abilities are associated with each other (e.g., individuals with the fastest speed of processing may also have the best working memory performance). Findings of relationships between performance on different tasks have led to appreciation of domain-general aspects of cognitive aging. Such an approach emphasizes that declines occur consistently across multiple abilities rather than affecting distinct abilities to greater or lesser degrees (e.g., Salthouse, 2017; Tucker-Drob, 2011; Tucker-Drob et al., 2014).

1.3 Cognitive Neuroscience of Aging Theories

An initial brain-based theory of cognitive aging, the **frontal aging hypothesis**, predated much of the cognitive neuroscience movement. This emerged from a neuropsychological approach, guided largely by older adults' impaired pattern of performance on tasks thought to be mediated by the frontal lobes, in conjunction with observations of exaggerated structural decline in the frontal lobes and reduced dopamine in the region (West, 1996). The literature has largely moved away from this hypothesis. This shift has occurred because cognitive neuroscience methods have uncovered complex patterns with age, sometimes indicating reorganization and change, in the conditions under which frontal lobes are engaged by tasks. There is also great variability in the rates at which different regions of the frontal lobes decline.

1.3.1 Increased Activity and Compensation with Age

One of the initial observations identified changes in the **bilaterality** of brain activation patterns with age (Cabeza et al., 1997; Grady et al., 1995; Reuter-Lorenz et al., 2000). That is, whereas younger adults largely activate the left *or* right prefrontal cortex during tasks, older adults tend to activate the same region in both hemispheres. Roberto Cabeza and colleagues identified two frameworks to characterize the pervasive patterns of changes in neural activity with age. The hemispheric asymmetry reduction in older adults, or **HAROLD**, model (Cabeza, 2002) emphasizes the increased bilaterality with age. Another change in the pattern of brain activity with age, a posterior–anterior shift in aging, or **PASA**, links age-related increases in frontal lobe activity with age-related decreases in occipital lobe activation (S. W. Davis et al., 2008).

Initially, there was much debate over the function of these patterns of activation, with some researchers claiming they were compensatory. That is, by recruiting the other hemisphere, older adults are able to harness additional cognitive resources and thus improve their performance relative to what it would be if supported by the younger adult pattern of unilateral activation. Data comparing high and low performers (e.g., Cabeza et al., 2002), differences in reaction time (e.g., Madden et al., 1997), and successful versus unsuccessful performance (e.g., Gutchess et al., 2005) were interpreted as supporting the notion that increased activation with aging is compensatory (see Figure 1.1). The claim of compensation is substantiated by a method that allows for the

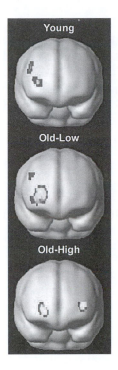

Figure 1.1 During a memory recall task, high-performing older adults (bottom) showed more bilateral prefrontal activity than lower-performing older adults (middle). This was interpreted as evidence that bilaterality is compensatory, as the pattern was linked to better performance for older adults, despite differing from the unilateral prefrontal activations seen in young adults (top).
Adapted from Cabeza et al. (2002), *NeuroImage*, Figure 2.

disruption of neural activity in a region. Older adults' performance is impaired when the second hemisphere is targeted (Rossi et al., 2004).

Whether increased activation serves a compensatory function became a more complicated question due to diverging findings in the literature when comparing across groups, including those with disorders associated with aging (e.g., Alzheimer's disease (AD)). Thus, models of cognitive aging began to consider task demands and differences across individuals and groups. This led Cabeza and Dennis (2013) to delineate criteria to differentiate successful compensation from mere *attempts* at compensation. Specifically, neural activity may initially increase as the brain atrophies, reflecting a compensatory attempt to respond to cognitive decline. As the brain continues to deteriorate with age, or as task demands exceed one's ability, it will no longer be possible to continue to increase activity in an attempt to compensate, so neural activity will decline. Furthermore, for neural activity to be considered evidence of successful compensation, the activity must be related to improved task performance and occur in neural regions known to support task performance in older adults. With limited ability to test the *causal* role of brain activity on behavioral outcomes (e.g., what happens to behavior when a region is impaired versus intact), it has been difficult to conclusively substantiate claims of compensation (for further discussion, see Section 1.4.2).

1.3.2 Changing Neural Responses to Task Demands

Whereas initial frameworks largely described the patterns of neural activity that occur with age, other frameworks emerged that emphasized how the demands on cognitive resources change with age. For example, the compensation-related utilization of neural circuits hypothesis (**CRUNCH**) purports that increased task demands should necessitate increased neural activity for older adults at lower levels of difficulty than is the case for younger adults (Reuter-Lorenz & Cappell, 2008). The scaffolding theory of aging and cognition (**STAC**) incorporates a similar perspective, whereby cognitive and neural challenges that accompany aging require additional resources (D. C. Park & Reuter-Lorenz, 2009). Life experience factors, such as fitness and social or intellectual engagement over the life span, can also shape the availability and engagement of resources (Reuter-Lorenz & Park, 2014). When these resources are available, through recruitment of additional neural regions or other processes that enhance neural systems (such as cognitive training and exercise), older adults will harness them to support cognitive performance. The STAC framework goes beyond the others in considering individual differences and contextual factors. For example, individuals may differ in how they respond to the challenges of aging or other neural insults (e.g., head injury, AD). This idea is encapsulated in the concept of **cognitive reserve**, whereby individual differences in neural systems or cognitive abilities, developed as a function of nature or nurture (e.g., educational attainment, leisure activities), could serve a protective function for those individuals with higher capacity (Stern, 2002, 2009). Another model suggests that age groups differ in *when* they engage resources to encounter task demands. This could allow younger adults to manage task challenges more successfully than older adults. Whereas younger adults engage in proactive control, planning ahead for challenging conditions, older adults display reactive control in response to task demands (Braver et al., 2009; Velanova et al., 2007).

1.3.3 Reduced Specificity of Neural Responses with Age

A final set of models proposed to account for cognitive changes with age focuses on the ways in which aging reduces the clarity of information processing with age. There is substantial evidence for **dedifferentiation** with age, meaning that neural regions respond in a less specific way for older than younger adults. This has largely been established for sensory regions, such that regions for processing visual information that are narrowly tuned in younger adults to respond to certain classes of stimuli, like faces or houses (places), respond more generally across categories for older adults (D. C. Park et al., 2004). Similarly, motor cortex response tends to be lateralized for each side of the body, with the left motor cortex responding to movement of the right side of the body, and vice versa. With aging, however, motor cortices respond bilaterally to movement on either side of the body, reflecting a loss of specialization with age (Carp, Park, Hebrank, Park, & Polk, 2011). Findings of greater dedifferentiation with age also extend to memory (e.g., St-Laurent et al., 2014). These findings are discussed further in Chapters 3 and 4.

Other processes also exhibit a loss of specificity with age. The **default network** is so named because these neural regions tend to be more engaged when at rest than when performing cognitive tasks (e.g., solving math problems presented on a computer screen). Older adults do not suppress this network as much as younger adults during tasks that demand external attention (Grady et al., 2010; Persson et al., 2007). This may indicate difficulty in alternating between cognitive states with age. In addition, neural transmission may be noisier in older adults, with a reduced signal-to-noise ratio (Backman et al., 2006; S. C. Li et al., 2001). This could make it difficult to distinguish representations, such as one item from another similar one. Failure to suppress the default network during tasks or to distinguish the relevant neural signal from noise could increase older adults' vulnerability to making errors as a result of poorer-quality representations of information.

1.4 Cognitive Neuroscience Methods

There are two broad classes of measures: those that measure the physical structure of the brain, and others that measure the function or dynamic engagement of the brain over time or task demands.

1.4.1 Measures of Structural Integrity of the Brain

One approach to studying the brain is to investigate the integrity of and changes in structural measures of anatomy. This includes measures of gray matter (consisting of the cell bodies of neurons) as well as white matter (consisting of bundles of myelinated axons from neurons and glial cells). By considering structural measures, one can assess the physical changes of the brain and relate these to performance on cognitive tasks. Such comparisons largely adopt an individual differences approach to determine whether greater loss of volume in a specific region is related to poorer cognitive performance.

Magnetic Resonance Imaging (MRI)

This technique involves imaging the anatomy of the brain with magnetic fields and radio waves. Because the magnetic properties of soft tissue allow it to be differentiated from bone, blood, or other substances within the head, high-resolution images can be produced that distinguish gray from white matter in the brain. MRI is preferred to other 3D imaging measures, such as CT (X-ray computed tomography), because it has higher resolution and is safer due to the lack of ionizing radiation. Measures of brain structure have the longest history of application to the study of cognitive aging, and have illustrated the ways in which aging impacts gray and white matter. As will be discussed in Chapter 2, individual differences in the volume of particular regions can be linked to how well individuals perform on a task (e.g., is a bigger brain region associated with better performance on a memory task?). But because these measures convey static information about an individual's anatomy, MRI cannot be directly linked to trial-by-trial task performance.

Diffusion Tensor Imaging (DTI)

Diffusion is a measure of how much water spreads from a point, and is used to assess white matter pathways. When unconstrained, water is equally likely to flow in all directions from a point. White matter fiber tracts restrict the flow along that pathway, much as paved roads direct the flow of traffic; the presence of white matter fibers is inferred through diffusion measures. One measure of diffusion is fractional anisotropy (FA), which characterizes how strongly water molecules diffuse in a particular direction. Aging can break down the microstructure of tissue, decreasing FA (Alexander et al., 2007; Gunning-Dixon et al., 2009).

Although the study of aging has a longer history of focusing on measures of gray matter, there is increasing recognition that white matter changes can be profound, and may explain much age-related decline in cognition (Gunning-Dixon et al., 2009).

1.4.2 Measures of Brain Function

Measures of brain function provide information about what parts of the brain are engaged over time. The approach typically is used to investigate which regions of the brain are involved during tasks (e.g., viewing attractive versus unattractive faces), but some of these methods are used to evaluate which regions communicate with each other, with or without an ongoing task. One of the limitations that applies to all of the methods discussed in this section is the fact that the data are largely correlational. This means that the results of different studies illustrate how the brain responds for younger adults versus older adults, but the current methods are largely unable to establish causality (e.g., is this region responsible for memory impairments with age?). In order to determine causality, it would be necessary to independently increase or decrease levels of neural activity and then measure the effect on behavior. The inability to determine causality is an important caveat to keep in mind when reading about studies relying on methods such as fMRI and ERP, as well as recognizing the difficulty posed for testing theories based on neural data.

Functional magnetic resonance imaging (fMRI) relies on the same imaging properties as MRI, but requires additional hardware and software that allow the scanner to track neural activity over time. This allows us to assess brain activity during cognitive tasks, such as attending to some information while ignoring other information, or holding a series of numbers in mind. Thus, neural activity can be linked with tasks, and the resulting performance (e.g., success or failure on a trial; better or worse performance than other individuals). The technique does not directly measure the activity of the brain (e.g., the firing of neurons) but instead capitalizes on the differences in the magnetic properties of oxygenated versus deoxygenated blood. The BOLD (blood oxygenation level dependent) signal detects active brain regions based on the inference that oxygenated blood is drawn to active regions of the brain and deoxygenated blood flows away. Although fMRI has reasonable temporal sensitivity, on the order of seconds, it is not instantaneous because the BOLD response is slow, allowing a signal to peak approximately 6 s after the neural activity occurred. Despite its imperfect temporal resolution, the method has good spatial resolution, on the order of mm (and this can be increased with methods such as high-resolution imaging).

fMRI methods are the most common in the study of cognitive aging, due to their good spatial resolution, relative cheapness, and ready availability, compared to some other methods. Still, it is important to realize the shortcomings of this method, including the potential for age-related changes in the very signal that is being measured. For example, research suggests that the BOLD response may lag with age, or even reach a flatter peak for older than younger adults (D'Esposito et al., 1999; Huettel et al., 2001). Studies comparing the effects of aging across conditions (e.g., difficult versus easy) sidestep this concern to some extent, because the overall effects of aging should impact both conditions. The comparison across conditions also highlights the fact that fMRI does not produce an absolute value that can be compared across conditions or individuals. Rather, it relies on *relative* comparisons, using subtractions of different conditions, such as assessing whether the neural response to a difficult arithmetic problem is *more* affected by aging than the neural response to an easy problem.

Positron emission tomography (PET) is a functional imaging technique much like fMRI in that it relies on blood flow to localize regions that are engaged during performance of cognitive tasks. The method involves injecting a participant with a radioactive tracer. Regions that use more or less of the compound (e.g., oxygen, glucose) labeled with the tracer can be identified as radioisotopes are emitted. These data can be used to create 2D or 3D images, showing the distribution of the tracer across brain regions. PET has been largely replaced by fMRI, which is a cheaper method that is less invasive for human participants (no injections of radioactive substances), while also offering superior spatial resolution and flexibility in the timing of experimental designs. Because PET can target specific neurotransmitter systems (e.g., dopamine), the method is having a resurgence, used even in combination with other methods.

Event-related potentials (ERP) use electrodes positioned on the scalp to measure electrical activity, typically reflecting the postsynaptic potentials emitted when neurotransmitters bind to receptors (Luck, 2014). These can be measured at the scalp when they are emitted simultaneously from many neurons that are oriented the same way. ERPs have particularly good temporal resolution, and this timing information can be used to identify specific components. Components are linked to specific mental processes (e.g., perceiving an oddball tone, committing an error when responding), and are identified by their timing, polarity (i.e., whether the waveform is positive- or negative-going), and distribution on the scalp (Luck, 2014; Luck & Kappenman, 2012). For example, the N400 is a negative-going ("N") potential that occurs around 400 ms, generally over central and parietal electrodes, and occurs when semantic expectations are violated (e.g., a sentence ends with an unexpected word). Components can be compared across age groups using measures such as **amplitude** (e.g., is the N400 waveform higher for younger or older adults?) and **latency** (e.g., does the N400 component occur earlier or later with age?). Although the method has excellent temporal resolution, its spatial resolution is limited. Because ERPs are measured from the scalp, it is difficult to determine precisely where the signal was generated within the brain. Although modeling techniques estimate the source of the signal, these methods are based on many assumptions. In general, methods like fMRI are best for spatial precision, and ERP is superior for temporal resolution.

There are many ERP studies of aging, but these may not converge well with cognitive aging theories that stem from behavioral literature, partially due to overreliance on a few paradigms (Friedman, 2012). The emphasis on identifying age-related changes in specific components, rather than focusing on age-related changes across domains and components, may thus far have limited the impact of ERP research on theories of the cognitive neuroscience of aging (Friedman, 2012).

1.5 Recent Methodological Advances

Recent advances include new data analysis techniques, and an increase in multimodal approaches (see Figure 1.2). Additional methods will be discussed as future directions in Chapter 8.

1.5.1 Structure–Behavior Relationships

Despite the loss of volume in many regions of the brain (e.g., Fjell, Westlye, et al., 2014; Raz et al., 2010), cognitive performance is not determined simply by the amount of brain volume. Thus, a bigger brain is not necessarily better, even in older age. One exception could be the entorhinal cortex, as its volume is related to memory performance in normal aging (Rodrigue & Raz, 2004). The entorhinal cortex atrophies substantially in AD, but also shrinks in nonclinical aging (Fjell, Westlye, et al., 2014). There is much interest in identifying biomarkers, such as the rate of atrophy, to predict neurodegenerative disease before its clinical manifestation. Preliminary evidence, however, suggests that only a few

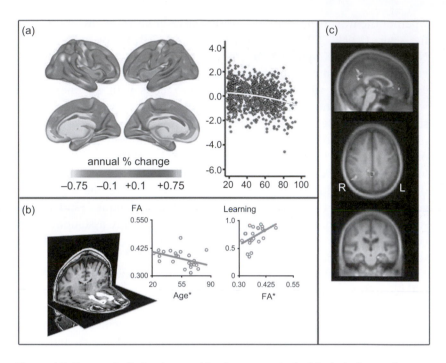

Figure 1.2 The panels display data resulting from recent methodological advances in cognitive neuroscience. The colored regions in the left side of panel A illustrate the widespread cortical thinning that occurs across the cortex with age. The hot colors (red and yellow) denote loss of volume, with the yellow regions showing the largest loss per year. The right side of panel A displays the loss of volume in the entorhinal cortex, which is exaggerated in later years (age is plotted on the x-axis) (from Fjell, Westlye, et al., 2014, *Cerebral Cortex*, Figures 5 and 2f). The left side of panel B highlights corticostriatal tracts. The graphs to the right show that the integrity of the tract (fractional anisotropy (FA)) declines with age and that greater integrity (FA, x-axis) is related to higher levels of reward learning (from Samanez-Larkin et al., 2012, *Journal of Neuroscience*, Figure 1d). Panel C shows that the default network (orange regions) is disrupted for participants with high beta-amyloid load, compared to those without (from Hedden et al., 2009, *Journal of Neuroscience*, Figure 4). *A black-and-white version of this figure will appear in some formats. For the color version, please refer to the plate section.*

brain regions, including the entorhinal cortex, exhibit greater atrophy with age; this atrophy occurs in both cognitively normal and clinical samples (Fjell, Westlye, et al., 2014). One possible explanation for the lack of overwhelming evidence of structure–function relationships may be that changes occur hand-in-hand; the same processes that lead to reductions in the size of structures also may foster plasticity, allowing for more flexible use and recruitment of multiple brain regions with age (Greenwood, 2007).

1.5.2 Structure–Function Relationships

Several studies unite structural measures of the brain, such as gray matter volume or thickness or white matter integrity, to functional activation patterns. Such an approach is particularly tantalizing for the prefrontal cortex, which evinces some of the greatest structural and functional changes. However, these measures have diverging trajectories, with functional increases while volume and thickness *decrease* (Greenwood, 2007). Comparing across individuals, findings suggest that *smaller* prefrontal volumes show greater activation, but *more* gray matter has been related to greater activation (Maillet & Rajah, 2013). White matter is increasingly being considered, as connections between regions are critical for communication and coordination of functions. From measures such as DTI, the integrity of white matter seems to be related to functional activation, as assessed with fMRI (see Figure 1.3). The relationship changes with age,

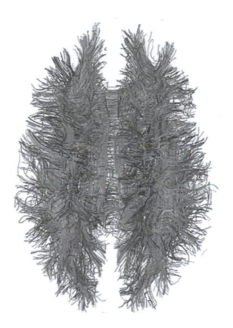

Figure 1.3 DTI image, with colors illustrating the different connected tracts of white matter across the brain. Figure from Gigandet, X., Hagmann, P., Kurant, M., Cammoun, L., Meuli, R., et al. (2008), Estimating the confidence level of white matter connections obtained with MRI tractography, *PLoS One* 3(12): e4006. doi:10.1371/journal.pone.0004006, via Wikimedia Commons. *A black-and-white version of this figure will appear in some formats. For the color version, please refer to the plate section.*

however, such that white matter integrity is associated with greater neural activity in younger but *reduced* neural activity in older adults (I. J. Bennett & Rypma, 2013). Variations in the combinations of methods and measures within a modality (e.g., gray matter volume versus thickness) employed across studies pose some challenges in uniting results, but meta-analyses should prove useful for integrating data.

1.5.3 Resting State fMRI (rs-fMRI)

Resting state fMRI (rs-fMRI) is another application of fMRI that does not rely on measuring neural activity induced by a cognitive task – participants can even have their eyes closed with this method. Instead, neural signal across regions of the brain is assessed over time, allowing the identification of regions that spontaneously fluctuate together, perhaps indicating a functional network of regions that work together. This approach is based on findings that spontaneous fluctuations in brain activity are organized systematically, such that activity in one region is related to other regions in the same network (Buckner et al., 2008). Note that this is not the only method to investigate networks in the brain – one can also attempt to identify regions that work together during a task – but rs-fMRI is considered a potentially powerful method due to the large amount of data about communication between regions that can be acquired during a short scan. This feature makes it especially appealing in studying populations that may have difficulty lying still in the scanner for long periods of time (but note that the method is highly prone to artifact from movement (Power et al., 2012)) or cannot complete cognitive tasks.

rs-fMRI studies often focus on the default network (see Section 1.3), which comprises regions most active during rest and suppressed during tasks requiring attention to the external world. Compared to younger adults, older adults' ineffectiveness in "turning off" this network during attention-demanding tasks (Grady et al., 2010) and weaker connectivity between regions (Ferreira & Busatto, 2013) suggest that aging disrupts how well regions cohere, or work together within a network, even in the absence of a task (e.g., Campbell et al., 2013).

1.5.4 Beta-Amyloid (Aβ)

The default mode network also is of interest because Aβ tends to be deposited disproportionately in these regions. These plaques are a hallmark of AD; previously only identified at autopsy, they are now amenable to study *in vivo* by PET imaging. Surprisingly, even 20–30% of people not diagnosed with AD have Aβ accumulation. This finding has generated intense interest in understanding the effects of Aβ on cognition and its potential to serve as an early marker of AD (K. M. Kennedy et al., 2012). Amyloid burden is associated with poorer cognitive performance and disrupted neural activity, particularly in the default mode network (Ferreira & Busatto, 2013). This pattern is true for older adults without an AD diagnosis (Hedden et al., 2009), as well as younger adults (K. M. Kennedy et al., 2012). Amyloid burden was associated with a greater likelihood of cognitive decline over 3 years in a cognitively normal sample (Donohue et al., 2017).

1.5.5 Neurotransmitters

Changes to dopamine occur with age, including in the density of receptors and potential for binding. This neurotransmitter has been implicated in age-related cognitive changes, perhaps accounting for noisier information processing with age (Backman et al., 2010). Molecular imaging allows the measurement of dopamine receptor binding during cognitive tasks. Although challenging task conditions vary the amount of binding in younger adults, this is not the case for older adults (Karlsson et al., 2009). Novel approaches combining fMRI and PET (e.g., Backman et al., 2011), even simultaneously, allow the measurement of a precise neurobiological mechanism (PET) alongside the temporal flexibility to study the brain on task (fMRI).

1.5.6 Future Directions

Powerful computational methods are charting new directions to explore complex data. Rather than studying brain regions in isolation, there is greater emphasis on the networks connecting disparate regions, be they structural ones relying on white matter tracts or functional ones in which a task jointly drives regions. A connectomic approach is one that explores the interactions of billions of neural connections within a brain, and how these connections contribute to function, including with age (Filippi et al., 2013). Pattern classification approaches identify different cognitive states (e.g., remembering versus forgetting) by using high-resolution data to detect an organization and structure not apparent to the human eye (Norman et al., 2006). Even the variability (Garrett et al., 2011; Garrett, Samanez-Larkin, et al., 2013) from one measurement to another may be useful for studying the aging brain, with younger brains exhibiting more variability than older brains, perhaps reflecting a broader range of brain states that flexibly support tasks (Garrett, Kova-cevic, et al., 2013). As discussed in Section 1.4.2, the methods so far are largely correlational, illustrating how the brain responds under different task conditions, rather than causal, allowing one to determine that the neural activity conclusively leads to behavioral changes. Nonhuman animal models allow the use of more invasive methods to determine how lesions, or damage, to different parts of the brain affect behavior or turning on or off different circuits. Methods in humans are inherently limited due to concerns about the safety and comfort of participants in research, but newer methods to address causality will be discussed in Chapter 8.

1.6 Introduction to the Rest of the Book

The remaining chapters in this book will review studies investigating the ways in which aging impacts the brain. The chapters will be organized by different processes, such as memory or emotion, to illustrate what has been discovered thus far about how the brain changes during the aging process. Some abilities have received far more attention from a cognitive neuroscience perspective than others; as a consequence, I will highlight some of the unanswered questions and debates to be resolved with future research, particularly in Chapter 8. The chapters will present research based on the methods explained in this chapter, with an emphasis on fMRI data. For those readers unaccustomed to reading about the brain, Box 1.1 describes some common directional terms that will appear in the names of different brain regions and includes an illustration of the major lobes of the brain and some internal structures. Regions can be localized by different conventions, such as Brodmann's areas (numbers used to distinguish regions based on cytoarchitecture, or different cellular structure), 3D coordinates in space (e.g., 20, –10, 30), or directional terms (e.g., *dorsolateral prefrontal cortex* (DLPFC)). I will focus on the naming convention to discuss regions in Box 1.1.

Chapter Summary

- The growth of cognitive neuroscience has changed the way we think about aging, emphasizing plasticity and reorganization rather than simple loss.
- Theories have moved away from one-factor explanations for age-related changes, given the rich array of patterns in neural activity across brain regions and methods.

Box 1.1 Navigating the Brain

Direction terms:

Anterior versus posterior: forward versus back of the brain

Rostral versus caudal: head versus tail

Superior versus inferior: higher versus lower

Medial versus lateral: towards the midline (division between hemispheres) versus the outer edges

Dorsal versus ventral: back (spine) versus belly*

These terms make more sense for humans if you imagine them walking on all fours.

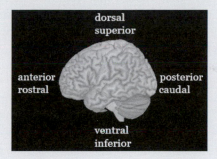

Lobes and structures of the brain:

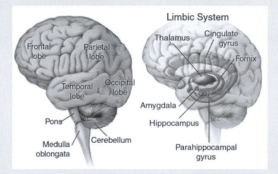

Source: artlessstacey/artlessstacey (artlessstacey) [Public domain], via Wikimedia Commons.

- Theories based on cognitive neuroscience emphasize challenges, due to brain deterioration or task difficulty, and the potential neural responses to those challenges (as well as the limitations of the aging brain).
- Cognitive neuroscience methods allow for the investigation of the ways that aging affects the neural response and information processing.
- However, more work is needed to integrate findings across methods and systems, with a goal of establishing causality.

Discussion Questions

1. What are the different theories of cognitive aging? How has the addition of cognitive neuroscience methods altered these theories?
2. What are compensation and dedifferentiation? How do they differ from each other?
3. What is an example of a type of question that is well suited to be answered through the use of fMRI methods? ERP methods?
4. Which method is best for spatial localization of *where* activity differs between tasks? Which has the best temporal resolution?
5. What are some of the limitations of the currently available methods?
6. What types of advances are needed in future work?

For Further Reading

Backman, L., Lindenberger, U., Li, S. C., & Nyberg, L. (2010). Linking cognitive aging to alterations in dopamine neurotransmitter functioning: recent data and future avenues. *Neuroscience and Biobehavioral Reviews*, *34*(5), 670–677. doi: 10.1016/j.neubiorev.2009.12.008

Cabeza, R., & Dennis, N. A. (2013). Frontal lobes and aging: deterioration and compensation. In D. T. Stuss & R. T. Knight (Eds.), *Principles of Frontal Lobe Function* (2nd edn, pp. 628–652). New York: Oxford University Press.

Friedman, D. (2012). Components of aging. In S. J. Luck & E. S. Kappenman (Eds.), *The Oxford Handbook of Event-Related Potential Components* (pp. 513–536). New York: Oxford University Press.

Greenwood, P. M. (2007). Functional plasticity in cognitive aging: review and hypothesis. *Neuropsychology*, *21*(6), 657–673. doi: 10.1037/0894–4105.21.6.657

Park, D. C., & Reuter-Lorenz, P. A. (2009). The adaptive brain: aging and neurocognitive scaffolding. *Annual Review of Psychology*, *60*, 173–196.

Key Terms

amplitude
beta-amyloid (Aβ)
bilaterality
cognitive control
cognitive reserve
common cause hypothesis
compensation
CRUNCH
dedifferentiation
default network
diffusion tensor imaging (DTI)
event-related potentials (ERP)
frontal aging hypothesis
functional magnetic resonance imaging (fMRI)
HAROLD
inhibition theory
latency
magnetic resonance imaging (MRI)
PASA
positron emission tomography (PET)
processing speed theory
resting state fMRI (rs-fMRI)
sensory function
STAC
working memory

CHAPTER TWO

Brain Mechanisms of Aging

Learning Objectives

- How do gray and white matter change with age? How do their trajectories differ?
- In what ways are gray and white matter changes associated with behavior?
- What other brain changes occur with age? These changes include consideration of connectivity, the default mode, neurotransmitters, and dedifferentiation.
- How do individual differences shape neural changes with age? These factors include genetics, intelligence, sex, personality, stress, bilingualism, and culture.

2.1 Introduction

How does the brain change with age? This chapter introduces many of the mechanisms that underlie changes to brain and behavior with age. This includes considerations of the ways in which the structure of the brain is affected by aging. For example, is the loss of gray and white matter widespread throughout the brain, or limited to particular regions? How are these structural changes linked to behavior? Beyond the changes to the structure of the brain, it seems that the way in which regions work together, via specific connections or as a network, also changes with age. Other mechanisms accounting for widespread changes in function with age, such as the default mode (introduced in Chapter 1), neurotransmitter systems, and the loss of specificity in neural responses, will be explained. The second half of the chapter will attempt to answer the question of who ages well. In these sections, we will consider individual differences that modify the aging process through structural and functional effects.

2.2 Structural Changes in the Brain: Gray Matter

At the most fundamental level, brain structures change with age. The volume of the brain is reduced, and the cortex thins. The overall weight of the brain decreases and spaces in the brain, including the **sulci**, the grooves between different parts of cortex, and the **ventricles**, spaces through which cerebrospinal fluid passes, become enlarged. Despite these gross changes, losses do not occur at a consistent rate with age across all regions of the cortex. Some regions, such as the prefrontal cortex, are particularly vulnerable to the loss of gray matter although other regions, including the primary sensory cortex, are better preserved with age (Raz, 2000). The anterior cingulate, a region in the prefrontal cortex, exhibits an unusual pattern, in that some data suggest that it gets thicker with age (Salat et al., 2004), whereas other data indicate that the anterior cingulate and the orbitofrontal cortex may not decline as much as other regions with age (see further discussion below concerning methods) (Fjell, Westlye, et al., 2014).

Structural changes to the brain can be striking over even relatively short periods of time. In one study over a 5-year time span, the volume decreased in nearly every region measured, save for the primary visual cortex (Raz et al., 2005). Follow-up studies noted changes in even shorter periods, such as between two 15-month follow-ups (Raz et al., 2010). Although most of the research on aging relies on cross-sectional comparisons, which contrast different individuals from multiple age groups at one point in time (e.g., today's 20-year-olds versus today's 80-year-olds), some of the research employs longitudinal designs, studying aging in the same individuals over time. Box 2.1 discusses these types of research designs. According to longitudinal data, substantial losses with age occur in the caudate and the cerebellum (Raz et al., 2005), and the rate of loss in these regions appears stable across middle and older age (Raz et al., 2010; see Figure 2.1). Results generally converge across the use of cross-sectional and longitudinal methods, although *higher* rates of cortical thinning seem to emerge when studying the same individuals over time, compared to cross-sectional methods (Fjell, Westlye, et al., 2014). There is, however, some divergence in the patterns across the two methods. For example, cross-sectional data suggest an increase in the thickness of the anterior cingulate (shown in Figure 2.2) whereas longitudinal data indicate thinning in this region of the cortex (Fjell, Westlye, et al., 2014). This pattern potentially reflects sampling bias in cross-sectional samples such that older groups comprise the healthier individuals who are still able to participate in the study. As a

Box 2.1 Is It Aging?

One of the challenges to the study of aging is whether we are, in fact, actually studying differences due to age. That sounds like a fairly basic question, but isolating effects as due to age is surprisingly difficult to do.

One challenge is that experimental designs rely on randomly assigning participants to the different groups to test the effect of a particular variable (e.g., is drug 1 or drug 2 more effective for treating cancer?). Experiments are the reference standard of research methods because they allow us to infer that a variable *causes* differences in behavior. The logic is that groups should start out the same, if enough people are randomly assigned to each group. Therefore, any difference between the groups at the end of the study is a result of the manipulation (e.g., which drug was administered). However, it is impossible to randomly assign people to be "young" or "old," making studies of aging quasi-experimental.

Cohort effects cause another challenge to comparing today's 20–30-year-olds to today's 60–80-year-olds. Because older and younger adults have lived their lives during very different times, it is difficult to isolate differences due to age rather than other differences between the groups. Perhaps the groups would exhibit dramatic dissimilarities if directly compared at the same age, meaning that the differences between groups reflect nothing about age itself. For example, growing up during World War II and during difficult economic times, compared to being surrounded by the plethora of technology available today, could sculpt the brain in different ways across age groups due to the effects on personality, affect, or cognition.

In addition, multiple changes occur across the life span that reflect effects that are comorbid with aging – that is, processes distinct from aging but inherently associated with it. For example, the incidence of disorders such as diabetes, heart disease, or dementia increases with age, but is separable from the effects of age *per se*.

When studies compare extreme age groups of younger and older adults, with different individuals in each age group (**cross-sectional designs**), it is impossible to rule out cohort effects or entirely eliminate the contribution of factors that are comorbid with aging. **Longitudinal studies**, which study the same individuals over time, or even cross-sequential designs, which study multiple cohorts of individuals over time, are better able to unravel the effects of aging from other factors. Studies comparing adult development across the entire life span are also helpful at revealing when and how age-related changes emerge.

Given the relatively recent proliferation of cognitive neuroscience methods, most of the research discussed in this book relies on cross-sectional methods.

Box 2.1 (cont.)

Although effects are discussed as due to "aging," it would be most appropriate to call these patterns "age-related," allowing for the possibility that factors other than age may contribute to the effects. This is an important point to keep in mind throughout the different topics and findings reviewed in this book. More research employing longitudinal and life-span designs will lead to better understanding of what constitutes aging.

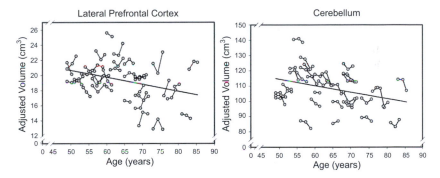

Figure 2.1 Declines in the volume of gray matter occur with age across most of the brain, including the lateral prefrontal cortex (left panel) and the cerebellum (right panel). However, note the difference in the measurements within the same person, depicted by the spaghetti plots – the two or three points connected with a line. These plots show the within-individual changes over a 30-month period. Whereas in the cerebellum nearly all of the spaghetti plots go down over time, the pattern is far more variable in the lateral prefrontal cortex.
Adapted from Raz et al. (2010), *NeuroImage*, Figures 3 and 5.

consequence, age-related changes could be underestimated in cross-sectional samples because less healthy older adults with higher rates of atrophy may not be represented in the sample.

High rates of shrinkage also occur in the **hippocampus** (Raz et al., 2005), a brain region associated with memory, and the rate of decline increases in this region in late life (Raz et al., 2010). The adjacent **entorhinal cortex** also exhibits loss with age (see Figure 2.3), although this may not begin until around age 70 (Raz et al., 2010). Caution is warranted in interpreting changes with age in medial temporal regions such as these, as they could reflect dysfunctional, rather than typical,

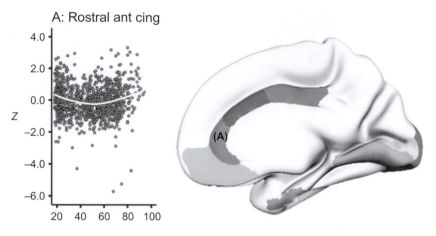

Figure 2.2 The anterior cingulate (rostral ant cing) is one of the few regions to show increases in volume over the life span. The left panel depicts measures of cortical thickness from the region (labeled A in the right panel), with each dot plotting the standardized mean thickness (Z-score, on the y-axis). Note the U-shaped pattern, indicating a decrease in thickness from young to middle-aged, and then an increase from middle-aged to older adult (age, from 20–100, is denoted on the x-axis). The increase in anterior cingulate with age may be limited to cross-sectional methods, as it does not extend to longitudinal measures.
Adapted from Fjell, Westlye, et al. (2014), *Cerebral Cortex*, Figure 2.

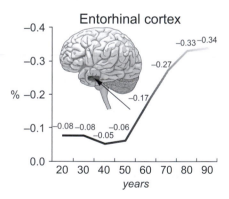

Figure 2.3 The entorhinal cortex, denoted by the arrow, undergoes accelerated thinning later in life. The graph depicts the estimated annual change in volume, estimated from cross-sectional data.
Adapted from Fjell, Westlye, et al. (2014), *Cerebral Cortex*, Figure 4.

changes with age. Although participants are screened for evidence of AD or other dementia, it is possible that the neuropsychological screening measures employed lack the sensitivity to detect early changes from disease and thus some participants in the sample could exhibit early neural changes from disease (for further discussion, see Chapter 7). Although the entorhinal cortex exhibits an exaggerated rate of thinning in AD, the region exhibits notable thinning over merely a 1-year period even for older adults at very low risk of developing the disease (Fjell, Westlye, et al., 2014).

It is important to note that not all individuals exhibit volume losses at the same rate, and there is much interest in uncovering the factors that improve outcomes with age. Regions vary in terms of how much individuals differ in their age-related trajectories of change, with the cerebellum exhibiting high variability across individuals in contrast to the inferior parietal lobe, which exhibits little variability (Raz et al., 2005). Some specific individual difference factors will be considered in the latter part of this chapter. Much more research is needed on this topic, particularly in terms of health status and outcomes.

2.2.1 Relationships between Gray Matter and Behavior

There has been considerable interest in how gray matter volume relates to behavior (e.g., do people with larger hippocampi, or less atrophy with age, perform better on memory tests?). Unfortunately, these relationships have not been as pervasive as one might expect. It is hard to say whether this reflects limited sample sizes, insensitive measures of behavior, the involvement of multiple neural regions in tasks, the potential for compensation or changes in strategy usage, or the complex interactions between neural structure and function.

Despite this, some relationships have emerged, with a focus on memory. When assessed longitudinally, greater reductions in hippocampal volume over 6 years are associated with greater declines in memory over 20 years (Persson et al., 2011). Memory declines over time also were related to how much the activation of the hippocampus decreased over time during a longitudinal fMRI study. The entorhinal cortex is of particular interest for memory outcomes over time. Greater loss of volume in this cortex over 5 years predicts poorer memory performance (Rodrigue & Raz, 2004), hippocampal atrophy relates to episodic memory decline over time (Gorbach et al., 2017), and greater thinning of the entorhinal cortex correlates with larger changes in learning over time (Fjell, Westlye, et al., 2014). Medial temporal lobe volume, encompassing the entorhinal cortex as well as the hippocampus and parahippocampal gyrus, also relates to memory for everyday events (e.g., dining at a restaurant) (H. R. Bailey et al., 2013). Everyday memory differs from other types of memory because it often relies on pre-existing knowledge (e.g., what happens when I walk into a restaurant?) and relies on **event segmentation**, which is breaking complex information into discrete scenes (e.g., talking to the host, placing an order with the waitstaff, paying the check). Segmenting events in a more typical manner, in agreement with peers, is related to better memory of videos of everyday events. This relationship seems to be partially determined by having greater medial temporal lobe volume (H. R. Bailey et al., 2013).

The volume of the prefrontal cortex also relates to task performance, including how participants self-initiate the use of memory strategies. One common strategy when attempting to learn word lists is to cluster words together by meaning (e.g., organizing all of the animals together). The use of this strategy decreases with age, and this relationship is **mediated** by the amount of gray matter volume in the bilateral middle and left inferior frontal regions (shown in Figure 2.4) (Kirchhoff et al., 2014). This means that older adults with greater volume in these regions would be expected to use the clustering strategy more than those with less volume. In turn, using this strategy should improve memory for information. A clustering strategy likely draws on **executive function**, the ability to coordinate multiple cognitive processes to work together (see Section 3.3 for more discussion of this construct). Gray matter volume in the prefrontal cortex relates to performance on executive function tasks, but this relationship does not systematically vary across the life span, according to the results of one meta-analysis (Yuan & Raz, 2014).

To summarize the findings about gray matter, many regions lose volume with age. The rate of these reductions varies across regions, on the basis of whether the changes are measured longitudinally or cross-sectionally, and probably as a function of individual difference factors, including neurodegenerative disease. Relationships with behavior have not emerged in studies as robustly as one might expect, although the volumes of the hippocampus and entorhinal cortex are associated with memory ability and change in memory performance over time.

2.3 Structural Changes in the Brain: White Matter

Even though aging research initially focused predominantly on the effects on gray matter, white matter may be even more important to consider. This is due to some suggestions that the effects of aging on white matter may be more pronounced (Salat et al., 2005). There are also different trajectories of change across the life span. Gray matter volume

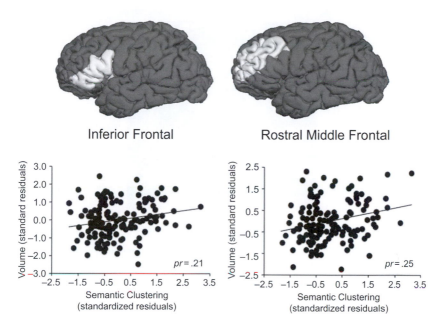

Figure 2.4 The more gray matter available in the prefrontal cortex, including the inferior and middle frontal regions depicted in the top row, the greater the use of a semantic clustering strategy thought to improve memory performance (bottom row). Each dot represents a participant. Data are standardized residuals controlling for sex, gross cognitive status, and semantic processing ability. *pr*: partial correlation coefficient controlling for sex, gross cognitive status, and semantic processing ability.

Adapted from Kirchhoff et al. (2014), *NeuroImage*, Figures 1 and 2.

loss seems to begin in early adulthood, whereas the volume of white matter continues to increase until midlife – then a loss begins (e.g., Coupe et al., 2017; Hedden & Gabrieli, 2004). White matter changes with age include the loss of **myelin**, the fatty substance that surrounds the axons of neurons, and the presence of **white matter hyperintensities**, which appear as "bright spots" on MRI and likely reflect white matter damage (Raz, 2000).

Although white matter changes are pervasive with age, they are not consistent across all tracts in the brain. An anterior-to-posterior gradient of white matter deterioration emerged in early work (Head et al., 2004), with changes more pronounced in the anterior **corpus callosum** (see Figure 2.5) and frontal lobes than in the posterior corpus callosum or the temporal, parietal, and occipital lobes. Other studies converge to suggest that white matter is particularly disrupted in frontal regions, particularly in ventromedial and deep prefrontal regions (Salat et al., 2005). Greater loss of white matter volume in the prefrontal cortex also occurs in comparisons

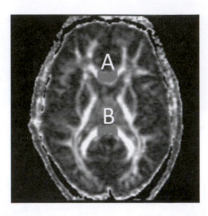

Figure 2.5 The location of relevant white matter tracts on an anisotropy image. The anterior corpus callosum (A) declines more with age than the posterior corpus callosum tracts (B).
Adapted from Head et al. (2004), *Cerebral Cortex*, Figure 2.

within the same individual over 5 years (Raz et al., 2005). Although the anterior-to-posterior gradient does not emerge across the whole brain in all studies (e.g., K. M. Kennedy & Raz, 2009), the gradient does emerge *within* regions. Within frontal and parietal tracts, the most disruption with age occurs in the anterior portion of these tracts (S. W. Davis et al., 2009). The temporal lobes, however, do not exhibit this pattern.

One hypothesis to explain the anterior-to-posterior gradient is the principle of "first-in, last-out." This idea suggests that the regions that develop first in infancy, or are older evolutionarily, are the most resistant to late-life changes due to age. Conversely, those regions that develop later in childhood, or evolutionarily, will be impacted early by aging (last-in, first-out) (Raz, 2000). While some aspects of white matter development are in line with this hypothesis, others are not (S. W. Davis et al., 2009). It may be that additional factors, such as those related to health, lead to different patterns and rates of decline in white matter with age. For example, hypertension, elevated blood pressure, is a risk factor with aging. Hypertension, and even pre-hypertension, has been linked to more shrinkage in the corpus callosum and other white matter microstructure abnormalities (Raz et al., 2010; Suzuki et al., 2017).

2.3.1 Relationships between White Matter and Behavior

To some degree, white matter deterioration probably reflects the degeneration of myelin (S. W. Davis et al., 2009). Myelin contributes to speeding the transmission of impulses, so it is not surprising that white matter is most commonly associated with behavioral measures of speed of processing.

One of the first studies to link white matter integrity to behavioral performance examined reaction times during a visual attention task. Using DTI, (Madden, Whiting, Huettel, White, MacFall, & Provenzale, 2004) identified regions where the measure of fractional anisotropy (FA) (see Chapter 1) related to reaction time differently for younger and older adults. Greater FA in the anterior limb of the internal capsule, a connection between subcortical regions (including the thalamus and the striatum) to prefrontal regions, correlated with faster reaction times for older adults. The pathway may reflect the role of attention in executing responses with age. For younger adults, greater FA in the splenium of the corpus callosum was associated with faster reaction times. This was thought to implicate a large role for visual processing, particularly in transferring information between the hemispheres, in the target detection task for younger adults. These findings illustrate the importance of white matter tracts in the transfer of information, informing quick decisions. Much like the fMRI literature, these findings indicate potential changes in neural structures with age that lead younger and older adults to rely on different subprocesses.

Another study investigated white matter pathways involved in the speed of retrieval from memory. Memory relies on the interplay of a number of processes distributed across the brain. This observation led Bucur and colleagues (2008) to speculate that white matter pathways play an important role in preserving the coherence of memories through the intact transmission of information across neural regions. DTI measures indicated that the integrity of white matter in the genu, an anterior portion of the corpus callosum, and in the pericallosal frontal tract, located in the anterior horn of the lateral ventricles, is related to reaction times for episodic memory decisions. Thus, impaired white matter integrity, particularly in frontal regions, can result in a disconnection syndrome, in which the various regions supporting subprocesses in memory cannot coordinate activity or share information effectively. Disconnection between regions ultimately slows reaction time during retrieval.

Studies report a variety of links between different tracts and task domains. S. W. Davis and colleagues (2009) found that FA in anterior tracts is associated with executive function and that FA in posterior tracts is linked with visual memory. Another study measured white matter integrity manually (rather than with automatic detection using software). Findings indicated that a number of cognitive abilities are associated with measures of white matter, and that white matter integrity and age each make distinct contributions to performance (K. M. Kennedy & Raz, 2009).

Age-related decline in anterior (largely prefrontal) regions is related to speed of processing and executive function performance. In contrast, inhibitory performance is related to age-related decline in posterior regions. Yet other areas, including temporal and central regions such as the internal capsule, are related to performance on episodic memory tasks. Results largely converge across studies and methods, such that the white matter tracts implicated in specific abilities are located in the vicinity of gray matter regions known to contribute to these tasks.

Although the integrity of white matter is related to aging to some degree, white matter hyperintensities appear to be linked to health status, as they are elevated in individuals with cerebrovascular conditions (e.g., hypertension, stroke). White matter hyperintensities are associated with cognitive abilities, such that individuals with more hyperintensities perform more poorly on tests of executive function, speed of processing, fluid intelligence, and memory. Furthermore, the presence of white matter hyperintensities seems to affect performance separately from the effects of prefrontal volume (Gunning-Dixon et al., 2009) and from the effects of white matter integrity (Salat et al., 2005).

To conclude, white matter changes with age can be quite dramatic, despite the later onset of decline (in midlife) compared to gray matter changes. Deterioration may occur in anterior more than posterior pathways in the brain, and this anterior-to-posterior gradient may even occur within regions, such as the frontal and parietal lobes. White matter integrity has some of the strongest relationships with speeded measures of behavior, including attention and memory retrieval.

2.4 Connectivity

While I have discussed research on gray matter and white matter separately, they are, of course, inherently linked. The loss of white matter integrity likely affects the ability of the prefrontal cortex to work in conjunction with other regions, such as the hippocampus and the striatum (Hedden & Gabrieli, 2004). Recent work has devoted more attention to the network properties of the brain, rather than looking at single regions in isolation. A network approach considers how regions work together by considering either **structural connectivity**, the white matter pathways that connect regions of gray matter, or **functional connectivity**, the regions that activate together (e.g., when the left motor cortex activates, the right motor cortex typically activates as well). **Oscillations** reflect coordinated activity across regions within particular frequencies, or time frames.

In one study assessing the ways in which the different types of connectivity work together, S. W. Davis et al. (2012) found that older adults show bilateral activation of prefrontal cortex regions during task performance. This pattern of greater functional connectivity between left and right regions of the prefrontal cortex was found to be related to the integrity of white matter in the corpus callosum. Taken together, these findings suggest that the pattern of greater bilateral recruitment with age (e.g., HAROLD; see Chapter 1) could reflect greater functional connectivity across the hemispheres in the prefrontal cortex with age, relying on the structural connectivity provided by intact white matter tracts in that cortex.

The pattern of increased functional connectivity with age in prefrontal regions converges with other work indicating stronger anterior connectivity with age. However, it is important to note that there are many, if not more, findings of reduced connectivity with age, such as between medial temporal and posterior regions (see Sala-Llonch et al., 2015 for a review). Long-range connections, across more widespread regions of the brain, seem to be more affected by aging, including frontotemporal and temporoparietal regions implicated in memory (L. Wang et al., 2010). Other age-related changes, such as increases in the length of the shortest path or changes in the centrality of regions in a network, may also indicate reduced network efficiency for older adults (L. Wang et al., 2010). Investigations of network changes with age indicate shifts in the role of subcortical and cerebellar regions, possibly contributing to changes in life satisfaction over the life span (Voss, Wong, et al., 2013).

Some research takes a much broader network approach to consider how the brain is organized into distinct and coordinated subsystems with age. Younger adults appear to have tightly organized and distinct modules for different brain systems, allowing for strong organization within a system while also having the ability to coordinate with other systems via sparser connections. With age, the distinction of brain systems breaks down, such that there are weaker connections within a system and stronger connections between systems (Chan et al., 2014). Although these changes appear to occur gradually across the life span for sensory-motor systems (e.g., vision), there is a sharper decline for systems that link up with primary sensory systems (e.g., control systems; see Figure 2.6). These patterns of changes to connections have implications for memory performance, as better segregation of the association systems relates to better memory performance (Chan et al., 2014).

The effects of aging on connectivity may well differ across individuals, indicating better or worse cognitive outcomes. For example, a study of

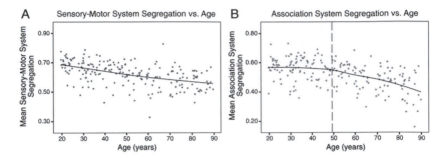

Figure 2.6 Although the segregation of sensory-motor (panel A) and association (panel B) systems decreases with age, changes are exaggerated after age 50 in the association systems. Each dot represents a participant.

Adapted from Chan et al. (2014), *Proceedings of the National Academy of Sciences of the United States of America*, Figure 3.

"supernormals," those older adults with high levels of cognitive ability who perform more like young or middle-aged adults on cognitive tests, showed that patterns of oscillations across several brain regions are impervious to the effects of aging in this group (X. Wang et al., 2017). Such findings indicate that research adopting a network approach may be a fruitful line of work with which to study individual differences.

2.5 Default Mode Network

Much of the research about changes in networks with age has centered on the **default mode network**. This may be because it appears to be intricately involved in a wide variety of thought, from self-referential reflection to spontaneous mind wandering, and deactivated by tasks demanding external attention, as is the case for most cognitively demanding processes. The network is widespread across the brain, encompassing both medial prefrontal cortex and parietal regions, and the network's relationship with other networks may also be of great importance.

One of the first studies implicating the default mode network in cognitive changes with age used a semantic classification task (i.e., "does this word represent a living thing?"). Compared to younger adults, older adults failed to deactivate, or reduce the activity of, relevant regions during judgments (Lustig et al., 2003). Additional studies (e.g., Grady et al., 2010; Persson et al., 2007) also found that older adults experience more difficulty in suppressing the default mode network than younger

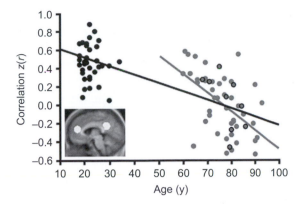

Figure 2.7 Anterior–posterior connectivity is higher for younger than older adults. Age is depicted on the x-axis, such that young adults are plotted with the dots on the left and older adults with the dots on the right. Even within the older group alone, the strength of the connection between the regions (depicted in the brain panel) decreases with advancing age. Adapted from Andrews-Hanna et al. (2007), *Neuron*, Figure 1.

adults. Early results also began to probe the network properties of the default mode, establishing that long-range connections across the brain, particularly in the anterior–posterior direction, are disrupted with aging, as shown in Figure 2.7 (Andrews-Hanna et al., 2007). Disruptions in the default mode network with age also emerge during rest (Damoiseaux et al., 2008).

Subsequent research further probed the subregions of the default mode network as well as the ways in which the network works together with other networks. Across networks, long-range connectivity in the default mode and the dorsal attention networks decreases with age, although the functional connectivity density increases in sensorimotor networks (Tomasi & Volkow, 2012). Other work (Campbell et al., 2013) probed the subregions implicated in the default mode network, identifying some dissociations in the effects of aging on the different regions. The ventral posterior cingulate cortex and the dorsomedial prefrontal cortex exhibited weaker connectivity with age, indicating a vulnerability in this system. In contrast, older adults had stronger connectivity in the dorsal posterior cingulate system, which is implicated in cognitive control.

A promising extension of the work on the default mode network investigated the way that this network couples with others depending on task demands. The contributions of the default mode, attention, and control networks were compared for different tasks. For young adults, the control network coupled with the default mode network during an autobiographical planning task but with the attention network during a visuospatial planning task (Spreng & Schacter, 2012). Older adults, in contrast, did not deactivate the default network during the visuospatial planning task. The observation that the default network is not dysfunctional under all circumstances led the authors to suggest that aging impacts the *interaction* of the networks rather than the default mode network *per se*. These observations were extended into the study of executive function failures with age, leading to the default-executive hypothesis of aging (Turner & Spreng, 2015). This hypothesis suggests that older adults have difficulty modulating network activity in response to increased task difficulty, affecting both default and control networks. Moreover, the default network couples with lateral prefrontal regions with age in an attempt to cope with cognitive control demands.

2.6 Perception and Sensation

Overall, younger adults engage perceptual regions, such as the occipital cortex, more robustly than older adults (see meta-analysis by Spreng et al., 2010). Dedifferentiation, a major theory positing that processes and neural regions are less specialized and respond more generally with age, emerged from the perceptual domain. Building on behavioral findings indicating that a number of different cognitive abilities are highly related to each other with age and that sensory function predicts ability on more complex cognitive tasks with age (Lindenberger & Baltes, 1994), D. C. Park and colleagues (2004) predicted that neural signatures would be less distinct in older adults. In their study, younger and older adults viewed different categories of stimuli (e.g., faces, houses), known to engage specialized neural regions in the ventral visual cortex in younger adults. As in prior research, younger adults showed a pattern of specialization, with neural regions responding more to one type of stimuli than the others; this pattern was pronounced in regions recognized as category selective (e.g., fusiform for faces; parahippocampal gyrus for places). As seen in Figure 2.8, older adults' pattern was less distinct, providing evidence of neural dedifferentiation with age. Dedifferentiated neural representations also have been shown within a category, with the fusiform face area of older adults responding less selectively to individual faces compared to morphs of those faces (Goh et al., 2010). The original D. C. Park et al. (2004) data were reanalyzed with **multivoxel pattern analysis (MVPA)**, a method that is more sensitive to neural representations by

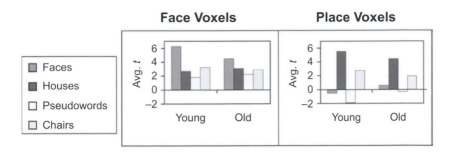

Figure 2.8 The response of voxels in the fusiform face area (left) and parahippocampal place area (right), measured by mean *t* values (y-axis), illustrate that the more specialized response in young adults is reduced with age. That is, the heightened response of the fusiform to faces and parahippocampal gyrus to places relative to other stimulus types is reduced with age.

Adapted from D. C. Park et al. (2004), *Proceedings of the National Academy of Sciences of the United States of America*, Figure 3.

comparing patterns of activation distributed over space rather than being constrained to comparing focal and contiguous activations. Results revealed that the older adults' less distinct neural activation pattern occurred not only in the ventral visual cortex but also in the early visual cortex and regions that are outside the visual system, such as the parietal and frontal cortex (Carp, Park, Polk, & Park, 2011).

A question arising from the dedifferentiation literature is *how* neural representations become less distinct with age. Do neurons respond more broadly, such that neurons in younger adults that are tuned to respond to very specific stimulus properties (e.g., faces) respond more loosely to other types of stimuli (e.g., the neurons also respond to houses)? Or does neural attenuation occur, such that the neural responses are not as strong (e.g., the response of face-selective neurons is weaker to faces)? A study across the adult life span found support for changes in both of these mechanisms with age (J. Park et al., 2012). In the core regions of the face network, such as the fusiform face area, there was evidence of broadening, with a greater response to houses in the region across the life span. A pattern of attenuation emerged in the extended face network, with less activity over the life span in response to faces in some regions. Another recent finding suggests that dedifferentiation may reflect properties of network connectivity. The distinction between nodes within a system (e.g., visual; semantic) and those that connect across systems is less distinct with age and this may affect patterns of connectivity during rest as well as during tasks (Chan et al., 2017).

Beyond the extensive work on dedifferentiation with aging, the neural literature on perception and sensation is rather impoverished. Although perceptual and sensory changes with age are robust in the behavioral literature (Lindenberger & Baltes, 1994), such fundamental differences have been difficult to study by neural measures. This may be because it is difficult to study lower-level processes separate from higher-order cognitive processes such as attention and memory (see Chapter 3), as fMRI studies require comparison across conditions and often occur in impoverished sensory conditions (e.g., restricted viewing conditions; loud noise from the scanning sequences) in the scanner.

Some work has illustrated these challenges. For example, one study investigating neural markers of visual acuity differences with age suggests that differences in P1 and N1, ERP markers of early attentional processing (see Section 1.4.2 for a discussion of the naming of ERP components), may simply reflect poor visual acuity rather than differences in attention *per se* (Daffner et al., 2013). Initial age differences in latency that indicate delays for older samples in the P1 and N1 components were eliminated once visual acuity was accounted for in analyses. With correction, an age difference emerged for the amplitude of the P1 component, indicating a larger effect in older than younger adults; no age differences emerged in the initial analyses that were uncorrected for visual acuity. Thus, changes in the effects of basic sensory processes with age highlight the challenges of studying components in more complex cognitive tasks without accounting for sensory differences.

The distractions introduced by the scanning environment for fMRI studies could impact participant behavior and results in multiple ways, particularly with age. Compared to younger adults, older adults were disproportionately impaired on a long-term memory task administered in the scanner compared to those participants tested in the laboratory, although the decrements did not extend to a working memory task (Gutchess & Park, 2006). The response of the auditory cortex also may serve as a potential marker of the distracting scanner environment, with older adults engaging the region more than young on trials that they failed to encode into memory (Stevens et al., 2008). The region was functionally connected to the default network, and this was interpreted as suggesting that the activity represented monitoring of one's environment.

2.7 Neurotransmitters

Neurotransmitter systems can experience widespread changes with age. The literature suggests that systems mediating dopamine, serotonin, and acetylcholine decline with age, losing as much as 10% per decade in terms of receptors or other markers (as reviewed by S. C. Li et al., 2013). The dopamine system has been most studied with aging, and has been linked to widespread processes including cognition, motor abilities, and response to reward. Aging has been shown to affect a number of aspects of neurotransmitter systems, including the number of some subtypes of dopamine receptors and dopamine transporters, and there is evidence of changes in dopamine metabolism (see Volkow et al., 1998).

PET scanning is typically used to investigate particular neurotransmitters *in vivo*. One such study assessed the effects of aging on D_2 receptors and linked this with performance on motor and cognitive tasks, with a focus on tasks assessing frontal lobe function (Volkow et al., 1998). This study found that the number of D_2 receptors in the striatum decreases with age and that the availability of dopamine receptors correlates with performance on the neuropsychological tests of motor and cognitive function. Another PET study revealed that D_1 receptor binding potential is reduced with age in the caudate nucleus and the DLPFC (Backman et al., 2011). This reduction appears related to poorer modulation of frontal and parietal regions across different working memory loads in older adults. Other work demonstrates healthy older adults' increased dopamine synthesis capacity compared to young adults and links this with cognitive flexibility (e.g., adapting to changing task rules), which is reduced with age (Berry et al., 2016). Chapter 8 will discuss contributions of dopamine to motivated behavior, including reward learning.

Research connecting neurotransmitters to the effects of aging on brain structure and function is sparse, but it is a direction of great interest. Backman and colleagues (2006) have argued that dopamine may provide the critical link to understand age-related declines in cognition. Although many neurotransmitter studies have been cross-sectional, longitudinal work is underway to test the effects, as well as assess the importance of individual difference factors such as lifestyle and genes (e.g., Nevalainen et al., 2015).

Another approach to assess the role of neurotransmitters in cognitive aging is through pharmacological intervention. Findings with nonhuman animals show that dopamine enhances memory via the hippocampus (Lisman et al., 2011). Chowdhury and colleagues (2012) enhanced dopamine by having older adults ingest **levopoda (L-DOPA)**, a dopamine precursor. The behavioral performance and activation of neural regions were compared for participants receiving L-DOPA as opposed to a placebo. Older adults' memory for neutral scenes improved with the medium level of the dose of L-DOPA, but this was not reflected in

hippocampal engagement. The authors suggest that the failure to implicate the hippocampus may reflect the long period over which memory
traces are formed in the brain. Another study used a similar approach to
investigate the contributions of dopamine to reward learning in older
adults (Chowdhury et al., 2013). Administering L-DOPA did improve
learning, such that some older adults performed comparably to younger
adults. The neural response of the nucleus accumbens tracked reward
prediction error, and the signal for older adults was restored after
receiving L-DOPA. Furthermore, the strength of the nigrostriatal white
matter tracts, assessed with DTI, predicted individual differences in the
expected value response of the nucleus accumbens. These studies highlight the potential benefits to cognition as a result of boosting the
available dopamine. The findings, however, underscore the importance
of considering basal levels of dopamine, as individual differences in the
functioning of the system and the importance of identifying the optimal
dose can greatly shape responses (see also Berry et al., 2016).

2.8 Individual Differences

In the remainder of the chapter, we will consider individual difference
factors that have been shown to affect brain and behavior with aging.
Although I will sample only a few research findings from each of these
domains, it is important to keep in mind that much of this research is in
the initial stages. This means that many of the findings are based on
preliminary links, potentially with modest sample sizes and limited
measurements.

2.8.1 Genes

Genes exert a large effect on neurotransmitter systems, contributing to
the types of processes discussed in the preceding section. Several genes
affect neurotransmitter levels, including the *COMT* gene that affects
dopamine signaling in the prefrontal cortex, in addition to dopamine
transporter and receptor (DRD2) genes (for a review, see S. C. Li et al.,
2013).

In terms of learning and memory, BDNF (brain-derived neurotrophic
factor) has emerged as an important factor. Individuals who have the
Met allele, as opposed to those who are homozygous (have two copies)
for the Val allele, have less BDNF, and this is linked to greater age-related
decline in some memory tasks including item and prospective memory
(K. M. Kennedy, Reese, et al., 2015). Another gene that impacts memory

function, *APOE*, is linked to risk of developing AD. Relevant findings regarding *APOE* will be discussed further in Chapter 7.

A gene that affects serotonin transporters is implicated in emotional reactivity. Individuals with the short allele are more vulnerable to depression and anxiety, perhaps due to their poorer ability to regulate emotion. One study (Waring et al., 2013) found that older adults' task performance was unaffected by whether they had the short or long allele. However, the functional connectivity between regions implicated in regulating emotional conflict (the dorsal and pregenual anterior cingulate cortex) was reduced for older adults carrying the short allele.

Epigenetics allows for life experiences to alter genetic transcription, thus allowing the environment to shape genetic expression. The plasticity of the hippocampus may make it particularly subject to alteration through epigenetic processes. Thus, experiences would be able to shape memory function, and some research with rodents supports this possibility (see Penner et al., 2010; Spiegel et al., 2014). This is an exciting area for future research, not only to understand aging processes but even to uncover the epigenetic changes that are possible in younger brains.

2.8.2 Intelligence

A chance discovery spurred research on the effects of early-life intelligence on cognitive aging. Voluminous archives of standardized testing data from children tested in 1932 and 1947 were discovered in Scotland, allowing for childhood intelligence to be linked to later life outcomes (Underwood, 2014). Older adults who completed these standardized tests in the Lothian region near Edinburgh have participated in extensive studies, revealing findings such as the large contribution that childhood intelligence makes to cognitive performance in old age (e.g., Gow et al., 2011), even as late as age 90 (Deary et al., 2013). High intelligence in childhood does not seem to slow the *rate* of cognitive change in old age, but, rather, affects the *level* of cognitive ability later in life (Gow et al., 2011).

Recent studies have begun to incorporate biological measures into assessments of the role of childhood intelligence in cognitive aging, and some results suggest that there is a large genetic contribution to intelligence (Deary et al., 2012). One approach links early-life intelligence (from ages 3 to 11) to midlife biological age, using a host of measures such as perceived facial age, heart age, and telomere length (repeating sequences of DNA at the ends of chromosomes), as well as an algorithm incorporating multiple biomarkers that together predict mortality (Schaefer et al., 2016). Being biologically older was associated with lower levels of intelligence across these measures, although the associations were weaker for the telomere measure. The relationship between intelligence and biological age held whether intelligence was measured at midlife (at the same time as the biological aging measures), late childhood, or early childhood, suggesting the pervasive effects of early-life cognition.

Other interesting uses of the available childhood data on intelligence is to better understand the meaning of cortical thickness with age and to better match samples. Whereas many studies suggest that preserved cortical thickness indicates better outcomes of aging through the relationship with higher cognitive performance, measures of cortical thickness correlate strongly with childhood intelligence (Karama et al., 2014). This finding suggests that higher levels of cortical thickness in old age may reflect higher levels of cortical thickness at a young age, rather than different rates of loss as a function of age-related cognitive decline. Another study used childhood intelligence, alongside measures of socioeconomic background, to match samples of 73-year-olds to 92-year-olds. Results revealed that white matter hyperintensities and total cortical surface, rather than measures of cortical thickness or volume, were associated with cognitive declines across the two age groups (Ritchie et al., 2017). Importantly, the studies discussed in this section reveal how measuring the same individuals across the life span plays a critical role in disambiguating the effects of aging from other factors (see Box 2.1), and suggest that changes to cortical thickness with age may not be the predominant factor in cognitive decline.

2.8.3 Sex Differences

Sex differences in cognition occur in young adults, with women performing better on verbal tasks and men performing better on spatial tasks. However, it is not well established whether these patterns of sex differences extend into older adulthood (for a review, see Gur et al., 2002). Furthermore, there are few links to neural measures. Age-related declines in cortical cerebral blood flow and tissue volume seem to be comparable across the sexes in some data sets (as reviewed by Gur et al., 2002), although other studies suggest slightly greater loss of volume in older males than females (e.g., Carne et al., 2006). In terms of specific lobes, the parietal lobe showed marked reduction in volume with age for males but not females, whereas the temporal lobe showed a larger tendency to be reduced in females than males (Carne et al., 2006).

The effects of the loss of **estrogen** in menopausal women are one particular consideration in studying cognitive aging. In menopause, the production of **estradiol** declines, with the potential to impair memory and executive function. Estradiol works in opposition to the effects of **glucocorticoids**, which are released in response to stress and can impair memory and executive function. As estradiol, which benefits cognition, declines with menopause and allows glucocorticoids to exert a stronger effect, the net effect is harmful to cognition (for a review, see Herrera & Mather, 2015). In terms of neural regions affected by levels of estrogen, the prefrontal cortex and hippocampus are vulnerable to damage from glucocorticoids, in contrast to the protective effects offered by estradiol. Although these studies are largely based on work with animals, neural activation patterns in humans change as a result of glucocorticoid and estradiol exposure (as reviewed by Herrera & Mather, 2015). In addition, administering estradiol over 3 months, compared to a placebo or lower dose of estradiol), increased hippocampal gray matter volume for postmenopausal women (K. Albert et al., 2017). Interestingly, some research has suggested estrogen use for long periods of time (>10 years) could have deleterious effects (Erickson, Colcombe, Elavsky, et al., 2007). Whereas using estrogen in old age initially seems to offer a protective effect, with greater gray and white matter volume compared to women who did not take estrogen, the effects may reverse over longer durations. Fitness level is another important factor to consider. As discussed in Chapter 3, high fitness levels are associated with better outcomes in old age, including greater tissue volume. High levels of fitness may supplement the effects of estrogen at shorter durations of use and mitigate the deleterious effects over longer terms (Erickson, Colcombe, Elavsky, et al., 2007).

2.8.4 Personality

A small body of work has explored how personality could impact the brain with age. Some research has focused on the **Big 5 personality traits**, a theory suggesting that five dimensions – extraversion, neuroticism, agreeableness, conscientiousness, and openness to experience – account for much of the variation in personality across individuals (Costa & McCrae, 1987). For example, Jackson and colleagues (2011) examined how the personality traits of neuroticism, conscientiousness, and extraversion related to the volume of gray and white matter in a sample of 44–88-year-olds. Their approach allowed them to look at both the overall effects of personality on brain volumes and the effects of personality

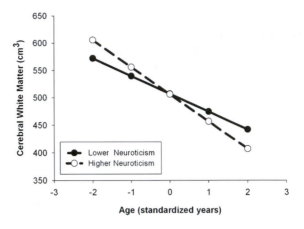

Figure 2.9 Whereas higher levels of neuroticism are related to decreased gray matter volume across younger and older adults, the effects of neuroticism on the volume of white matter change across the life span. Higher levels of neuroticism (white dots with dashed line) relate to greater loss of white matter with age compared to lower levels of neuroticism (black dots with solid line).

Adapted from Jackson et al. (2011), *Neurobiology of Aging*, Figure 2.

on age-related changes in volumes. Neuroticism seemed to have the largest negative effects. Overall cerebral gray matter volume was lower in individuals high in neuroticism, and this relationship did not change with age. This pattern was pronounced in regions of the prefrontal cortex (i.e., the ventrolateral prefrontal cortex (VLPFC), the dorsolateral prefrontal cortex (DLPFC), and the orbitofrontal cortex). For overall cerebral white matter volume, however, the loss in volume with age was greater for individuals high in neuroticism than for those with lower levels, as shown in Figure 2.9. Another study (Wright, Feczko, Dickerson, & Williams, 2007) found converging results, with individuals with high levels of neuroticism having thinner cortex in regions such as the superior and inferior frontal cortex (although the anterior temporal cortex showed *increased* thickness).

In terms of the personality trait of conscientiousness, highly conscientious individuals showed less decline with age in white matter volumes. Specific gray matter regions exhibiting the effects of conscientiousness included VLPFC/DLPFC and orbitofrontal cortex volumes, which were higher in conscientious individuals (Jackson et al., 2011). Furthermore, individuals with higher levels of conscientiousness exhibited less decline in the volume of the amygdala and parahippocampal gyrus.

Although extraversion did not have strong effects on gray and white matter volume in the Jackson et al. (2011) study, at least one other study found such a relationship. Older adults with high levels of extraversion had thicker volumes in frontal cortex (i.e., the superior and middle frontal cortex.) In addition, they reported negative effects of openness, with reduced cortical thickness in older adults with high levels of this factor (Wright, Feczko, et al., 2007).

Although the results from (Wright, Feczko, Dickerson, & Williams, 2007) seem to suggest negative effects of openness on cortical thickness, the story diverges when examining *functional* brain data. Measures of resting state brain activity, assessed with PET, revealed that adults older than 55 years who had high levels of openness exhibited greater activity in the orbitofrontal cortex (Sutin et al., 2009). Interestingly, specific regions showing this relationship differed across men and women. Whereas openness correlated with activity in the orbitofrontal cortex for both men and women, there were additional relationships with activity in DLPFC for women and with the anterior cingulate for men. The results illustrated how one factor, such as the personality trait of openness, could be manifested in brains differently based on one's sex. These findings were thought to reflect the different processes (e.g., working memory versus attention and reward) that are impacted by openness for women and men, respectively.

Different ways of thinking about oneself can also shape brain aging. Levels of self-esteem and internal locus of control, the extent to which one feels in control of the outcomes in one's life, have been related to the brain in both younger and older adults. Hippocampal volume was larger in those younger and older adults with higher levels of self-esteem and higher levels of internal locus of control (J. C. Pruessner et al., 2005). A modest relationship between hippocampal volume and self-esteem also emerged in a sample of middle-aged men (Kubarych et al., 2012). Although the size, generalizability, and even presence of a relationship between self-esteem and hippocampal volume have varied across some studies (e.g., Engert et al., 2010; Kubarych et al., 2012; M. Pruessner et al., 2007), there remains great interest in establishing a connection. This is because one's level of self-esteem has the potential to influence the experience of stress, which is known to have deleterious effects on hippocampal volume.

Taken together, the neuroimaging results converge with other behavioral data to illustrate the potentially harmful effects of high levels of neuroticism with age, and the beneficial effects of high levels of conscientiousness, self-esteem, internal locus of control, and potentially extraversion.

2.8.5 Stress

Exposure to chronic stress results in the release of glucocorticoids, and exposure to these over years can impact the functioning of glucocorticoid receptors and the **hypothalamic-pituitary-adrenal (HPA) axis**, increasing glucocorticoid levels (see review by Prenderville et al., 2015). Stress also appears to be related to atrophy in the hippocampus, which could contribute to memory impairment (see review by McEwen, 2006). Some studies show effects of even acute stressors on memory in older, but not younger, adults (e.g., Hidalgo et al., 2014), although this finding is not universal (e.g., Pulopulos et al., 2013). These memory impairments may be related to dysregulation of the stress system, assessed through markers such as **cortisol** (Hidalgo et al., 2014). The magnitude of the cortisol response may be related to memory performance with age, even when memory was not assessed during a period of stress (Almela et al., 2014). High cortisol responsivity may indicate a well-functioning HPA axis, which may help to preserve memory with age. However, prolonged activation of the HPA axis, as through chronic stress, may be linked to dysregulation and development of neurodegenerative diseases such as AD (Prenderville et al., 2015). Aging is also associated with increased inflammation, metabolic changes, and oxidative stress, all of which may contribute to cognitive dysfunction. Many of the same factors thought to contribute to cognitive changes with aging are also associated with depression and anxiety, conditions that could exacerbate dysfunction in the aging brain (Prenderville et al., 2015).

Recent work has investigated the effects of stress on decisions with age. Willingness to take risks is one aspect of decision making that could vary with age. Younger and older adults were exposed to either a stress condition (placing hands in ice water) or a control condition. They then completed a driving task in which more points were accumulated by continuing to drive on a yellow light until the red appeared, at which time points were lost if participants were still driving (Mather et al., 2009). Whereas younger and older adults exhibited similar cortisol responses to stress, the stress condition impaired older adults' performance on the subsequent driving task. Stress altered older adults' decisions under risky conditions by making them more conservative in the way that they approached the task (e.g., stopping more, rather than driving).

Individuals differ in their chronic responses to stressors, and **trait anxiety** may be one determinate of this response. The structural connections between the amygdala and the ventral prefrontal cortex may be important in regulating the response to emotion, including anxiety, such that prefrontal regions can help to downregulate the response of the amygdala. The integrity and volume of these tracts were examined by DTI in younger, middle-aged, and older adults in a study investigating the effects of aging and anxiety (Clewett et al., 2014). Multiple measures of white matter showed declines for the older adults. Somewhat surprisingly, the connectivity between the amygdala and the ventral prefrontal cortex was associated with *higher* levels of anxiety, a pattern inconsistent with the idea that the pathway would reflect regulation of anxiety. Thus, the results suggest that the losses in this white matter pathway with age may be related to lower levels of anxiety in older adults.

One stressor that may be of particular importance with age is loneliness. Perceived loneliness is associated with a number of risk factors, including blood pressure, HPA activity, and a number of psychological and physiological conditions and behaviors (for reviews, see Cacioppo et al., 2010; Wilson & Bennett, 2017). Several studies link perceived loneliness in later life to depression (Cacioppo et al., 2006), with loneliness predicting depression, rather than the other way around (Cacioppo et al., 2010). Interestingly, *perceiving* oneself as lonely seems to be the critical factor in these health outcomes, rather than objective social isolation or a lack of social support (Cacioppo et al., 2010; Cacioppo et al., 2006). One study investigated the effect of loneliness on long- and short-range functional connectivity during resting state scans in older adult males (Lan et al., 2015). Higher levels of loneliness impacted short-range functional connectivity in the lingual gyrus, a region potentially contributing to social cognition. The authors furthermore argued that loneliness and depression might exert separate effects on the brains of older adult males. Given the dearth of literature on this topic, much more research is needed on the effects of loneliness on neural pathways with age, and how potential neural changes contribute to depression later in life.

2.8.6 Bilingualism

Speaking multiple languages may protect cognition against some age-related declines. The constant demands of switching between languages and inhibiting the language not in use could improve executive control. Behavioral evidence supports the idea of advantages for bilinguals, including older adults, for tasks invoking executive function demands, such as inhibiting, switching, and monitoring conflict (for reviews, see Bialystok et al., 2012; Grant et al., 2014).

How does bilingualism change older adults' brains? In terms of structural changes, gray matter volume is higher in the left anterior temporal pole (Abutalebi et al., 2014) and the inferior parietal lobules bilaterally for bilingual compared to monolingual older adults (Abutalebi et al., 2015). Monolingual older adults evidenced thinning of the left temporal pole across older adulthood whereas bilinguals showed more preservation with age (Olsen et al., 2015). Furthermore, proficiency in the language affects the pattern of findings, with better ability to name items in the second language associated with greater volume in the left anterior temporal pole (Abutalebi et al., 2014) and the left inferior parietal lobule (Abutalebi et al., 2015).

Given the distributed nature of the language system, the effects of bilingualism on white matter are of great importance. Bilingual older adults have more white matter volume in the frontal lobes than monolinguals, and more frontal white matter is associated with better performance on measures of executive function and resistance to interference (Olsen et al., 2015). Bilingual older adults have more white matter integrity in the corpus callosum that connects regions involved in language (Luk et al., 2011). They also show increased functional connectivity in a frontal-posterior network, in what could indicate a more efficient tightly coupled network. In contrast, monolinguals show heightened functional connectivity between regions in the frontal lobes. These findings indicate that long-range connections, extending across disparate regions such as the frontal lobes and parietal and occipital lobes, may fare better in bilinguals than monolinguals. However, it is important to note that this pattern of increased white matter integrity for bilinguals is not consistent across the literature, with some studies even finding *reduced* integrity for bilinguals compared to monolinguals (Gold, Johnson, & Powell, 2013).

Finally, a few effects of bilingualism have emerged from the fMRI literature. Bilingual older adults may activate frontal regions less than monolinguals, potentially reflecting efficiency (Gold, Kim, Johnson, Kryscio, & Smith, 2013). That is, compared to monolinguals, bilinguals can achieve the same level of task-switching performance, or even perform faster, while requiring less brain activation to do so. Another study probed the effects of bilingualism on older brains at rest. Grady and colleagues (2015) compared two networks implicated in executive control – the frontoparietal control system, implicated in switching among networks, and the salience network, which unites sensory experiences and internal states – as well as the default mode network, which is deactivated for externally focused tasks. Results indicated higher levels

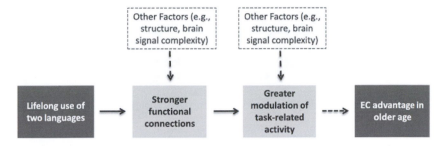

Figure 2.10 A model depicting a number of processes that may contribute to enhanced executive control (EC) ability in bilinguals, with age.
From Grady et al. (2015), *Neuropsychologia*, Figure 8.

of functional connectivity in the frontoparietal control and default mode networks for bilinguals compared to monolinguals. The authors interpreted their results as in line with prior findings of better integrity in relevant white matter pathways and behavioral advantages in executive control tasks for bilinguals.

Across the literature, a few models have attempted to explain how bilingualism alters brain systems. One model argues that bilingualism strengthens the connection among regions. As shown in Figure 2.10, Grady and colleagues (2015) suggest that stronger connections allow for better modulation of the brain across tasks, benefiting executive control. Another model focuses on the preservation and activation of particular neural regions, with a nod to connectivity. Grant and colleagues (2014) propose that preserved posterior (e.g., parietal and temporal) regions, increased prefrontal function, and strengthened frontal-posterior connectivity enhance the functioning of the bilingual brain with age, as depicted in Figure 2.11. A third model builds on observations of preserved activations of posterior regions to suggest that bilinguals rely more on subcortical and posterior regions than monolinguals (Grundy et al., 2017). Although this pattern is the opposite of that described by the PASA model (see Section 1.3), this pattern is thought to reflect a decreased need for top-down processing in bilinguals compared to monolinguals, which could help to mitigate the deleterious effects of aging.

2.8.7 Culture

There is but a small body of work investigating cross-cultural differences beyond language. Thus far, studies primarily address patterns of structural change with age. Aging appears to largely affect brains similarly

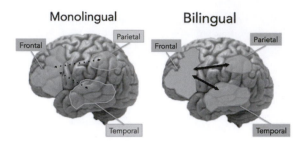

Figure 2.11 A second model of bilingualism emphasizes the potential for more preserved frontal, parietal, and temporal regions (indicated by less transparent shading of those regions, compared to the monolingual brain) as well as enhanced connectivity of posterior regions (indicated with solid arrows, compared to the dashed arrows in the monolingual brain) in bilinguals, with age.
From Grant et al. (2014), *Frontiers in Psychology*, Figure 2.

across cultures, such that East Asians tested in Singapore and a predominantly Caucasian sample tested in the United States exhibit comparable total cerebral volume decreases with age (Chee et al., 2009). The volume of the hippocampus is similarly reduced with age across cultures (Chee et al., 2009), consistent with age-related reduction in hippocampal activation across cultures when binding objects to scenes (Goh et al., 2007).

Despite the similar trajectories for the aging brain across cultures, direct comparisons of cortical thickness reveal some regions that differ with age. Compared to Singaporeans, young Americans have thicker cortex in a number of regions of the polymodal association cortex, including in the frontal, parietal, and medial temporal lobes (Chee et al., 2011). Cultural differences generally did not emerge for older adults, aside from thicker volume in the left inferior temporal gyrus for Singaporeans compared to Americans, a pattern that emerged for both younger and older adults (Chee et al., 2011). Despite the convergence of the cultures with age, it would be premature to conclude on the basis of a single study that cultural differences are reduced with age. There is substantial variability in older adults' brain volumes, which might make it difficult to detect effects of culture. Notably, comparing only the high-ability subsamples of Americans and Singaporean older adults yielded a pattern of cultural differences similar to the pattern that emerged for younger adults. This finding indicates that caution is needed in interpreting differences across groups as entirely reflecting the influence of culture, as the groups could differ in other inadvertent ways (e.g., poor matching of the samples on cognitive ability). If structural differences do reflect the role of culture, they could be due to a combination of multiple factors, including genetic as well as environmental factors, such as bilingualism or cross-cultural differences in strategies (Chee et al., 2011).

In terms of differences in functional activation patterns with age, older East Asian participants showed a reduced response to the repetition of objects, whereas the neural response was robust for Americans across the life span (Goh et al., 2007). This finding indicates that cultural differences can be exacerbated across the life span, perhaps emerging later in life due to prolonged differences in cognitive strategies or constraints on resources with age. Although this was the only study to directly compare younger and older adults across cultures, an interesting direction for future work might be to compare the effects of culture on resting state activity across the life span, as cultural differences in this network could have pervasive effects on a number of processes. One prior study of young adults (Goh, Hebrank, et al., 2013) reported cultural differences in the default mode network, such that Americans suppressed activity in the network more than East Asians. This suppression may have paralleled Americans' greater activation of task-positive regions during a task that was more challenging for them compared to East Asians. Future work will allow us to investigate the ways in which networks differ across cultures, during rest as well as during tasks.

2.8.8 Summary

Understanding individual differences requires large, diverse samples, as well as potentially studying these individuals over time. Research with cognitive neuroscience methods has only begun to achieve this, particularly as multisite, longitudinal, and life-span studies incorporate measures of brain structure and function. The insights afforded by such approaches are nicely illustrated by the studies of the effects of childhood intelligence (Section 2.8.2). Thus, our understanding of individual differences should expand rapidly in the coming years.

Chapter Summary

- Gray matter volume decreases with age, although the rate of loss varies across regions. The entorhinal cortex, a region linked to memory, undergoes substantial change even in healthy aging. Measurement is also sensitive to whether change is measured within the same person, which reveals higher rates of loss, or across different groups.

- White matter integrity is disrupted with age. The pattern of loss begins in middle age, which is later in life than the changes to gray matter.
- The ways in which aging affects how regions and networks work together may be more important than the changes in activity in isolated regions, in order to understand how aging affects the brain.
- Difficulty in suppressing the default mode network, reduced specificity of neural responses to different types of stimuli, and decreased dopamine may account for a wide variety of age-related changes in behavior.
- Early-life intelligence, measured in childhood, is a strong predictor of cognition in late life.
- Work to understand individual differences is generally in the early stages, and much more investigation is needed to understand which abilities may lead to particularly good or poor outcomes with aging.

Discussion Questions

1. How does the pattern of age-related change differ between gray and white matter?
2. To what extent do structural changes seem to account for behavioral changes with age?
3. What is the default mode? Why is it important in explaining age-related changes in cognition?
4. What is dedifferentiation? Why is it important in explaining age-related changes in cognition?
5. What individual differences seem particularly important to consider with age? With the current state of the literature, which ones do you think are critical to consider in understanding how the brain ages?
6. Although longitudinal studies are ideal to study the effects of aging, what are some of the challenges to using these designs? In the study of age-related changes, which processes would benefit the most from a longitudinal design? What processes would be the most challenging to study with a longitudinal design?

For Further Reading

Davis, S. W., Dennis, N. A., Buchler, N. G., White, L. E., Madden, D. J., & Cabeza, R. (2009). Assessing the effects of age on long white matter tracts using diffusion tensor tractography. *NeuroImage*, *46*(2), 530–541.

Fjell, A. M., Westlye, L. T., Grydeland, H., Amlien, I., Espeseth, T., Reinvang, I., . . . Alzheimer Disease Neuroimaging Initiative. (2014). Accelerating cortical thinning: unique to dementia or universal in aging? *Cerebral Cortex*, *24*(4), 919–934. doi:10.1093/cercor/bhs379

Park, D. C., Polk, T. A., Park, R., Minear, M., Savage, A., & Smith, M. R. (2004). Aging reduces neural specialization in ventral visual cortex. *Proceedings of the National Academy of Sciences of the United States of America*, *101*(35), 13091–13095.

Raz, N., Lindenberger, U., Rodrigue, K. M., Kennedy, K. M., Head, D., Williamson, A., ... Acker, J. D. (2005). Regional brain changes in aging healthy adults: general trends, individual differences and modifiers. *Cerebral Cortex*, *15*(11), 1676–1689.

Key Terms

Big 5 personality traits
corpus callosum
cortisol
cross-sectional designs
default mode network
entorhinal cortex
epigenetics
estradiol
estrogen
event segmentation
executive function
functional connectivity
glucocorticoids
hippocampus
hypothalamic-pituitary-adrenal (HPA) axis
levopoda (L-DOPA)
longitudinal studies
mediated
multivoxel pattern analysis (MVPA)
myelin
oscillations
structural connectivity
sulci
trait anxiety
ventricles
white matter hyperintensities

CHAPTER THREE

Cognition and Aging

Learning Objectives

- Discuss the effects of aging on cognitive processes including attention executive function, motor control, and language, using methods including functional and structural MRI, resting state fMRI, ERP, and DTI.
- Understand the ways in which cognitive demands for older adults may be greater than for young adults, and how these demands may necessitate additional neural activity at lower levels of task difficulty. This may make it impossible for neural activity to increase at higher levels of difficulty.
- Gain an appreciation for the number of ways that executive function and cognitive control may intersect with other cognitive processes.
- Learn about potential cognitive and neural effects of training programs for older adults, as well as challenges to establishing the effectiveness of interventions.

3.1 Introduction

Many people may appreciate that cognition declines with age, but which specific abilities are affected? And is there anything that we can do to minimize the effects of aging? Cognition is widely disrupted with age, but different abilities are affected to various degrees. For example, some components of attention, including searching for a particular stimulus or detecting an "oddball" stimulus in an array, are impaired with age. Executive functions, including working memory and inhibition, can be affected by aging. Because these abilities intersect with a number of other ones, the effects of age can be widespread. These changes with age also affect *when* cognitive control processes are engaged such that engaging these processes late may be less effective than doing so early. To capture the breadth of cognition, the chapter will briefly review literature on motor control and language. Age differences in even relatively basic motor processes can cascade to affect a number of other cognitive processes. In contrast, language is preserved with age, though there can still be changes to the underlying neural system. Despite a great deal of interest in cognitive training programs, evidence for *effective* programs is limited thus far. The chapter will review evidence on the effects of cardiovascular exercise programs, the approach that has emerged as the most promising thus far, as well as some cognitive training regiments.

3.2 Attention

Attention allows one to focus on external stimuli and information in the outside world. This external focus is in contrast to the internal focus of the default mode network discussed in Chapter 2 or the internal refreshing of information discussed in Chapter 4. The frontoparietal network supports external attention. A variety of tasks have been used to assess different aspects of attention, and a handful of them will be discussed in this section. Because attention plays a role in focusing on particular information as well as ignoring distraction from irrelevant information, it has strong links with other processes, including interference and inhibition (reviewed in Section 3.3) and memory (reviewed in Chapter 4).

One function of attention is to search for information as quickly as possible, as in a visual search task. In these tasks, the selection could be based on a single feature, such as looking for an X in an array of Os. These are known as **feature searches**. **Conjunction searches** require searching for an item that is the combination of two features, such as a green X in an array of Xs and Os that are green or red. See Box 3.1 for an example of the task. Conjunction searches take longer than feature searches. Aging disproportionately slows conjunction search, perhaps due to greater difficulty ignoring irrelevant distractors (Madden et al., 2014). In the visual search task, older adults engaged frontoparietal regions associated with attention more than younger adults. Counter to what might be expected, the increased activity occurred across all conditions rather than only for the most attention-demanding ones (Madden et al., 2014; Madden et al., 2007). Higher levels of activity, however, were associated with longer reaction times for both younger and older adults (Madden et al., 2014). Another visual search study indicated age differences in the regions related to performance for searching for single unique items, with activity in the frontal eye fields and the superior parietal lobule linked to longer reaction times in older adults (Madden et al., 2007). Taken together, these results indicate the importance of the frontoparietal network in attentional tasks and illustrate the convergence between neural and behavioral measures, such that increased

Box 3.1 Tasks Used to Measure Attention and Interference

Visual Search Task

In this task, participants search for a particular stimulus (here, a green X) and respond as quickly as possible. Searching for a conjunction of features (e.g., green and X) takes much longer than searching for a single feature (a lone X or green stimulus).

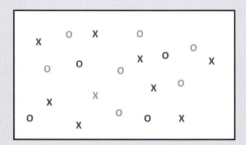

Stroop Task

In the Stroop Task, participants name the color of the font as quickly as possible. Reading color words that are incongruent with the color of the font ("incongruent" column) is slower than control trials or congruent words (the word "red" in red font)

Control Task	Incongruent	
XXXXX	YELLOW	← Response: "Red"
XXXXX	GREEN	← Response: "Blue"
XXXXX	BLUE	← Response: "Yellow"
XXXXX	RED	← Response: "Green"

Go/No Go Task

In the go/no go task, participants respond quickly to some stimuli, (here, letters), but they are instructed to withhold responses to a particular letter (here, X).

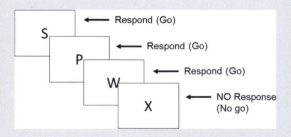

Box 3.1 (cont.)

Flanker Task

In the flanker task, participants respond quickly to the central stimulus (here, the sign <) by pressing the corresponding key. The central item is flanked by either congruent items or incongruent items; this should slow responses due to interference.

Congruent trial

<< < <<

Incongruent trial

>> < >>

A black-and-white version of this figure will appear in some formats. For the color version, please refer to the plate section.

---

activity in frontoparietal regions occurs alongside slower reaction times for older adults.

White matter changes with age also impact performance on attentional tasks. As measured with DTI, older adults generally evidence reduced integrity of white matter with age (Madden, Whiting, Cabeza, & Huettel, 2004) (see Chapter 2 for a broader discussion of white matter changes with age). Breakdowns in white matter integrity with age, assessed with DTI, may account for some of the increases in frontoparietal activity with age on a visual search task (Madden et al., 2007). Moreover, different white matter tracts may be related to performance across the age groups. On an **oddball task**, in which an infrequent stimulus required a different button press than standard stimuli, reduced integrity of the splenium predicted slower reaction times for younger adults (Madden, Whiting, Cabeza, et al., 2004). This pathway is involved in transferring visual information across the two hemispheres. In contrast, reduced integrity of the internal capsule predicted slower reaction times for the older adults (Madden, Whiting, Cabeza, et al., 2004). This pathway is thought to connect the prefrontal cortex and subcortical structures. Thus, quick transfer of information across hemispheres may be most important for young adults to perform well whereas frontal control processes may be most important for older adults.

In measuring distraction with ERPs, Getzmann and colleagues (Getzmann et al., 2013) employed an auditory distraction task in which participants responded to standard tones but ignored deviant tones. The study compared young adults to high- and low-performing older adults. Three stages of processing are captured by different ERP components. The **mismatch negativity (MMN)** occurs in frontocentral sites when a deviant tone is detected, and this is thought to occur without attention (e.g., the different tone is detected even if someone is engrossed in reading a book rather than listening for the tones). This component decreases with age, but the decrement was most pronounced in low-performing older adults compared to young adults. The next component is the P3a, which reflects automatic attention-switching. Compared to young adults, the amplitude of this component was reduced in the high-performing older adult group, and its latency was longer for the low-performing older adult group (see Chapter 1 for explanation of amplitude and latency). Finally, reorienting negativity occurs as a participant returns to the original task after distraction, and is reflected in frontocentral sites. Compared to young adults, the amplitude of this effect was reduced and the latency later with age. The ERP components were related to performance: individuals more vulnerable to distraction exhibited weaker MMN and stronger P3a responses. These results showed that distraction, orientation, and refocusing are all affected by aging. Even high-performing older adults were impacted, underscoring the heighted vulnerability to distraction with age.

Attentional selection can affect which aspects of complex information are attended to and processed further, interacting with other systems and processes. In one study investigating selective attention, participants viewed transparent pictures of faces and places that were superimposed over each other (Schmitz et al., 2010). Participants made judgments about the faces, making places irrelevant for the task. Consistent with the task selection demands, younger adults exhibited **adaptation**, or reduced responsivity over repeated trials, in their neural response to faces (occurring in the fusiform face area), but not to the unattended places. Older adults, however, showed adaptation in both regions, including to the unattended places (in the parahippocampal place area). The fact that older adults responded to both types of information reflected older adults' difficulty inhibiting, or ignoring, the irrelevant information. In addition, there was some evidence for later attentional selection processes in older adults. Rather than successfully suppressing initial activity in visual regions, older adults engaged the middle frontal cortex, perhaps in an attempt to control the competing visual place information that they continued to process rather than ignore. These results are in line with the idea that early attentional selection processes support more effective ignoring of information (i.e., the places). With aging, early selection is impaired, contributing to older adults' vulnerability to distraction. See Section 4.2.1 for discussion of related memory processes and findings.

Expectations may allow people to prepare to attend to the relevant aspects of information. In the case of motion, younger and older adults can detect the onset of motion faster when they have expectations about the direction of the motion. In research using ERP methods, the N1 component, an early (~100 ms) sensory and attentional component that has been localized to motion-selective areas of visual cortex, was larger for trials that violated expectations. Furthermore, the N1 response tracked the magnitude of the expectation violation (Zanto et al., 2013). With age, the N1 response was reduced when horizontal motion was expected, possibly reflecting the need for communication across both hemispheres. White matter tracts between hemispheres degrade with age more than those within a single hemisphere. Overall, the results indicated that expectations affect early processes, indexed by the N1, and that expectations of horizontal motion are disproportionately impaired with age, perhaps due to disrupted connections between hemispheres.

In summary, there is evidence that a variety of attentional processes are disrupted with age. Frontoparietal networks are important for visual search, including the speed of searches. The contribution of different white matter pathways suggests that different processes (e.g., transfer of information across hemispheres; frontal control mechanisms) may have the strongest links to performance for younger versus older adults. ERP data demonstrate age-related impairments in distraction, orientation, refocusing, and expectation. Early selection may also be disrupted with age, preventing older adults from ignoring irrelevant information. Failing to suppress information early instead necessitates the late recruitment of frontal control processes.

3.3 Executive Function

Executive function generally supports the controlled processing of information, which is important for many tasks. Several subprocesses contribute to executive function: updating and monitoring which information is in mind, suppressing irrelevant information, and shifting between tasks or mental states (Hedden & Yoon, 2006; Miyake et al., 2000). Together, these subprocesses allow some information to be attended to and manipulated while other information is kept online but out of focus. Executive function operates like a cook, switching among pots and pans to attend to the one requiring focus at any moment while other pots and pans simmer on back burners. In this way, you can see that the attentional processes reviewed above can be a part of executive function; the distinction drawn in this chapter between these processes is not a firm one. Moreover, executive function can intersect with any other ability, such as memory (e.g., how does one control what information is retrieved from memory? How are different numbers juggled in the mind during mental arithmetic) or language (e.g., how are different languages kept distinct in a bilingual's brain?).

A large meta-analysis (Turner & Spreng, 2012) compared the effects of aging on two different processes related to executive function: working memory and inhibition. Working memory, introduced in Chapters 1 and 2, involves keeping information in mind and active for a particular period of time. While the process is discussed in more detail in Chapter 4, it is also discussed here in order to contrast the effects of aging to other executive functions. Across nineteen studies of the effects of aging on working memory, older adults evidenced more activation of anterior and dorsal regions of the prefrontal cortex, while young activated a more posterior region of this cortex as well as frontal eye fields and posterior visual regions (Turner & Spreng, 2012; see Figure 3.1). **Inhibition** is the ability to exert control over strong responses or thoughts that are automatic or dominant, perhaps as the result of prior learning and experience (e.g., a native English speaker inhibiting the English word for "book" when attempting to retrieve the Spanish word "libro"). A frontoparietal network, including ventral prefrontal, motor, and parietal cortices, is implicated in attention-demanding tasks or executive

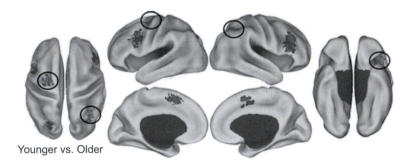

Younger vs. Older

Figure 3.1 Regions exhibiting age differences in working memory, based on a meta-analysis. The circled regions note those areas activated more by younger than older adults, and the other activity reflects regions activated more by older than younger adults. See text (Section 3.3) for discussion of the regions.

Adapted from Turner and Spreng (2012), *Neurobiology of Aging*, Figure 1.

Box 3.2 Neural Regions Associated with Executive Function

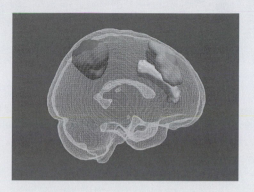

A black-and-white version of this figure will appear in some formats. For the color version, please refer to the plate section.

The frontoparietal network implicated in executive function includes the parietal cortex (dark orange), the DLPFC (light orange), and the anterior cingulate (yellow).

Figure created with software from Madan (2015), Creating 3D visualizations of MRI data: a brief guide, *F1000Research, 4,* 466.

function (as reviewed by Turner & Spreng, 2012; see Box 3.2.) In the comparison of age differences across thirteen studies, younger adults engaged visual association areas more than older adults, whereas older adults engaged frontal regions, including the right inferior frontal, left medial superior frontal, and presupplemental motor regions more than younger adults (Turner & Spreng, 2012; see Figure 3.2). A direct comparison of inhibition and working memory regions reveals that the underlying networks are distinct for both younger and older adults, indicating that the functions continue to be specialized and distinct with age. The patterns of activity, however, differ somewhat with age. Whereas inhibition is characterized by greater activation of the same network with age, working memory is marked by the recruitment of additional regions, particularly bilaterally, with age.

For tasks used to assess inhibition, behavioral data tend to show increased reaction time and errors with age, though neural data show variable patterns. In the Stroop Task, people experience interference

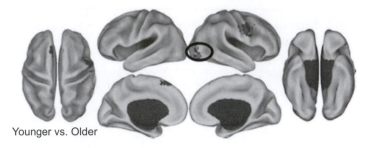

Younger vs. Older

Figure 3.2 Regions exhibiting age differences in inhibition, based on a meta-analysis. The circled region marks an area activated more by younger than older adults, and the other activations reflect regions activated more by older than younger adults. See text (Section 3.3) for discussion of the regions.
Adapted from Turner and Spreng (2012), *Neurobiology of Aging*, Figure 2.

when attempting to read the color of a font rather than the word itself (e.g., the word, "blue," printed in green font, to which one should respond "green"). See Box 3.1 for examples of all of the tasks discussed in this section (Stroop, go/no go, and flanker). Older adults recruit many of the same regions as young adults during the Stroop Task, with one study finding heightened activation of the left inferior frontal cortex (Langenecker et al., 2004). Another study of the Stroop Task reported that older adults activated the DLPFC and some parietal regions less than young adults, while activating other regions, including the inferior frontal and anterior cingulate, more than young adults (Milham et al., 2002). The pattern of increased activation with age, particularly in prefrontal regions (Nielson et al., 2002) as well as in the putamen/globus pallidus (Langenecker et al., 2007), also occurred for a go/no go task (Nielson et al., 2002). This task requires that participants should respond only to some stimuli, or particular combinations of stimuli (e.g., alternating letters, but not to a repeated letter), but they should withhold responses to other stimuli. The flanker task is another inhibitory paradigm in which participants respond to a central target (e.g., the sign <) that is flanked by either congruent (e.g., < < < < <) or incongruent items that would necessitate an opposing response (e.g., > > < > >). For the incongruent trials, older adults engaged the bilateral middle prefrontal gyrus more than younger adults, who engaged the region in the right hemisphere only (Colcombe et al., 2005). Poorer-performing older adults exhibited more bilateral prefrontal cortex activity than better performers, so the pattern of heightened activation with age was interpreted as dysfunctional rather than compensatory (see Figure 3.3). White matter density differed in task-relevant regions across age groups

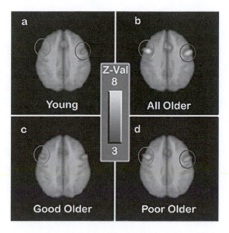

Figure 3.3 Older adults exhibited engagement of the middle prefrontal cortex more bilaterally than younger adults, who showed activation of only the right prefrontal cortex. Poor-performing older adults also evidenced more engagement bilaterality (note the brighter activation pattern, denoting the peak Z-score (Z-Val)) than good performers.
From Colcombe et al. (2005), *Psychology and Aging*, Figure 1.

and was linked to performance, leading the authors to suggest that white matter integrity may contribute to patterns of functional activation.

Despite some inconsistent results, these studies overall suggest that older adults rely on regions of the prefrontal cortex more than young adults during inhibitory tasks. This pattern of greater recruitment may reflect greater difficulty resolving interference with age.

Another component of executive control is **task switching**, the ability to alternate between different task demands (e.g., responding based on spatial position versus color in complex stimuli that include both types of information). Task switching engages the frontoparietal attention network, with the network engaged more during task switching than when performing only one type of task. The effects of aging on this network are mixed. One study of aging found that older adults engage the prefrontal cortex for single trial blocks as well as blocks in which the tasks alternated (DiGirolamo et al., 2001). Another study reports a different pattern, with a more spatially constrained network engaged by younger compared to older adults (Gold et al., 2010). In line with the DiGirolamo et al. (2001) study, the switch condition did not produce larger age differences in neural activity. The integrity of white matter pathways, however, was more strongly coupled with performance. This was assessed with DTI, measuring the integrity of the left superior longitudinal fasciculus, a white matter pathway between frontal and parietal regions, using the fractional anisotropy (FA) measure. Higher FA in this pathway predicted lower switch costs. This pattern indicated that younger and older adults who had more integrity in their white matter pathways were less disrupted by switching. As the measure of integrity explained much of the age effect, the authors suggested that perhaps the loss of integrity in this tract degraded information transfer between frontal and parietal regions, thus slowing older adults' task performance.

Another study (Madden et al., 2010) investigated switch costs on back-to-back trials, as opposed to performing the same judgment on two trials in a row. Although there were no significant age differences in the neural regions engaged during switch trials, relative to repeat trials, other measures differed across the age groups. In a comparison of sustained activity, assessed across an entire block of trials rather than treating each trial individually, younger adults activated the left inferior frontal gyrus more than older adults. Furthermore, measures of functional connectivity, assessing the interdependence of regions in the network, indicated that higher levels of connectivity were related to better performance. This measure of connectivity accounted for the majority of the effects of aging on decision reaction time in the task. These data suggest that functional connectivity may be a particularly sensitive assay of individual differences in performance. This measure may prove more useful than comparing the activation levels of specific neural regions, which show inconsistent effects of aging across the literature.

To summarize the fMRI literature on task switching, it was initially surprising that the effects of aging are no larger for switch trials than with no-switch trials. The use of additional measurements and methods may help to explain that finding, in that state effects (e.g., sustained activity over several trials) or connectivity between regions, be it functional or structural (e.g., white matter integrity), are more tightly linked to task performance than are trial-by-trial measures of cortical activation. Recent work with a network approach has focused on these regions as part of the dorsal attention network. This network tends to be more activated by older adults and sometimes in conjunction with additional regions (Eich et al., 2016). The dorsal attention network tends to be anticorrelated with the default mode network, although the distinction between the networks is weakened with age (Spreng et al., 2016).

With ERP, task-switching demands are reflected in a heightened P3 component, measured over the parietal cortex (West & Moore, 2005). Aging reduced the parietal P3 component in a comparison of switch and no-switch trials (see Figure 3.4). This age difference could reflect poorer learning of the switch cue at the beginning of the trial or difficulty updating working memory to reflect the current task demands.

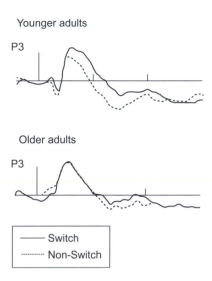

Figure 3.4 Younger adults exhibit a larger P3 (denoted by the difference between the two lines, with switch > non-switch) at a posterior midline channel during task switching than controls.
Adapted from West and Moore (2005), *Cortex*, Figure 3.

A follow-up study (West & Travers, 2008) capitalized on the potential for ERP to differentiate distinct subprocesses of task switching due to its excellent temporal resolution. Several processes were affected by aging, indicating overall that older adults have difficulty applying the correct task set up front, perhaps related to the suggestion that older adults employ later and less effective control strategies than young adults.

fMRI studies support the idea that younger adults implement control early and more effectively than older adults. Younger adults engage the lateral prefrontal and posterior parietal cortex in response to cues, potentially allowing them to prepare for the task (Jimura & Braver, 2010). Older adults engage these same regions later, perhaps to resolve the conflict they experience. This study additionally offered a novel approach by investigating temporal dynamics, rather than simply age differences in the magnitude of activity. By employing a mixed blocked/ event-related design for their fMRI study, Jimura and Braver (Jimura & Braver, 2010) could distinguish activity sustained across trials from transient trial-by-trial neural activity (Jimura & Braver, 2010). The anterior prefrontal cortex response illustrates the complex and complementary information offered by these measures. Whereas young adults exhibited sustained activity in this region that was higher for mixed blocks (multiple different judgments) than single task blocks, older adults did not show sustained activity in either condition. This finding was thought to reflect older adults' diminished cognitive control abilities during task switching, and was suggested to be a pervasive pattern across the aging brain. However, in comparisons of the transient activity, the same region was more responsive for older adults: the anterior prefrontal cortex was more engaged for older than younger adults and responded more to switch than no-switch trials in older but not younger adults. The pattern of sustained activity showed different relationships with performance across the age groups, with greater sustained activity related to smaller switching costs in younger but not older adults. In contrast, the transient activity was related to *larger* switch costs for older adults. Across these different levels of analysis, younger adults seemed to exhibit more of a proactive, or "up-front," control style, reflected in the sustained activation of regions. Proactive control is ultimately more effective in dealing with cognitive conflict than older adults' deployment of reactive control, as reflected in the later transient activation of the regions.

Cognitive control deficits with age may belie difficulty maintaining goal states, challenging one's ability to maintain relevant information and suppress irrelevant information. The lateral prefrontal cortex is thought to support this ability. These ideas were tested in a study that probed the effects of aging on the different elements of keeping a goal in mind (Paxton et al., 2008). When the task required participants to maintain a goal in order to respond correctly, older adults committed more errors than young adults. Conversely, when maintaining the goal could lead to errors, older adults performed better than young adults. In terms of neural activity, older adults engaged prefrontal regions more than the young but over longer delays, failed to activate the critical frontal regions of the dorsolateral prefrontal and inferior frontal cortex as much as the young, although they activated other frontal regions more than the young. Thus, older adults experienced the most difficulty maintaining goals over time, and the DLPFC may be important for this ability (see Figure 3.5).

A longitudinal study following the same individuals over an approximately 3-year time span substantiated that changes in the neural response to task switching occur with age, even over such a brief period (Hakun et al., 2015). Older adults activated premotor (peak in the middle frontal gyrus) and ventrolateral prefrontal cortical regions more during the later session than the earlier one. In contrast to the pattern of increased fMRI activation, DTI measurement of the FA of white matter tracts showed the expected pattern of decline with age. In the later session, FA decreases were pronounced in frontal commissures,

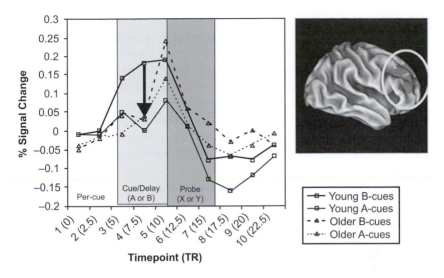

Figure 3.5 Younger adults engage cognitive control processes early (the x-axis displays time, in terms of the number of scans (TR) and seconds), denoted by the arrow indicating the difference between the solid lines during the cue/delay period of the task, rather than waiting until the probe appears. The right DLPFC (region circled in the right panel) subserves control processes.
Adapted from Paxton et al. (2008), *Cerebral Cortex*, Figure 4.

including the genu and anterior portion of the body of the corpus callosum. The breakdown in white matter with age could lead to the increases in fMRI activity, as more decrease in FA in the body of the corpus callosum was related to higher increases in activity in ventrolateral prefrontal regions. Furthermore, increases in activity in a posterior region of the left VLPFC related to slower reaction times. The results converge with other literature to suggest that increases in prefrontal activity with age may reflect the higher levels of conflict that older adults experience on demanding tasks, and their attempt to harness additional resources to support performance.

Recent studies target the effects of age on *resolving* interference, which required comparison of correct and incorrect responses (based on K. Murphy & Garavan, 2004). Overall, the frontoparietal network was more active for incongruent than congruent correct flanker trials (D. C. Zhu et al., 2010). Older adults exhibited less activity than younger adults, with the frontal regions of activation shifted slightly with age. Compared to previous studies, these results suggest that the inclusion of error trials may contribute to reports of age differences.

Another study (Salami et al., 2014) investigated interference resolution by a multivariate partial least squares approach which considers all of the conditions simultaneously (rather than a subtraction of a subset of conditions). This method is more sensitive to distributed patterns of activity in regions operating as a network rather than discrete focal activations. In addition to the dorsolateral prefrontal and parietal regions discussed throughout this section, conflict resolution also relies on the dorsal anterior cingulate. A network including the left DLPFC and anterior cingulate cortex exhibited heightened responses to interference for older than younger adults across multiple types of interference. The results again highlight the importance of considering performance, as high-performing older adults tended to engage the same network as young, indicating that in interference tasks, a young adult pattern of brain activity may be optimal with age.

Response inhibition, withholding the strong urge to make a response, is disrupted with age, consistent with other impairments in inhibitory processes. One study found that the effects of aging on the neural markers of inhibition varied based on the task demands (Sebastian et al., 2013). Older adults activated core inhibitory regions, including the middle and inferior frontal, presupplementary motor, and parietal cortices, more than young adults on the most basic of the tasks (go/no go), which requires withholding an action. As demands increased (i.e., with a spatial component of the task that required inhibition), older adults recruited additional inhibitory control regions. However, at the highest level of task difficulty, which required canceling an action that was prepared for execution, older adults exhibited *lower* levels of activation than young adults, potentially reflecting that the task exceeded their capacity (see Figure 3.6). The data seem consistent with the CRUNCH and STAC models (see Section 1.3), in that older adults increased recruitment of neural resources until their capacity is exceeded.

The overall takeaway from the study of executive function is that the effects of age can appear in multiple guises, including increases or decreases of the activity in regions, or the recruitment of smaller or broader networks and regions. The nature of age differences depends on many factors, such as which aspects of executive function are targeted by tasks and whether measures identify effort/interference or success. The heterogeneity of changes to the frontal cortex with age is nicely illustrated in a study (Goh, Beason-Held, An, Kraut, & Resnick, 2013) that compared the effects of aging on frontal engagement across a variety of tasks, including components of executive function. Whereas higher activity in various frontal regions was associated with better performance for some

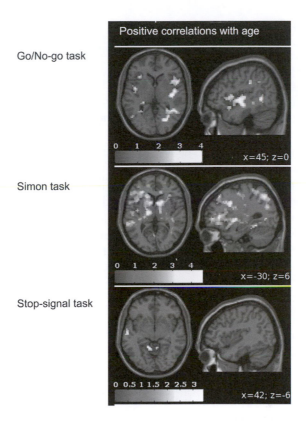

Positive correlations with age

Go/No-go task

0   1   2   3   4

x=45; z=0

Simon task

0   1   2   3   4

x=-30; z=6

Stop-signal task

0 0.5 1 1.5 2 2.5 3

x=42; z=-6

Figure 3.6 Older adults activate inhibitory regions more than younger adults for the go/no-go and Simon tasks (top two panels). The figure displays regions (axial views on the left and sagittal views on the right; x- and z-coordinates in MNI (Montreal Neurological Institute) space) that are more active with increasing age. When a task exceeds inhibitory capacity, as in the stop-signal task (bottom panel), older adults do not engage inhibition regions more than young.

Adapted from Sebastian et al. (2013), *Neurobiology of Aging*, Figure 3.

tasks, higher levels of activity in other frontal regions indicated *poorer* performance on other tasks. Which processes are evoked by a task critically determines the regions implicated and whether aging is associated with increases or decreases in activity. Recent work has also considered the role of the frontoparietal control network as a "switch" coupling with either the default mode or dorsal attention network depending on the goals of the task. With aging, these networks seem to be less segregated (Grady et al., 2016; Ng et al., 2016).

3.4 Motor Control

Although a large body of research has probed cognitive deficits with age in a number of different abilities, less work has been conducted on the effects of aging on motor performance. Declines in motor abilities with age, including difficulty coordinating movements, slowing, and challenges integrating multiple cues, may demand more cognitive resources to support motor tasks (Seidler et al., 2010). These greater demands are harder to meet as neural regions supporting movement, such as the motor cortex and the cerebellum, decline, alongside cognitive regions. For example, motor learning is associated with the volume of the caudate, a region of the basal ganglia, as well as the lateral prefrontal cortex. People with larger volumes learned to perform mirror-drawing better than those with smaller volumes (K. M. Kennedy & Raz, 2005). Similarly, the volume of motor regions predicted which older adults better learned to play a strategic video game. Faster game playing time was related to having larger volumes in a number of frontal regions, including the anterior cingulate and supplementary motor areas, the postcentral gyrus, and the cerebellum. (Basak et al., 2011). The involvement of these regions reflects improvements in motor learning of the task, such as complex skill acquisition (e.g., learning to use a mouse), sensory and motor feedback, and cognitive control.

White matter changes with age may affect motor task performance. Abilities such as **bimanual coordination** rely on transferring information across both hemispheres. As the corpus callosum contains the majority of the connections between the two hemispheres, this bundle of white matter plays a major role in motor abilities. Disruptions of the neurotransmitter systems also contribute to motor changes with age. Norepinephrine changes, related to neuron loss in the locus coeruleus, impacts motor learning mediated by the cerebellum. Dopamine changes have been linked to a number of aspects of motor tasks, including balance, gait, and fine motor control. Little work, however, has investigated tasks that are primarily motor with direct connections to cognition (as reviewed by Seidler et al., 2010).

In terms of the activation of neural systems, changes occur with age in even seemingly basic motor processes. Whereas motor processes are largely lateralized in young adults, with **contralateral** organization (e.g., the right hemisphere cortical regions controlling movement on the left side of the body), activation is more bilateral in older adults. During a button press task, older adults showed greater activity in the same contralateral motor regions as young adults, as well as in **ipsilateral** regions

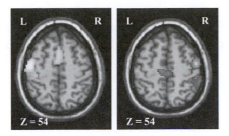

Figure 3.7 Younger adults activate left motor regions more than older adults (left panel) whereas older adults activate right motor regions more than young adults (right panel). The literature overall suggests some differences in laterality of activation for movement with age, although the literature is inconsistent regarding whether age differences occur predominantly ipsilateral or contralateral to the moving hand.
From Riecker et al. (2006), *NeuroImage*, Figure 5.

(on the same side of the body as the hand) that were not implicated for young adults (Mattay et al., 2002). These regions had bilateral activations in the sensorimotor cortex, the putamen, and the cerebellum as well as contralateral premotor and supplementary motor areas. Because more activation was linked to faster reaction times, the age-related changes were interpreted as compensatory. However, the effects of aging are not consistent in the literature, as another study reported that older adults activated core contralateral motor regions *less* than young adults, with increases in activation with age occurring primarily in ipsilateral regions (sensorimotor and premotor cortex) (Riecker et al., 2006; see Figure 3.7). Even though this was a simple finger tapping task, the findings were interpreted as suggesting strategy differences across the age groups. A similar finding emerged in a study of finger tapping employing an MVPA approach. The results demonstrated that older adults show more dedifferentiation in the motor system than young adults such that neural distinctiveness, how distinct the pattern is for left versus right finger taps, is reduced across a number of motor regions with age (Carp, Park, Hebrank, et al., 2011). Another study directly pitted compensation versus dedifferentiation explanations, finding that older adults engaged basic motor control regions as well as higher level sensorimotor and frontal regions for a task requiring coordination of both limbs (Heuninckx et al., 2008). More engagement of the higher level sensorimotor and frontal regions was linked to better performance, supporting a compensation interpretation. Increased motor activity with age is a pervasive finding, even when task performance (i.e., on a memorized sequence of finger movements) is automatic (Wu & Hallett, 2005b).

Taken together, these studies indicate that older adults consistently recruit more neural activity during motor tasks than young adults. This is in contrast to many other domains, in which older adults often exhibit patterns of underactivation. This increased activation with age is especially striking in that it occurs on basic motor tasks (e.g., button presses, finger tapping), meaning that age-related disruption to the motor system could impact a number of different processes, particularly because studies – be they emotional, affective, or social – often rely on motor responses. As noted in the review by Seidler and colleagues (2010), the typical motor demands of tasks may further deplete cognitive resources, exaggerating the effects of aging.

3.5 Language

Language is generally well preserved with age, with older adults having intact comprehension and better vocabularies than young adults (Shafto & Tyler, 2014; Wingfield & Grossman, 2006). The preservation with age is somewhat surprising, given the rapid stream of speech that a listener must disambiguate. One might expect language comprehension to be impaired in older adults as a result of cognitive losses with age that lead to slowing and reduced working memory capacity, increased incidence of hearing loss with age, and the demands that effortful listening makes on cognitive resources (Shafto & Tyler, 2014; Wingfield & Grossman, 2006).

In their review, Wingfield and Grossman (2006) discuss two networks involved in language comprehension. The first is a core sentence processing network that encompasses the left ventral inferior frontal cortex (including **Broca's area**) and a left posterolateral temporal region (including Wernicke's area). The second is an extended network spanning both hemispheres and some subcortical structures. This network supports processes such as working memory and executive functions that are necessary for language comprehension under demanding conditions (Wingfield & Grossman, 2006). In a study substantiating this model that employed a task including difficult sentence structures, the data showed that younger adults relied on the core network, whereas high-performing older adults supplemented that network by recruiting the homologous right hemisphere region of the posterior temporal site (Grossman et al., 2002a). The low-performing older adults, in contrast, recruited prefrontal regions from the extended network. Their recruitment pattern reflects the working memory demands of the task and an attempt to compensate via general executive function rather than language-specific systems (Grossman et al., 2002b). Related results emerged from a study of functional connectivity (Antonenko et al., 2013). In young adults, the functional connections to a region of Broca's area occurred predominantly in the left hemisphere syntax network, and the coherence of this network related to better task performance. Connectivity was reduced in this network for older adults and did not relate to their performance. As an alternative, older adults had increased connectivity in a broader set of regions, including in the right hemisphere, though this pattern was associated with poorer performance.

Wingfield and Grossman (2006) also discuss the potential for older adults to recruit additional processes at a late time point for challenging linguistic tasks. This idea is similar to the tendency for older adults to recruit late rather than early control processes (e.g., Jimura & Braver, 2010).

In order to determine how aging affects the neural network across the life span, a study investigated four different groups aged 20–65 (Manan et al., 2015). The same network was generally implicated across the life span for speech perception, including the superior and middle temporal gyri, the pre- and postcentral gyri, **Heschl's gyrus** (primary auditory cortex), and the cerebellum. Interestingly, the pattern of activation increased from the 20s to the 30s, but then declined for the age groups 40+. Calculations of laterality indicate that activations become more right-lateralized for the oldest group of participants (50–65 years old). These results suggest that the reorganization of the neural response in response to aging unfolds over multiple stages, with an initial increase in activity occurring in earlier adulthood and a shift in lateralization occurring later.

Functional connectivity has proved useful in investigating alterations with age in speech regions. One study used a **verbal fluency task**, during which participants generated exemplars for a given category (semantic) or first letter (orthographic). This task engaged a network consistent with previous studies of speech production, which encompassed the inferior and middle frontal, supplementary motor, precentral, inferior temporal, and inferior parietal cortices, the insula, and the cerebellum in both younger and older adults (Marsolais et al., 2014). Despite similar behavioral performance, age differences emerged within subnetworks. Older adults had reduced connectivity in portions of the semantic fluency and orthographic fluency networks. The results suggest that even if some regional activations are age-equivalent, as in the core language network described by Wingfield and Grossman (2006), the connectivity of the regions may still be impacted by aging.

In their review, Shafto and Tyler (2014) contrast the age-related preservation of syntactic processing to age-related impairments in word production. An example of these difficulties occurs in "**tip of the tongue states**" (TOTs), the familiar experience of being unable to retrieve a word even though it feels highly accessible, perhaps due to recalling some of its features (e.g., the first letter). TOTs increase with age, potentially due to weakened phonological access. Whereas younger adults engage cognitive control regions during TOTs, older adults generally do not, although higher performers look more like younger adults than lower performers. The authors suggest that perhaps harnessing additional neural regions at a lower level of difficulty limits older adults' ability to engage the regions during TOTs.

As language processing should be tightly linked to the ability to perform a number of other cognitive tasks, a few studies have examined the intersection of language and cognition. Young and middle-aged participants judged whether two words were from the same or different category, in an ERP study that took place in the presence of distracting speech (speech noise throughout the experiment) (T. M. Davis & Jerger, 2014; T. M. Davis et al., 2013). The researchers first compared the **N400** component of the auditory ERP across age groups to assess the effects of aging (T. M. Davis et al., 2013). The N400 tends to be larger for semantically unrelated information, possibly reflecting the extent of additional linguistic processing needed for unrelated information. The amplitude of the N400 was greater (i.e., more negative) for younger than middle-aged adults in response to word presentation. However, in a difficult condition in which words were semantically unrelated, middle-aged adults were more sensitive to distracting speech presented on the right side than the left. This finding reflects the **right ear advantage**, in that people tend to better understand speech presented to the right ear than the left. Middle-aged adults showed greater N400 negativity when there was competition on the right than on the left, suggesting that the right ear advantage is affected in middle-aged adults with relatively normal hearing. Thus, with aging, individuals may be more affected by speech competition at a lower level of difficulty, depleting cognitive resources required for more difficult tasks. Another study targeted the **late positive component (LPC)**, considered to be a marker of context updating and additional evaluation and processing of meaning, and assessed 700–800 ms after stimulus presentation in this study (T. M. Davis & Jerger, 2014). Although the LPC was similar across the age groups for trials drawn from the same category (e.g., horse – mouse), the trials drawn from different categories (e.g., horse – lamp) revealed age differences, with a greater LPC peak amplitude for middle-aged than younger adults. The pattern of the electrodes also differed with age.

Whereas the LPC amplitude was greatest at posterior sites and decreased more anteriorly for young adults, it was more consistent across all of the midline electrodes for middle-aged adults. It is possible that the increased frontal response in middle-aged participants represents an attempt at compensation, but comparisons of performance and electrophysiological signal with (as in the case of this study) and without distraction would be necessary to further evaluate this idea.

The effects of aging on speech comprehension in a noisy environment were further probed to assess individual differences. In this task, there were multiple speakers, simulating a "cocktail party" setting (Getzmann et al., 2015). The listener had to monitor for stock prices which were presented across different speakers with varying spatial locations. A number of components differed among young, old-high performers, and old-low performers. Although a group of young adults was matched to the old-high group on performance, age differences still emerged. For older compared to younger adults, the latency of the **P2** was delayed, reflecting poorer attentional control, and the N400 was absent, reflecting impaired semantic processing. Comparing groups of older adults on performance, the old-high group had larger amplitudes than the old-low group for the P2–N2 complex, indicating that the high performers increased their allocation of attention and inhibitory control in an attempt to compensate for losses in the system.

3.5.1 Language and Hearing Loss

A handful of studies have begun to investigate how the brain is affected by changes to hearing acuity, which typically declines with age. During a task in which individuals listened to a sentence and made a judgment about who performed the action, older adults with good hearing activated the primary auditory cortex in the left and right hemispheres more than older adults with poorer hearing (Peelle et al., 2011). Poor hearing acuity was associated with disruption of the auditory cortex, a primary sensory processing area, in conjunction with the effects on the **thalamus**, a critical region for transferring information to other cortical regions. The combination of these regions signifies the pervasive nature of hearing loss, as it affects both sensation and transfer of information. The impairment of these processes intimates how hearing loss could broadly impact cognitive processes.

Another indicator of the central role of hearing in cognition emerges from a longitudinal study of hearing impairment. Following up their prior behavioral research indicating links between hearing loss and poor cognitive outcomes, Lin and colleagues (Lin et al., 2014) evaluated the neural basis of these effects. Brain volumes at baseline from participants from the Baltimore Longitudinal Study of Aging were compared to volumes approximately 6 years later to assess the rate of change for those with normal hearing compared to those with hearing impairment. Although the two groups did not differ at baseline, those older adults with hearing impairments at baseline exhibited more atrophy over the next 6 years across the entire brain, particularly in the gray matter in the temporal lobes (Lin et al., 2014). This pattern of greater atrophy marked superior, middle, and inferior temporal gyri on the right hemisphere only. Converging with functional results (Peelle et al., 2011), these results further illustrate the potential cognitive vulnerabilities and challenges that emerge from even mild levels of hearing loss.

In summary, even though language processes are relatively well preserved with age, age differences nevertheless emerge in the underlying neural activity. The pattern and magnitude of these age differences reflect the impact of the highly related factors of hearing loss, cognitive ability, and task difficulty. Low-performing older adults recruit neural regions more broadly but less selectively, sometimes including cognitive regions that may reflect higher working memory demands. High-performing older adults exhibit more bilateral recruitment of language regions, although it is important to note that functional connectivity data indicate the hemispheres may be less integrated with age. Furthermore, older adults' tendency to recruit additional regions at lower levels of task difficulty than young adults may impact their ability to respond in more difficult tasks. Although fMRI studies of language do not seem to identify patterns of greater activity with age in the same regions that young adults engage, there are findings of increased amplitude and increased latency in ERP components with age. These patterns, alongside greater network recruitment, may indicate increased task demands with age. Such demands may exaggerate aging effects at higher levels of task difficulty, in line with CRUNCH and STAC models.

3.6 Training Cognitive Ability

Interest in training programs to improve cognitive abilities and stave off the deleterious effects of aging has soared in recent years. This is partially due to the rise in the number of older adults, as baby boomers reach late adulthood, but it is also related to the sometimes aggressive marketing and inflated claims of improving "brain health" through video or computer games. Despite the rise in interest in training, rigorous research has supported relatively few programs thus far. In part, this reflects the need to develop programs that train cognitive ability broadly. For example, doing hundreds of word search puzzles over several months may make one quite skilled at word search puzzles but does that training **transfer** to other domains, such as memory? Limited evidence of transfer has dampened enthusiasm for many training regimens investigated thus far. Although I will review the training outcomes linked to neural changes with age, the reader should keep in mind the paucity of converging studies on any given ability and the few training regimes that have demonstrated transfer to broader cognitive abilities (Hertzog et al., 2008).

3.6.1 Physical Activity

Exercise and physical training are the most robust programs studied thus far, with potential beneficial effects on cognition with age. Aerobic training has shown the most reliable changes to neural circuits thus far. Initial studies relied largely on survey and self-report methods, which were useful to compare larger samples of individuals across wider ranges of natural behavior. For example, older adults reporting higher levels of physical activity performed better on some cognitive tasks and had higher levels of gray and white matter volume (Benedict et al., 2013). In recent years, studies that employ true **interventions**, in which participants are randomly assigned to an experimental (e.g., aerobic exercise) or control group, have proliferated. Impressively, one of the first papers (Colcombe et al., 2004) to establish that increased cardiovascular fitness in humans is linked to improved cognitive functioning included both self-report and intervention data. In the first experiment, high-fit was compared to low-fit older adults and there was enhanced activity in the frontoparietal attention network with higher levels of fitness (see Figure 3.8). This pattern emerged again for participants randomly assigned to an aerobic training program compared to a stretching and toning control group for 6 months in the second experiment. In both studies, performance on the flanker interference task, responding to a cue embedded among congruent or incongruent stimuli, benefited from higher levels of exercise or fitness. This initial study both demonstrated neural changes related to fitness and suggested that an intervention as short as 6 months could begin to sculpt the brain and improve cognitive performance.

The same intervention, assigning sedentary older adults to an aerobic training group or a toning and stretching control group, impacted the

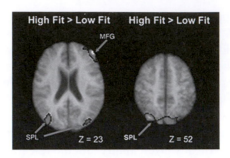

Figure 3.8 Older adults with higher levels of fitness exhibited greater activation of the frontoparietal network (including the middle frontal gyrus (MFG) and superior parietal lobule (SPL), displayed here) than those with lower levels of fitness. The images reflect the difference in activation across the groups (high fit > low fit).
From Colcombe et al. (2004), *Proceedings of the National Academy of Sciences of the United States of America*, Figure 2.

volume of the brain (Colcombe et al., 2006). The increases in volume affected not only cortical gray matter but also white matter for older adults, particularly in the frontal cortex. Gray matter increases occurred in a region of the anterior cingulate cortex that extended into the supplementary motor cortex, right inferior frontal gyrus, and left superior temporal gyrus, regions implicated in attentional and memory processes. White matter increases emerged in anterior tracts of the corpus callosum. These increases were limited to older adults; younger adults were unaffected. A later study employed DTI to probe how exercise changed the integrity of the microstructure of white matter. Training in a walking program for 1 year increased older adults' FA in frontal and temporal lobe white matter tracts compared to the control group, although the increases were not directly associated with improved scores on a working memory task (Voss, Heo, et al., 2013). Although it is unclear how changes to volume and microstructure impact behavior, the increases are notable given the tendency for gray matter volume and white matter integrity to decrease with age (see Sections 2.2 and 2.3). Converging evidence suggests that white matter microstructure may be the mechanism linking higher levels of cardiorespiratory fitness with higher levels of performance on a spatial working memory task (Oberlin et al., 2016), suggesting that structural brain changes related to exercise could result in improvements to cognition.

Another exercise intervention study examined changes to the hippocampus in sedentary older adults who completed a 1-year aerobic

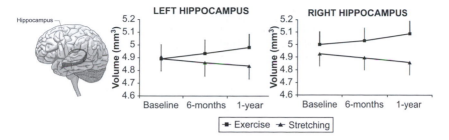

Figure 3.9 An aerobic exercise intervention program (top lines, with squares) increased the volume of the hippocampus bilaterally for older adults, compared to a stretching control group (bottom lines, with triangles), over 1 year. The hippocampus is noted in dark grey on the image.

Adapted from Erickson et al. (2011), *Proceedings of the National Academy of Sciences of the United States of America*, Figure 1.

exercise program, compared to those who completed stretching and toning (Erickson et al., 2011). At the conclusion of the 1-year program, anterior hippocampal volume had increased 2% from baseline in the exercise group. This is particularly striking in contrast to the control group, which exhibited a 1.4% decline in volume over the year (see Figure 3.9). Thus, aerobic exercise has the potential to offset 1–2 years of volumetric loss associated with aging. Based on research with rodents, it is thought that **brain-derived neurotrophic factor (BDNF)** may be the molecular pathway through which exercise affects the brain (Erickson et al., 2013). In the Erickson et al. (2011) study, volumetric increases in the anterior hippocampus bilaterally were matched by increases in serum BDNF levels, perhaps reflecting cell proliferation or dendritic expansion that contribute to the volume of the anterior hippocampus. Such an explanation is consistent with research across mice and human models showing that exercise increases cerebral blood volume in the dentate gyrus region of the hippocampus, consistent with **neurogenesis**, the growth of new neurons (Pereira et al., 2007).

Individual differences may also reveal who will benefit the most from exercise interventions. A polymorphism in a gene that affects levels of BDNF impacts the effects of exercise on working memory performance (Erickson, Banducci, et al., 2013). There is less secretion and distribution of BDNF in individuals with the methionine-specifying (Met) allele in comparison with those with the valine-specifying (Val) allele. A sample of over 1,000 middle-aged adults (ages 30–54) provided information on their level of weekly physical activity and were genotyped. For lower levels of physical activity, the Met carriers (those with at least one copy of the Met allele) performed worse on measures of working memory than the Val homozygotes. At higher levels of physical activity, the groups were equated. These data converge with the idea that BDNF is a factor in how exercise benefits memory and brain aging.

In an attempt to separate cardiorespiratory fitness from activity levels, one study employed accelerometers to measure physical activity over 1 week as well as measures of oxygen consumption during an exercise test (Burzynska et al., 2015). These measures were related to the variability in brain activity during a resting state scan. Results revealed that older adults with higher levels of physical activity, whether it was for light, moderate, or vigorous activity, exhibited higher levels of variability across cortical regions including prefrontal, anterior cingulate, hippocampal, and temporal regions. Higher variability is considered a marker of healthy brain functioning (see "Future Directions," Section 1.5.6), and tends to decline with age (Grady & Garrett, 2017). Surprisingly, cardiorespiratory fitness did not have a direct relationship with brain variability in this study (Burzynska et al., 2015), potentially meaning that the most important factor is to have an engaged, physically active lifestyle rather than one associated with high levels of cardiorespiratory fitness. If true, that would support programs that are easier for sedentary older adults to implement (e.g., increasing activities such as walking or gardening). Given that greater variability in brain states may contribute to a number of different cognitive functions, these results identify a potential effect of physical activity that could have widespread effects on brain fitness and cognitive ability. Other research, however, indicates the importance of high levels of cardiovascular fitness, but not physical activity, in having higher levels of functional integrity of networks with age (Voss et al., 2016). These discrepancies underscore the early state of the literature and the future work that is needed to clarify the complex relationships among many factors.

Although the data suggest that aerobic exercise is one of the most beneficial interventions for aging, several questions remain. Many of the studies thus far have investigated sedentary older adults in interventions up to 1 year long. Undoubtedly, there is little downside to recommending a program of exercise for those physically able but currently sedentary. But how much do older adults who exercise a moderate amount stand to benefit from continuing exercise at the current rate or increasing it? Although a year-long intervention is impressive from a research perspective, how do these gains unfold over several years? Some research provides hope for the longevity of gains due to training. In a

follow-up 2 years after the conclusion of a year-long exercise intervention, older adults who remained active after a physical activity intervention performed better on a speed of processing task and engaged regions
of the frontoparietal attention network, including the DLPFC, more than
sedentary participants from the control group (Rosano et al., 2010). It
may be that the studies so far have captured the largest possible gains
from exercise by targeting older, out-of-shape populations who stand to
benefit the most by going from no exercise to some. In addition to
questions of dose (how much exercise?) and individual differences (for
whom?), research must be done to identify which types of exercise
programs are most beneficial for cognitive and brain health (Erickson,
Gildengers, et al., 2013). It is also of interest to note that the neural
changes thus far seem to occur largely in frontal and hippocampal
regions that are related to higher-order cognition. Whether these regions
emerge because they are more malleable and flexible than other regions
or because they are more prone to age-related atrophy is unknown at
this time (Erickson, Gildengers, et al., 2013). Although direct links
between increased brain volume and task improvement are rare in
studies thus far, the impacted regions are the ones expected to play a
large role in cognition. The lack of findings thus far may reflect constraints of the study methods, in that large samples may be needed to
detect small effects emerging over a long period of time.

3.6.2 Meditation

Research has been burgeoning on the potential benefits of meditation
and mindfulness. Because much of this research initially studied people
who already practiced meditation or other mindfulness programs, the
samples naturally included middle-aged and older adults. As cortical
volume loss can begin during one's 20s, atrophy can be examined across
the life span rather than only in older adulthood. Samples from two early
studies had an average age of around 37, which allowed for tests of age
effects. Meditation has been suggested to slow the progression of brain
degeneration due to normal aging processes (Luders & Cherbuin, 2016).
The first study compared cortical thickness in experienced meditators to
control participants, finding thicker right middle and superior frontal gyri
in meditators. Furthermore, experienced meditators did not show
greater thinning for the older participants, although thinning occurred
with age for the control group (Lazar et al., 2005). In a study comparing
the brains of adults who practiced Zen meditation to a control group,
total gray matter volume decreased with age in the controls, although

this was not the case for the group of meditators (Pagnoni & Cekic, 2007). In addition, the volume of the putamen differed with age across the groups; the preservation of the region in meditators may reflect the benefits of meditation on tasks requiring cognitive flexibility. Increases in gray matter volume also emerged in a study examining the effects of a mindfulness-based intervention for older adults with sleep disturbances (Kurth et al., 2014). In this study, the volume of the precuneus increased over a 6-week intervention period in a small sample of older adults. Although it is surprising that volume decreases also occurred in a number of regions, particularly over such a short intervention period, the authors speculate that this may reflect the remediation of sleep disturbances in this sample.

In addition to changes to cortical volume, meditation affects resting state connectivity and cognition. Fluid intelligence, cognitive abilities that rely on logic and online processing, declined less across the sample with age in practitioners of yoga or meditation than in controls (Gard et al., 2014). Resting state measures indicated that networks were better integrated and more resilient to damage for people who practiced yoga or meditation compared to controls. Likewise, older adults reporting higher levels of mindfulness as a trait, based on a questionnaire assessing one's ability to focus and be present in the moment, exhibited greater connectivity of the default mode network than those reporting lower levels (Prakash et al., 2014). Heightened connectivity may reflect intact functioning of neural networks, and the potential benefits of focused attention. Specifically, results emerged in the posterior cingulate cortex and the precuneus, regions that may be particularly implicated in coordinating different nodes of the default mode network and interfacing this network with others, including the cognitive control network. Based on these potential connections between networks in this region, it has been proposed that long-term training in mindfulness may have the potential to ameliorate cognitive control deficits that occur with aging, improving performance and reducing rumination (Prakash et al., 2014).

The studies on mindfulness interventions such as meditation and yoga are tantalizing, but caution is warranted. This is particularly the case as many of these studies rely on very small samples or self-selected groups rather than random assignment to interventions (e.g., people who have been practicing meditation for years, rather than assigned to a controlled program as part of the research study protocol). It may be that individuals who pursue meditation or yoga differ in many ways from those who do not; their brains may differ beforehand rather than as a result of the mindfulness programs. Moreover, correlational studies that examine existing relationships among variables also cannot determine causality. For example, in the functional connectivity study described above (Prakash et al., 2014), it was not possible to determine that higher mindfulness *causes* greater connectivity of the default mode network. It may be that a more tightly integrated default mode network leads one to report higher levels of mindfulness, or that a third, untested factor causes both higher connectivity and higher scores. Experimental evidence is needed before suggesting that people practice meditation to improve their "brain health." Finally, claims about aging in the studies reviewed in this section are typically based on middle-aged samples and comparisons across individuals, rather than drawn from longitudinal studies of the same individuals experiencing neural and cognitive changes over time. The Kurth et al. (2014) study is notable in that it includes brain measurements pre- and post-training, but there were only six participants in the study.

3.6.3 Cognitive Interventions

In terms of training cognitive control abilities, one successful approach used a video game that trained multitasking ability as part of a racing game (Anguera et al., 2013). The game was designed to be adaptive, meaning that it would adjust to the user's skill level and become more challenging as the user improved. Older adult participants were required to play the game at home for 1 hour a day, three times a week, for 4 weeks. Multitasking typically impairs performance, particularly for older adults, but training reduced multitasking costs compared to control groups. Training benefits were maintained over 6 months post-training. Immediately after training, there was some transfer to untrained working memory tasks. Neural changes as a result of training were assessed with EEG. Multitask training improved older adults' midline theta power and functional connectivity (via long-range theta coherence), measures associated with cognitive control. Post-training, older adults' patterns of brain activity resembled young adults', unlike the patterns pre-training or from control groups. In another study, a training task to ignore auditory distractors in older adults also implicated frontal theta and theta coherence. The markers were thought to reflect reduced attention to the distracting information (Mishra et al., 2014).

Another study employed dual-task training in an attempt to improve attentional and executive control (Erickson, Colcombe, Wadhwa, et al., 2007). The trained group received 5 hours of practice on dual-tasks over 2–3 weeks in sessions that were adaptive and included feedback on performance. As a result of training, older adults' reaction times were faster and they were more accurate, and the benefits extended to dual-task conditions that were not trained. fMRI scans from pre- and post-training revealed changes as a result of training. The altered patterns of activations in the DLPFC and VLPFC reflected a combination of increases and decreases in activity with age, and overall were interpreted as evidence for plasticity in neural engagement with age. The degree of activation in some regions in the DLPFC and VLPFC correlated with the magnitude of the performance improvement in the dual-task condition. The study overall revealed benefits to behavior and neural activation, such that younger and older adults evidenced more equivalent prefrontal activity as the result of a fairly brief intervention.

Early attentional components may be amenable to training with age. One study trained older adults on a visual discrimination task for 10 hours over 3–5 weeks and found that training enhanced the N1 and N2 components for the more challenging condition (Mishra et al., 2015). These components measure early sensory processes, related to attentional control or early decision processes, and may contribute to selective attention. Furthermore, participants that had the largest increase in amplitude for the N1 component from pre-test to post-test exhibited most improvement on an untrained working memory task, suggesting transfer. Another study adopted a broad training approach over 4 months. Participants practiced tasks emphasizing speed, attention, and memory, and training effects were assessed on a visual search task (i.e., locating an arrow at a particular angle in a particular color in an array of other arrows) (Wild-Wall et al., 2012). In terms of ERP measures, trained participants had more pronounced N1 and P2 components than those in the control groups, suggesting that trained participants may have enhanced their attention to stimuli (N1), as well as their processing of relevant features (e.g., angle, color) of stimuli (P2).

Training impacts neural activity not only during tasks but also during rest. After 12 weeks of training in a strategy-based program to increase cognitive control by emphasizing attention, reasoning, and creative problem-solving, resting measures of brain activity were collected (Chapman et al., 2015). Compared to controls, the trained participants exhibited more cerebral blood flow and greater functional connectivity in the networks underlying the default mode and the executive function. DTI measures of fractional anisotropy (FA) indicated that the uncinate fasciculus, a white matter tract connecting the left middle temporal and left superior medial frontal gyrus, increased as a result of training. Changes to this white matter tract could impact the transmission of information, having widespread effects on cognition.

Thus, some cognitive training programs seem to produce robust effects with some evidence for transfer to other abilities. Successful programs broadly train a number of cognitive abilities (e.g., dual-task or multitasking performance) in an adaptive, challenging fashion. Neural measures reflect improved connectivity within networks, more "young-like" patterns of neural activity, and heightened markers of early attention. However, much work is needed to assess whether cognitive training programs can induce long-lasting benefits in abilities that affect performance in the real world.

3.6.4 Memory Training

Despite voluminous research investigating working memory training, there are few studies assessing neural effects with age. One study with 5 weeks of training employed an adaptive procedure for visuospatial and verbal working memory tasks in the training group compared to practice at only the lowest level of difficulty for the control group of older adults (Brehmer et al., 2011). In the fMRI scans post-training, activity decreased in regions of the frontal (including the DLPFC), temporal, and occipital cortex for trained older adults compared to controls. In some regions related to memory and attention, larger decreases in activation were related to larger increases in performance. Furthermore, there was evidence of transfer of benefits to untrained tasks. These results indicate the potential benefits of working memory training in older adults in comparison to a well-designed control condition. This study is also notable in that training supported the engagement of a more streamlined, efficient neural system in older adults, perhaps reflecting the reduced load on attentional networks when a working memory task is well trained.

Another fMRI study of working memory focused on transfer, predicting that transfer to other tasks would occur when both tasks relied on the same neural circuit (Dahlin et al., 2008). Training for 5 weeks on a regime focused on updating, the executive process that keeps the focus of working memory current, led to activation of the striatum during both the trained letter memory task and the n-back task (i.e., which number appeared "n" number of trials ago?; see Box 4.1) in young adults. Older adults showed more limited transfer, with no behavioral benefits on the 3-back task. The results suggest that the striatum may play an important role in transfer for young adults. However, aging may impair functioning of the striatum (it was not implicated in the task pre-training for older adults), possibly accounting for the limited transfer in older adults.

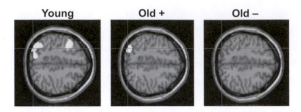

Figure 3.10 Memory training in the method of loci enhanced occipitoparietal activation in younger adults, and in older adults who exhibited a benefit in performance (old +), but not in older adults who did not show a performance improvement (old –).

Adapted from Nyberg et al. (2003), *Proceedings of the National Academy of Sciences of the United States of America*, Figure 3.

In addition to working memory training, there are programs training long-term memory in healthy older adults. Although memory is the focus of Chapter 4, we will briefly present findings relevant to the cognitive training literature. One of the earliest interventions suggested that older adults may experience difficulties in enhancing neural engagement in response to training. Nyberg and colleagues (2003) trained younger and older adults in the method of loci. This mnemonic relies on attaching new information to be learned (e.g., a grocery list) to an existing, well-known mental map (e.g., the layout of one's home). As we mentally "walk" along the known route, we "deposit" items to be remembered at landmarks along the way. The items can later be retrieved by mentally revisiting the route. Although overall age differences in memory performance were exaggerated post-training, older adults' performance varied widely with some showing no improvement. PET scans were used to evaluate neural changes as a result of training. Comparing activity post-training to pre-training revealed activity in the left DLPFC and a region of the left occipitoparietal cortex. Older adults engaged the occipitoparietal region, but this was apparent only for those whose performance improved from training. Frontal activity, in contrast, did not emerge for any of the subgroups of older adults (see Figure 3.10). These results indicate disruption with age in the higher-order, effortful strategic processes reflected in the prefrontal cortex, and in posterior regions likely reflecting visual imagery. Both of these patterns were thought to reflect limited cognitive reserve or plasticity with age, limiting older adults' potential for training benefits.

Later studies have yielded more robust neural activity in response to training, suggesting that older adults' brains have ample plasticity in the domain of memory. Training older adults to use memory strategies that emphasize thinking about the meaning of presented words (e.g., considering the pleasantness or personal relevance of a word; generating a sentence that includes the word) eliminated age differences in memory performance (Kirchhoff, Anderson, Smith, Barch, & Jacoby, 2012). Importantly, the training sessions increased the self-initiated use of strategies; whereas pre-training older adults reported using strategies less than younger adults, they reported more strategy usage post-training and the self-rated level matched that of younger adults. In terms of neural changes, older adults activated the medial superior and right precentral gyrus as well as the left caudate more after training. Notably, these enhancements were selective to a condition in which participants intentionally attempted to encode information in to memory. Improvements in memory performance after training were specifically related to changes in neural activity in the prefrontal and lateral temporal cortex, regions that reflected young adults' strategies to learn information. Furthermore, improvements in **recollection** (discussed in Section 4.3.3) – vivid re-experiencing of previously encountered information in memory – were reflected in increased hippocampal activity post-training (Kirchhoff, Anderson, Smith, Barch, & Jacoby, 2012). Right hippocampal activity during retrieval was related to activity during learning in the prefrontal and lateral temporal regions that seemed to underlie training benefits in the other study (Kirchhoff, Anderson, Barch, et al., 2012). Together, these papers demonstrate the ability to use memory training programs to remediate aspects of memory that are particularly vulnerable to aging, although research on the neural response to long-term memory training is in its infancy.

Chapter Summary

- Attention is often linked to greater activity in frontal regions with age when assessed with fMRI, but there were some declines in frontal components in ERP studies.
- Executive function demands often engage frontal regions more in older than younger adults. There can also be differences in the timing, with younger adults engaging these processes earlier and older adults later.
- Age-related declines in even basic motor abilities can have profound effects on a host of other abilities, as more cognitive resources may be depleted in supporting motor function.
- Language function is largely preserved with age. The core language comprehension network is similar for younger and older adults, although there is reduced functional connectivity with age. Word

production and language processes that interact with cognition are
more affected by aging, and hearing loss exacerbates cognitive and
neural changes.

- Although data are lacking to support the effectiveness of many types
of training programs, several studies have converged to demonstrate
the effects of cardiovascular exercise as well as some cognitive interventions, including video games, and training of attention and memory
processes.
- More research is needed to understand the mechanisms that lead to
changes from training programs and to substantiate additional promising interventions, such as meditation. This is particularly important
to resolve questions of who benefits and under what conditions.

Discussion Questions

1. What neural network underlies attention? What types of tasks have
   been used to investigate the effects of age on attention?
2. What types of processes fall under "executive functions"? How does
   aging affect these processes and the supporting neural regions? Why
   is it that engaging control processes later is considered to be less
   effective than earlier?
3. What aspects of language are more versus less affected by aging?
   What neural networks support language, and under what conditions
   do these show age differences?
4. How widespread is the support for different types of training programs? What is the biggest limitation to establishing the effectiveness
   of training? Why are researchers cautious about promoting interventions to the general public at this point?
5. What types of cognitive processes and brain areas are affected by
   exercise interventions? By cognitive training? What types of training
   programs do you think will prove most effective?.

For Further Reading

Erickson, K. I., Voss, M. W., Prakash, R. S., Basak, C., Szabo, A., Chaddock,
        L., ... White, S. M. (2011). Exercise training increases size of hippocampus
        and improves memory. *Proceedings of the National Academy of Sciences of
        the United States of America*, 108(7), 3017–3022.
Hertzog, C., Kramer, A. F., Wilson, R. S., & Lindenberger, U. (2008).
        Enrichment effects on adult cognitive development: can the functional

capacity of older adults be preserved and enhanced? *Psychological Science in the Public Interest*, *9*(1), 1–65.

Jimura, K., & Braver, T. S. (2010). Age-related shifts in brain activity dynamics during task switching. *Cerebral Cortex*, *20*(6), 1420–1431.

Turner, G. R., & Spreng, R. N. (2012). Executive functions and neurocognitive aging: dissociable patterns of brain activity. *Neurobiology of Aging*, *33*(4), 826.e821–826.e813.

Key Terms

adaptation
bimanual coordination
brain-derived neurotrophic factor (BDNF)
Broca's area
conjunction searches
contralateral
feature searches
Heschl's gyrus
inhibition
interventions
ipsilateral
late positive component (LPC)
mismatch negativity (MMN)
N400
neurogenesis
oddball task
P2
recollection
right ear advantage
task switching
thalamus
tip of the tongue states (TOTs)
transfer
verbal fluency task

CHAPTER FOUR

Memory and Aging

Learning Objectives

- Explore different subtypes of memory. How are these different types of memory affected by aging?
- Compare the effects of aging on the neural regions that support different types of memory.
- Within long-term memory, understanding which processes are more or less affected by aging.

4.1 Introduction

What part of cognition is most affected by aging? Many might answer that question with "memory." Indeed, research in this area supports the notion that many aspects of memory decline with age. This chapter will review the wealth of literature on how aging changes the neural regions that underlie memory, and discuss models informed by neural data to account for these differences. Not all types of memory, however, are similarly impacted by aging, and the chapter will pay attention to different domains of memory and subprocesses within long-term memory. Discussion of memory for social and emotional information is contained in Chapters 5 and 6 rather than the present chapter.

4.2 Working Memory

As discussed in previous chapters, working memory is the type of memory that involves keeping information in mind and active for a short period of time, such as when one rehearses a phone number before dialing it. This type of memory relies on passive storage of verbal (e.g., words) or visuospatial (e.g., a map) information, as well as a buffer that combines information into episodes, and executive control, which coordinates different demanding cognitive processes, as occurs when adding numbers in one's head (Baddeley, 2003). Aging seems to particularly impact the ability to manipulate information in working memory, as opposed to simple passive rehersal of the information (Craik & Jennings, 1992; Craik & Rabinowitz, 1984). This means that older adults may perform as well as young when information needs to be repeated back, but reordering or performing computations in one's head could be harder for older adults.

The neural organization of working memory changes with age. Whereas the young exhibit specialized activation of the left DLPFC for verbal working memory and the right DLPFC for visuospatial working memory (E. E. Smith & Jonides, 1998), this laterality breaks down with age. In an early PET study, older adults exhibited more bilateral prefrontal activations for both visuospatial and verbal working memory tasks, particularly in regions thought to support rehearsal of information (Reuter-Lorenz et al., 2000). This pattern of activity was suggested to reflect compensation for age-related declines in cognitive ability, as older adults who performed better on a working memory task activated the secondary hemisphere more than their lower-performing counterparts (Reuter-Lorenz et al., 2001; Rypma & D'Esposito, 2001).

Later work elaborated the ideas about compensation, testing working memory performance and corresponding neural activity across different levels of difficulty. This was manipulated by varying the working memory load, or how much information must be kept in mind at a given time (e.g., four items rather than two; see Box 4.1 for examples of working memory tasks). In the example tasks, load can be increased with more items in memory (e.g., in the set, or using a 3-back rather than 2-back task). Using fMRI, Cappell and colleagues (2010) found that older adults engaged additional regions of the DLPFC at lower levels of task difficulty than younger adults (See Figure 4.1). Furthermore, younger adults continued to increase levels of activity in the primary region to support task performance as task difficulty increased. In contrast, older adults' level of activity peaked at a lower load and did not increase much more for the higher load. These findings are consistent with the CRUNCH model, which purports that older adults need to recruit more neural resources than young, who require fewer neural resources to complete tasks (Reuter-Lorenz & Cappell, 2008). Similar findings have been reported with other methods such as EEG, showing increases with memory load for children, young adults, and older adults. However, only younger adults continued to increase activity for the highest load (Sander et al., 2012). Capacity limits are important to consider, as the highest load may be more than older adults can successfully hold in mind; age differences may be reduced when age groups are

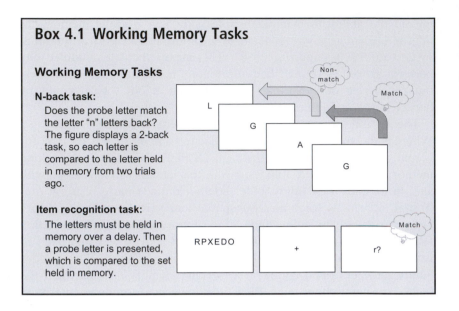

Box 4.1 Working Memory Tasks

Working Memory Tasks

N-back task:
Does the probe letter match the letter "n" letters back? The figure displays a 2-back task, so each letter is compared to the letter held in memory from two trials ago.

Item recognition task:
The letters must be held in memory over a delay. Then a probe letter is presented, which is compared to the set held in memory.

matched on capacity. In an fMRI study by Schneider-Garces and colleagues (2010), each participant's working memory span was assessed. Although older adults exhibited the expected pattern of higher activation at lower loads than young, the age groups looked similar when data were adjusted relative to the participants' spans. This finding underscores the importance of considering individual differences in ability, particularly when comparing neural activity across the age groups.

An interesting approach to evaluating the CRUNCH model married working memory load with assessments of dedifferentiation (Carp et al., 2010). The logic was that people rely on specialized neural resources for demanding tasks until the difficulty exceeds capacity. Whereas neural activity should be highly specialized as one approaches capacity, it will be less distinct at higher loads when people are unable to accurately perform the task. This study adopted a multivoxel pattern analysis (MVPA) approach to compare distributed patterns of activity across the brain during the period in which information was maintained in working memory. Indeed, older adults exhibited more distinct patterns of activity in the prefrontal and parietal cortex at a lower level of task difficulty than younger adults, consistent with the fact that this level of difficulty approached their capacity limits. But for higher task loads, younger

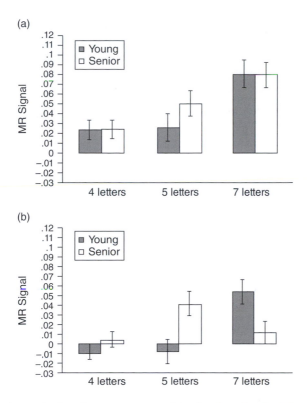

Figure 4.1 The graphs show how engagement of the dorsolateral prefrontal cortex (DLPFC) is affected by increasing working memory loads. The measure (y-axis) is the average MR signal change, in arbitrary units. Left DLPFC (panel *a*) activity increases as the task becomes more difficult (holding up to 7 letters in working memory), but does not differ with age. In the right DLPFC (panel *b*), older adults (white bars) recruit the region at a lower level of difficulty (5 letters), but underrecruit the region, compared to young adults (gray bars), at the highest level of difficulty (7 letters).
Adapted from Cappell et al. (2010), *Cortex*, Figures 3 and 4.

adults had more distinct patterns of activation than older adults, as the task was beyond the older adults' abilities. The authors concluded that both dedifferentiation and compensation should be considered, particularly in terms of task difficulty, when explaining the effects of aging on cognitive ability.

Marcia Johnson and colleagues suggest that another process even more fundamental than working memory may be disrupted with aging, that of **refreshing**, which is the ability to reactivate a stimulus in one's mind shortly after seeing it. For example, participants silently read words and on some trials were cued to think of a word that they saw half a second before (refresh), as opposed to seeing and reading the same word again or a new word (M. K. Johnson et al., 2004). An area of the left DLPFC supported refreshing in young adults, but not in older adults. This impairment in neural activity supporting refreshing is thought to contribute to deficits in more complex cognitive processes, including working and long-term memory, in older adults. In addition, older adults experience more interference from irrelevant items during refreshing (Raye et al., 2008). This finding highlights older adults' vulnerability to interference for even the most basic tasks of mentally reading or refreshing information.

4.2.1 Inhibition in Working Memory

Although Chapter 3 covered age differences in inhibition, its specific role in working memory will be discussed here. Some research has emphasized the important role cognitive control plays in preventing interference in working memory, in line with suggestions of deficits in inhibition with age (Hasher & Zacks, 1988; Zacks & Hasher, 1997). Gazzaley and colleagues (2005) developed an fMRI task that relied on attentional processes to enhance neural activity for information that was relevant, or to suppress it for irrelevant information. Participants viewed a stream of faces and scenes, and were directed either to remember the faces (ignoring the scenes) or to remember the scenes (ignoring the faces). This manipulation made some information relevant, and some irrelevant. A probe face or scene then appeared, and participants had to determine whether or not it had appeared in the previous set. Compared to passively viewing stimuli, younger adults exhibited the expected pattern of enhanced activation of regions related to scenes (left parahippocampal/lingual gyrus) when attempting to remember the scenes, and reduced activation of these regions when attempting to ignore scenes (see Figure 4.2). Older adults also showed enhanced activity of regions related to scenes when attempting to remember them. But when attempting to ignore scenes, the region responded no differently than for the passive view condition. Thus, Gazzaley and colleagues concluded that older adults' ability to suppress was selectively impaired. Moreover, the neural marker of suppression predicted performance on the working memory task, such that a reduced ability to suppress was related to poorer performance on the working memory task.

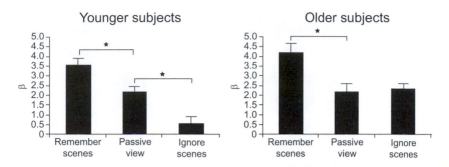

Figure 4.2 The graphs depict estimates of neural activity in scene-selective regions. Whereas younger and older adults both show enhancement (increase for the remember scenes condition, compared to passive view), only younger adults evidence suppression (decrease for the ignore scenes condition, compared to passive view).
Adapted from Gazzaley et al. (2005), *Nature Neuroscience*, Figure 2.

Subsequent research employed EEG and ERP measures, which have excellent temporal resolution. One study revealed age differences in the P1 amplitude and the N1 latency (Gazzaley et al., 2008). These findings indicate that aging may affect suppression through early perceptual processes that occur within the first 100 ms after a stimulus appears. Unlike younger adults, who showed suppression early in the task, older adults only evidenced suppression in the latest time window, at 500–600 ms. But the late suppression was not sufficient to overcome the early deficits, resulting in impaired working memory performance for older adults. Even warning participants in advance about which information should be attended to and ignored did not allow older adults to suppress irrelevant information (Bollinger et al., 2011).

4.3 Explicit Long-Term Memory

Explicit memory focuses on memory for information that one learns consciously. This encompasses learning which words were on a list studied in the lab, learning new vocabulary words or facts from the news, and memory for the episodes in one's life (e.g., the birthday you spent at the amusement park). Long-term memory spans a wide range of time frames, from memories from a few minutes ago to several decades in the past.

Box 4.2 Neural Regions Associated with Long-Term Memory

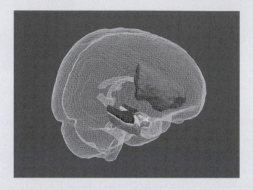

A black-and-white version of this figure will appear in some formats. For the color version, please refer to the plate section.

The bilateral inferior prefrontal cortex (medium green) and bilateral medial temporal regions, including the hippocampus (dark green) and parahippocampal gyrus (light green), contribute to explicit long-term memory, particularly for encoding information into memory.

   Figure created with software from Madan (2015), Creating 3D visualizations of MRI data: a brief guide, *F1000Research, 4*, 466.

The very first neuroimaging study of aging and memory, using PET, identified a pattern of age differences in prefrontal and medial temporal activations (Grady et al., 1995). Younger adults increased activation of left prefrontal and medial temporal regions more than older adults when forming memories of faces (see Box 4.2). Furthermore, these regions were strongly linked in young (i.e., if participants activated the hippocampus, they also activated prefrontal cortex), but not in older adults. Changes to prefrontal and medial temporal activations consistently emerged in the literature, including word learning (e.g., Cabeza et al., 1997), indicating that these regions are important to understand age differences in long-term memory.

4.3.1 Levels of Processing and Intentionality

Task instructions contribute to the magnitude of age differences in memory. **Encoding** occurs when people initially encounter information (e.g., studying a word list or entering a friend's new house for the first time), allowing memory traces to begin to be established as information is learned. During encoding, older adults benefit from explicit instructions and strategies, whereas age differences may be magnified when a strategy or task is not provided. Tasks that encourage people to think about the meaning of information (e.g., does this word denote something that is living or nonliving?), as opposed to a perceptual judgment (e.g., is this word italicized?), support deeper encoding of information into memory. This effect is known as **levels of processing**, through which information that is encoded in a deeper or more meaningful way is better remembered than information encoded more shallowly (Craik & Lockhart, 1972).

An early fMRI study (Logan et al., 2002) examined age differences in the engagement of prefrontal regions across different encoding conditions. **Intentional encoding** is a condition in which individuals know they should try to remember information, as opposed to **incidental encoding**, when individuals do not know to expect a memory test. For incidental tasks, participants often make judgments rather than passively viewing stimuli. When no strategy is provided during intentional encoding, participants must come up with their own strategies to remember information. Under these conditions, older adults underrecruited prefrontal regions compared to young adults. When a meaningful strategy was provided under incidental deep encoding conditions, older adults engaged prefrontal regions to the same extent as young (see Figure 4.3). These data were important in establishing the flexible patterns of neural activity with age. The pattern of underrecruitment was not a constant with age, but depended on how much the encoding conditions supported memory formation. In addition to the pattern of underrecruitment, older adults engaged additional prefrontal regions more than younger adults. This pattern emerged across conditions.

Not all studies converge with the results of Logan et al. (2002). Some find age deficits in prefrontal activity in the deep encoding condition (Daselaar et al., 2003; Grady et al., 2002; Grady et al., 1999; Stebbins et al., 2002). These studies also investigated medial temporal regions as a function of the level of processing. The results indicate deficits in older adults' medial temporal activity across conditions (Daselaar et al., 2003; Grady et al., 1999) and in the relationship of medial temporal lobe activity to behavior (Grady et al., 2002). Taken together, the results highlight the importance of considering the level of processing invoked by the task when interpreting commonalities or differences in the pattern of neural activity across younger and older adults.

Younger   Older

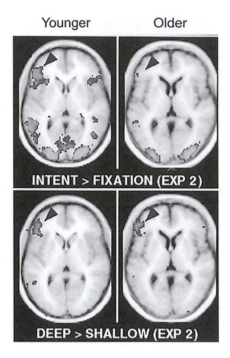

Figure 4.3 Older adults exhibited impaired activations of prefrontal cortex under intentional encoding conditions, denoted by the lack of an activation by the carrot (top row). However, incidental encoding that encouraged "deep" processing (bottom panel) eliminated these age differences. The activations in this condition are noted by arrowheads for younger and older adults.
Adapted from Logan et al. (2002), *Neuron*, Figure 3, depicting Experiment (EXP) 2 from that study.

4.3.2 Subsequent Memory

Subsequent memory paradigms compare those items successfully encoded into memory against those items later forgotten in order to investigate the neural regions linked to memory formation. Using this approach, Gutchess and colleagues (2005) found that older adults engaged prefrontal regions more than younger adults only when they successfully encoded scenes, but not when participants failed to encode the trials into memory. Older adults' increased prefrontal activity occurred with decreased engagement of medial temporal regions (e.g., parahippocampal gyrus), leading to the suggestion that perhaps prefrontal activity compensates for impoverished medial temporal activity.

Adapting the same paradigm to an ERP study led to a slightly different pattern of results, with younger and older adults exhibiting a similar frontocentral subsequent memory effect (Gutchess, Ieuji, & Federmeier, 2007). Subsequent memory effects also emerged for older adults in a verbal task (Friedman & Trott, 2000), although some studies failed to find subsequent memory effects in older adults (e.g., Friedman et al., 1996). Direct comparison of fMRI and ERP results using the same paradigm highlights some of the methodological differences across fMRI and ERP, such as the different neural regions that are amenable to measurement. For example, age differences in medial temporal lobe regions are difficult to assess with measurements from the scalp, which is how ERP data are collected.

A meta-analysis (Maillet & Rajah, 2014) across many subsequent memory fMRI studies of aging converged with some prior results while simultaneously offering new insights on the contribution of neural regions. This meta-analysis showed that medial temporal regions and prefrontal regions, specifically the inferior and middle frontal gyri, are linked to successful memory for both younger and older adults. Notably, a handful of studies reported a reduction in medial temporal activity with age for remembered versus forgotten items, although the findings for inferior and middle frontal gyri are more consistent in the literature. Posterior activations in occipital and fusiform gyri were largely consistent across the age groups, although there was some evidence that older adults underrecruited right hemisphere regions. In terms of age differences, a number of regions exhibited larger activations in older than in younger adults. Interestingly, many of these regions corresponded to regions linked to *unsuccessful* memory formation in younger adults. That is, engaging these regions during encoding may lead to forgetting. Maillet and Rajah (2014) speculate that aging may change the type of thought that occurs during encoding. Older adults could be more prone to off-topic thoughts that interfere with encoding, or they may reflect on different aspects of the stimuli during encoding. For example, older adults might engage emotional, self-relevant, and evaluative processes more than young, who focus on the perceptual details (see also Kensinger & Leclerc, 2009; and Chapters 5 and 6). More generally, age differences may reflect changes to the default network, indicating that older adults experience more difficulty "turning off" processes unrelated to encoding, and this disrupts memory formation (Grady et al., 2006).

4.3.3 Recollection

A large body of research has investigated differences with age in memory for specific qualities of information at retrieval. One major distinction is that between **recollection**, in which a participant can vividly re-experience initially studying an item (e.g., replay the thoughts they had when viewing the stimulus the first time; for example, "I remember thinking that face reminded me of a childhood friend"), and **familiarity**, a more general feeling of having encountered the stimulus before, but without reliving the experience or retrieving vivid details (Tulving, 2002). Paradigms often distinguish these by asking participants to decide whether they *remember* (recollect) or *know* (familiar) that they studied an item before. Many studies have shown that recollection, but not familiarity, is impaired with aging (e.g., Hay & Jacoby, 1999), although this finding is not universal (e.g., Duarte et al., 2010).

At retrieval, ERPs can robustly distinguish old from new items, and further distinguish remembered (or recollected) items from familiar ones. So-called "old/new" effects typically evoke two separate components: a mid-frontal component, occurring around 300–500 ms after the stimulus, responds to familiarity, and a parietal component, occurring around 500–700 ms after the stimulus, responds to recollection (as reviewed by Friedman, 2012). Note, however, there is not complete agreement on the interpretations of these components. The frontal component occurs regardless of whether participants make remember or know judgments or retrieve details, leading it to be labeled as reflecting familiarity. In contrast, the parietal component is thought to reflect recollection because it is larger for remember than know judgments and tracks the amount of information retrieved, and its later occurrence is consistent with retrieving more information than the faster signal of familiarity (Friedman et al., 2010).

In terms of the effects of age on these components, one life-span ERP study (Friedman et al., 2010), encompassing age groups from children to older adults, found the expected pattern of age effects based on the behavioral literature. Although the familiarity component (mid-frontal) was reduced for children, it was similar for adolescents through older adults (although more right-lateralized for older adults). The recollection component (parietal) evinced a different pattern, emerging robustly for childhood through young adulthood, but it was reduced for older adults. The pattern of spared familiarity and impaired recollection components with age was consistent with prior studies of younger and older adults (e.g., Nessler et al., 2007).

Notably, age differences in old/new effects do not always emerge. Supportive task conditions, such as using colored pictures, may help to equate the components in younger and older adults (Ally et al., 2008). High-performing older adults had intact recollection memory performance and robust early frontal and late parietal components, with scalp topography identical to the young adults (Duarte et al., 2006). In contrast, lower-performing older adults did not exhibit the same components as the other groups, instead showing a frontal negativity at 700–1,200 ms (Duarte et al., 2006). This pattern suggests that lower performers may drive the findings of age differences in the literature, as many studies treat older adults as one homogeneous group.

Unlike the variety of patterns that emerge in the ERP studies, fMRI studies tend to reveal age differences in the neural correlates for both recollection and familiarity (but see T. H. Wang et al., 2016). Age differences emerged across widespread regions in a number of studies of recollection (e.g., Angel et al., 2013; Duarte et al., 2010; Morcom et al., 2007) and familiarity (e.g., Angel et al., 2013; Duarte et al., 2010). Daselaar and colleagues (2006) focused on medial temporal activity. They reported that hippocampal activity, tracking recollection, is reduced with age, but rhinal cortex activity, indexing familiarity, increases with age. They also found corresponding network changes, with a network between a hippocampal/retrosplenial region and parietotemporal regions reduced with age, and a network between the rhinal cortex and frontal regions increased with age. Changes in connectivity may reflect more reliance on the rhinal cortex with age, which supports the processing of familiarity, as hippocampal networks that subserve recollection decline.

In summary, the literature on age differences in recollection and familiarity is somewhat mixed. Traditionally, older adults were thought to have intact familiarity but impaired recollection. ERP studies often align with that expectation, with the frontal component thought to reflect familiarity preserved with age, but the parietal component thought to reflect recollection impaired with age. However, fMRI studies show less consistent evidence for this pattern of preserved versus impaired processes with age.

4.3.4 Source Memory

The studies reviewed thus far have largely focused on memory for items (e.g., did I see the word "umbrella" before?), which can be determined to be "old" based on familiarity or recollection. For **source memory**, familiarity alone is not enough to make judgments regarding contextual details about where (e.g., I read it in *The New York Times*; Nancy told me about it) or how (e.g., it was in blue font; a female voice said it) information was encountered previously. Source memory is considered a more objective measure of what is remembered about an item, compared to judgments of recollection and familiarity. Despite being instructed on what type of information should be available to make a "remember" rather than a "know" judgment, people can differ in how they make judgments and how stringent they are in considering an item to be recollected, making those judgments more subjective.

Compared to item memory, source memory can be more impaired with age (K. J. Mitchell & Johnson, 2009; Spencer & Raz, 1995). During source memory judgments, parietal effects may be more intact with age, although a late-onset prefrontal component may be impaired with age (Trott et al., 1999). This seems to contradict the pattern reviewed above for the effects of aging on ERP markers of recollection (a parietal component that is larger in younger than older adults) and familiarity (a frontal component that is age-invariant). Determining source may invoke different processes than judgments of item memory, even when including judgments of recollection or familiarity.

Age differences in source versus remember/know judgments were directly contrasted in an fMRI study (Duarte et al., 2008). Lateral frontal cortex markers of source retrieval were impaired in both high- and low-performing older adults, whereas for "remember" judgments, only low-performing older adults exhibited deficits in behavioral performance and the parietal component. These findings indicate that different components support source memory and recollection. The prefrontal component invoked by source memory is a later-onset component that is extended in time and is right-lateralized in younger and older adults (Trott et al., 1999). This component is thought to index retrieval effort or retrieval mode, which may be invoked more for source memory than for old/new judgments. However, another study of source memory (Mark & Rugg, 1998) did not identify any age differences. It may be that more difficult tasks and lower levels of performance are necessary to elicit age differences. A subsequent study (Wegesin et al., 2002) assessed the importance of level of performance. The study built on the paradigm used in Trott et al. (1999), designed to enhance the performance of older adults. Under these conditions, the age differences in the late right prefrontal component persisted. Both groups exhibited the early parietal effect, although it was smaller and later in older adults (Wegesin et al., 2002). The high performance of older adults argued against the interpretation that the age differences in right prefrontal activity reflected retrieval success.

The importance of considering performance across the age groups was further underscored by J. Li and colleagues (2004). When they better equated the source memory performance of younger and older adults, removing "lucky guesses" that could dilute effects for older adults, age differences were not evident in the right parietal and late frontal components. The authors concluded that recovering information and assessing it, as indexed by these components, appear to be supported by similar neural regions with age.

There have been some suggestions that aging affects **post-retrieval monitoring**, which is the ability to evaluate the information that one has retrieved and select what is relevant to the present situation (e.g., if one retrieves the word "spoon," does it feel familiar because it was actually studied earlier or for another reason unrelated to the task?). Older adults show some dysfunction of monitoring activity, failing to increase activity in the right DLPFC as retrieval becomes more demanding (McDonough et al., 2013). In contrast, younger adults show increased recruitment of the region for word trials, which should demand more monitoring than picture trials, as pictures are more distinct. Another study, however, found no age differences in monitoring. This study examined monitoring by comparing "know" responses to "remember" responses, based on the logic that more monitoring is needed for the less certain "know" trials (T. H. Wang et al., 2016). The authors found that the same regions responded to monitoring demands across age groups, including the right anterior cingulate cortex, inferior frontal cortex, and DLPFC (see Figure 4.4). T. H. Wang and colleagues (2016) suggest that the demands of the retrieval task may drive age differences. As demands differ across studies, this has led to varying results in the literature.

Monitoring demands have been further probed with different materials, and the results underscore that age differences occur across different stimulus properties and demands (Daselaar et al., 2006; Dulas & Duarte, 2012; K. J. Mitchell et al., 2013). In an attempt to remediate age

Figure 4.4 Regions that respond to monitoring demands, defined as regions that respond more for "know" than "remember" responses in both younger and older adults. These include the right inferior frontal gyrus (the most anterior activation on the figure), insula (the most ventral), and dorsolateral prefrontal cortex (DLPFC) (the most dorsal).
Adapted from T. H. Wang et al. (2016), *Cerebral Cortex*, Figure 5.

differences in post-retrieval monitoring, Dulas and Duarte (2013, 2014) directed attention to the object alone or to its color. This manipulation improved source memory performance in both ERP and fMRI studies, but older adults continued to perform worse than younger adults. Directing attention seemed to reduce the demands on regions implicated in post-retrieval monitoring: a late right frontal component, as measured by ERP, and the right prefrontal region, as measured by fMRI. However, age differences still emerged. With ERP, older adults showed an impaired parietal old/new effect, consistent with age-related deficits in recollection (Dulas & Duarte, 2013). With fMRI, directing attention succeeded in engaging medial temporal lobe regions during the study, but older adults recruited the medial prefrontal cortex more than young adults during encoding (Dulas & Duarte, 2014). This pattern was thought to perhaps reflect a self-focus that detracts from effectively forming source memories (Dulas & Duarte, 2014).

Although this section has focused on source memory effects at retrieval, age differences have also been identified during encoding. Subsequent memory of source relies on the engagement of hippocampal and dorsolateral prefrontal regions, and older adults engage these regions less than younger adults (Dennis, Hayes, et al., 2008; see Figure 4.5). Inferior temporal activations were also impaired with age

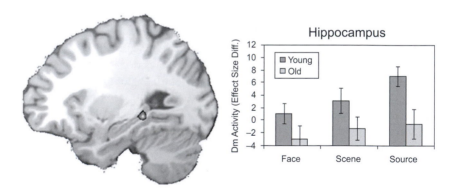

Figure 4.5 Age differences in the engagement of the hippocampus at the time of encoding. The bars depict the difference between successfully encoded items and forgotten items. This difference in this subsequent memory (Dm) effect is larger for younger (dark gray) than older adults (light gray). The age difference emerges across a variety of types of stimuli, including faces, scenes, and source memory. *A black-and-white version of this figure will appear in some formats. For the color version, please refer to the plate section.*
From Dennis et al. (2008), *Journal of Experimental Psychology: Learning, Memory, and Cognition*, Figure 2.

but these extended beyond source memory to item memory. Whereas functional connectivity for the hippocampus was strongest with posterior regions in younger adults, this pattern exhibits a PASA-like shift to anterior (including PFC) connectivity with age.

In summary, age differences emerge in most source memory studies, despite the variety of patterns of age differences that emerge. Although some studies find support for changes with age in retrieval success, post-retrieval monitoring, and the strength of memories, the evidence is mixed for any one of these interpretations. Carefully considering task demands so that comparable processes are compared across studies seems important for future work to reconcile divergent findings.

4.3.5 Associative Memory and Binding

Like source memory, **associative memory**, or **binding**, can be particularly impaired with age (Chalfonte & Johnson, 1996; Naveh-Benjamin, 2000). This type of memory can include remembering pairs of items (e.g., remembering shoe – blanket went *together* as a pair) as opposed to separately remembering the items (e.g., remembering that "shoe" and "blanket" were studied previously, without needing to know that they went together as a pair). The hippocampus supports associative memory and engagement of this region is reduced with age. For example, memory for objects in locations (K. J. Mitchell et al., 2000) and memory for face–name pairs (Sperling et al., 2003) are impaired with age, and these deficits are linked to reduced activation of the hippocampus. In additional to the reductions in activation, structural changes to the hippocampus with age may impact associative memory. Older adults with more atrophy in medial temporal regions, including the hippocampus, exhibit poorer performance on a test of visuospatial associative memory than those with less atrophy (Zamboni et al., 2013). Thus, the hippocampus plays an important role in associative memory, and may underlie deficits with age.

One question to emerge was whether age differences in binding occur above and beyond age differences in visual processing of objects and scenes (Chee et al., 2006). To answer this question, researchers adopted an approach that involved passively viewing object-backgrounds scenes with elements repeating four times in a row. The logic was that repetition should lead to adaptation, or reduced neural response, in the relevant neural regions. In order to isolate object and background processes, only the relevant dimension was repeated (e.g., for an object adaptation trial, a butterfly repeated against four different backgrounds). For binding trials, the combination of object and background was changed across all four repetitions in order to vary the associations. Binding was indeed associated with patterns distinct from object or background processing, with bilateral parahippocampal gyri and right hippocampus selective for binding in young adults but disrupted in older adults (Chee et al., 2006; Goh et al., 2007).

For memory tasks requiring relational processing, the hippocampus works in conjunction with ventrolateral prefrontal regions. When retrieving learned association, younger adults engaged hippocampal and ventrolateral prefrontal regions more than for items tested alone (Giovanello & Schacter, 2012). In contrast, older adults did not recruit these regions more for relational than item processing. Changes in relational processing may emerge by midlife, with middle-aged adults (ages 40–56) activating prefrontal and ventral occipitotemporal regions more than young adults during retrieval of context, a type of associative memory (Kwon et al., 2015).

Despite evidence for disruption in associative and relational processes with age, some work suggests that these impairments can be mitigated. Generating associations for unrelated words also engages the VLPFC, with activation increasing as the task became more demanding for younger, but not older, adults (Addis et al., 2014). Hippocampal activity was comparable for younger and older adults, perhaps indicating that providing appropriate strategies helps to ameliorate age-related deficits in hippocampal engagement. Similarly, creating a sentence to integrate unrelated pictures (e.g., spider and airplane) increased engagement of inferior frontal and hippocampal regions compared to related pictures (e.g., spider and ant), but this manipulation had the same effect for younger and older adults (Leshikar et al., 2010). Taken together, these results implicate frontal and hippocampal regions in binding tasks, but also suggest that supportive encoding strategies and contexts may help to facilitate memory performance and the engagement of neural regions for older adults. Older adults' activation of prefrontal regions also benefits from strategy training, as discussed in Chapter 3.

4.3.6 Semantic Memory

Semantic memory is another type of explicit memory that deals with remembering facts and stores of knowledge. Unlike episodic memory, which engenders a re-experiencing of an event, semantic memory is devoid of context. One might have a rich episodic memory that one could relive about attending one's first concert, including the setting, who was there, the set list, and details about the musicians. A semantic memory, in contrast, would consist of the knowledge that one attended this concert without replaying the experience. Semantic memory tends to be preserved with age (Light, 1992).

One study of semantic memory compared neural activity across the life span while people made living/nonliving judgments about words (K. M. Kennedy, Rodrigue, et al., 2015). Some of these were in the easy condition (e.g., "truck") whereas others were hard (e.g., "virus"). Comparing easy judgments to baseline revealed widespread brain regions typically implicated in semantic processes, including the left inferior prefrontal gyrus and the temporal and visual cortex, as well as deactivation of the default mode network. Activity increased with age, but these increases generally occurred in regions that were separate from the core semantic network. Activity in these regions increased gradually from young adulthood to very old age (i.e., 80s) in a linear fashion. For difficult, compared to easy, judgments, regions related to cognitive control (e.g., the frontoparietal and anterior cingulate cortex) were the primary regions where activity increased. However, the enhanced response for difficulty was most pronounced for younger adults; with advancing age, activity in these regions was not increased to the same degree. Results suggest that the core semantic network may vary little with age, consistent with behavioral findings. In contrast, older adults recruit more neural regions than younger and middle-aged adults and the changes with age in cognitive control regions are more pronounced with difficulty. Despite the relative preservation of semantic memory with age, patterns of neural changes largely converge with those for other cognitive processes.

4.3.7 False Memory

Erroneous or **false memories** describe memories for events that did not occur or are remembered with substantial alterations. Older adults exhibit false memories much more often than younger adults, particularly when new items (lures) are similar or related to the original item (e.g., mistakenly remembering "cow" was on the study list because other farm animals were studied) (Koutstaal & Schacter, 1997; Tun et al., 1998). Interestingly, much of the research indicates that false memories rely on the same neural regions as accurate memory, including visual regions responsible for perceiving features of items, frontal and temporal regions associated with semantic knowledge, and the hippocampus, which is involved in memory formation and integration of the various elements that constitute a memory (Gutchess & Schacter, 2012; Schacter & Slotnick, 2004). A recent meta-analysis highlighted the role of the left middle temporal gyrus and anterior cingulate cortex in the formation of false memories during encoding (Kurkela & Dennis, 2016).

There is some evidence that the neural correlates of false memory differ to some degree across younger and older adults. Older adults engaged the superior temporal gyrus more than younger adults when encoding related sets of words that would be later remembered as true *or* false memories (Dennis et al., 2007). This activity was thought to reflect the "gist," or shared categorical and thematic information across the items; the results indicate that older adults rely on these processes more than perceptual or other processes that would allow for specific items to be encoded with differentiating detail. Lateral temporal regions are also implicated when older adults endorse false memories at the time of retrieval (Dennis, Kim, & Cabeza, 2008). The precuneus responds to false memories more than to correctly identified new items, and this occurs for younger adults more than older adults (Duarte et al., 2010).

Varying the amount of "gist" by manipulating the number of related exemplars encoded (e.g., studying four versus twelve pictures of cats) also reveals changes in the neural response of older adults. They exhibit enhanced hippocampal activity for false memories when there are fewer, rather than many, related items (e.g., pictures of bicycles) studied in a set, perhaps reflecting errant attempts to reconstruct memories at low cognitive loads (Paige et al., 2016). Compared to younger, older adults also evidence reduced responses to false memories. For example, anterior cingulate activity tracks the amount of "gist" for younger adults, with the region responding less as more related exemplars are encoded. However, older adults do not exhibit this response (Paige et al., 2016). A related study used morphed faces to systematically vary the level of relatedness to studied items. Results with older adults highlighted the importance of considering individual differences, in that higher levels of false alarms were associated with more activation in regions including the middle and superior temporal gyrus, medial prefrontal cortex, and hippocampus (Dennis & Turney, 2018).

False recollection, which is the vivid but mistaken sensation of re-experiencing an episode, is also impacted by age. Despite a higher number of false recollections, older adults do not engage additional neural regions for these trials (Dennis et al., 2014). In comparison, younger adults engage prefrontal, parahippocampal, and occipitoparietal regions more than older adults for false recollections. This pattern is thought to reflect the idea that false recollections in young adults stem from reconstructive processes, in which a number of details and qualities are integrated across processes into a memory that is false.

Aside from gist-based errors, conjunction errors are another type of memory illusion whereby parts of words are recombined into a new word (e.g., "blackmail" and "jailbird"; "blackbird"). Giovanello and colleagues (2010) probed age differences in the neural correlates of this type of memory error, and found that older adults engage the parahippocampal gyrus more for errors than for accurately retrieved items. Young adults did not show greater activation of regions for false compared to true memory. Results suggest that older adults may commit conjunction errors due to reliance on information about familiarity, subserved by the parahippocampal gyrus. In contrast to younger adults, who engage the hippocampus during accurate retrieval, older adults fail to use relational information.

ERPs have also been used to distinguish age differences in true and false memories. Waveforms for hits (correctly recognized old items) and false alarms (new items mistakenly called "old") are distinct across early and late time windows for young adults during the recognition of scenes. However, older adults' waveforms are not distinct in any time window (Gutchess, Ieuji, et al., 2007; see Figure 4.6). Surprisingly, memory

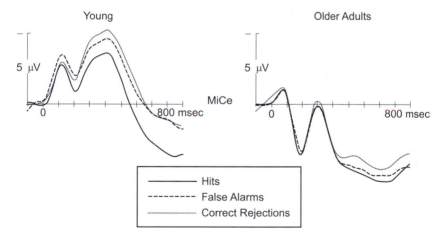

Figure 4.6 In younger adults (left) the neural signal reliably differentiates old items (hits; solid lines) from falsely remembered items (false alarms; dashed lines). Older adults (right) do not exhibit this difference as clearly. The plots show the ERP response at a midline central (MiCe) site, and are plotted against the response to new items (correct rejections) for comparison. Figure 6 from Angela H. Gutchess, Yoko Ieuji, and Kara D. Federmeier, Event-related potentials reveal age differences in the encoding and recognition of scenes, *Journal of Cognitive Neuroscience*, *19*(7) (July 2007), 1089–1103. © 2007 by the Massachusetts Institute of Technology, published by the MIT Press.

performance did not differ across the age groups. This makes the lack of distinct neural correlates for true versus false memories for older adults even more intriguing, perhaps suggesting that older adults form sufficiently detailed memories at encoding that the signal at retrieval is less diagnostic. Alternatively, the results could suggest that some essential retrieval processes are not amenable to measurement with ERPs.

4.3.8 Autobiographical Memory

Autobiographical memory is the rich memory of experiences in one's life, such as the memory of one's fifth birthday party or of a recent get-together with friends. With age, autobiographical memories become less detailed (Levine et al., 2002). This is particularly true for the episodic details, or the information about the experienced events. Semantic details, such as the names of friends and the knowledge of towns in which one resided during certain time periods, tend to be more intact with age. One fMRI study directly compared the effects of aging on semantic and episodic aspects of autobiographical memory. Age differences in the activation of the dorsal anterior cingulate reflected the tendency for younger adults to recruit the region more for episodic autobiographical memories (unique, one-time episodes) whereas older adults engaged the region more for semantic autobiographical memories (repeated or extended episodes, like the annual Christmas celebration at grandma's) (Martinelli et al., 2013). This pattern is consistent with declines in episodic details in autobiographical memory with age.

St Jacques and colleagues (2012) adopted a different approach, examining the different stages of autobiographical memory. In response to a word cue (e.g., dress), participants searched their memory for a specific event that occurred in their past, and then mentally elaborated the episode (e.g., remembering shopping for a prom dress). When searching for an autobiographical memory, both younger and older adults engaged a number of regions including the VLPFC, hippocampus, and parahippocampal gyrus, as well as temporal and retrosplenial regions. Only some of these regions, including the parahippocampal and retrosplenial cortex, continued to be engaged during the elaboration phase. A region of parietal cortex also contributed to the elaboration phase (see Figure 4.7). Although the activity during the search phase was more similar across the age groups, older adults exhibited reduced hippocampal, ventrolateral prefrontal, and parietal cortex activity during the elaboration phase. These reductions signify older adults' retrieval of less detailed autobiographical memories than young adults. Comparing only

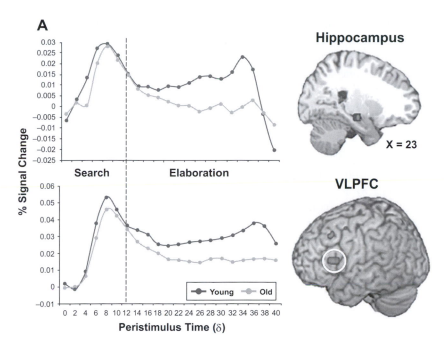

Figure 4.7 Autobiographical memory regions, including the hippocampus (top; the x-dimension for the displayed slice is in the Talaraich space) and ventrolateral prefrontal cortex (VLPFC; bottom), are similarly engaged by younger and older adults when searching for a memory (left part of graph labeled "search"). During elaboration of that memory (right side of graph), younger adults (dark gray) engage these regions more than older adults (light gray). *A black-and-white version of this figure will appear in some formats. For the color version, please refer to the plate section.*
From St Jacques et al. (2012), *Neurobiology of Aging*, Figure 2.

older adults' autobiographical memories that were relayed with rich episodic detail reduced age differences such that activation was equivalent for younger and older adults. Analyses to probe the relationship between prefrontal and hippocampal activity indicated that the VLPFC had a top-down influence on the hippocampus. This suggests that the prefrontal regions were responsible for producing detailed episodic memories, and that this mechanism may be disrupted with age. These results diverge somewhat from a report that right hippocampal activity *increases* with age during autobiographical memory retrieval (Maguire & Frith, 2003). However, the procedures differed substantially across these studies, with participants in the Maguire and Frith (2003) study answering "true" or "false" to questions about their autobiographical history that were created from an interview several weeks prior, rather than retrieving and elaborating autobiographical memories (as in St Jacques et al., 2012). It is also important for future work to probe the relationship between autobiographical and other types of episodic memory, as one study reports findings counter to these. During retrieval in an episodic memory task, age differences were pronounced during the search phase, with increased prefrontal and decreased posterior activations (Ford & Kensinger, 2017). Over time in the elaboration phase, however, older adults robustly activated posterior regions. Not only do these results diverge from those on autobiographical memory, but the elaboration phase results would not be predicted by the PASA model (Section 1.3).

Another study contrasted autobiographical memory for episodic and semantic memory, assessing the commonalities and differences in the networks subserving these different types of memory (St-Laurent et al., 2011). The analysis approach identified a network that distinguished the autobiographical task from the other types of memory, with neural regions largely converging with other studies of autobiographical memory. In terms of age differences, the networks for the different memory tasks were not as distinct for older adults as for younger adults. This indicated a pattern of dedifferentiation with age, with autobiographical and episodic memory in particular more distinct and differentiated in younger adults than in older adults. These findings are in line with behavioral work, suggesting relative preservation of semantic memory with greater impairments in autobiographical and episodic memory with age.

4.3.9 Memory and Future Thinking

A recent focus of research has been on the overlap between memory of past events and imagining the future. Many of the same brain regions responsible for memory, particularly of the richly detailed autobiographical variety, are involved in simulating the future (Schacter et al., 2007). This observation led to the suggestion that perhaps a primary function of memory is to prepare for the future. Such a function requires an adaptive, flexible system that can readily recombine information into new scenarios, and this also provides an account of why memory errors are so prevalent (Schacter et al., 2007; Schacter et al., 2011).

Although a number of behavioral studies have investigated the effects of aging on future thinking, few studies directly compare neural activity in younger and older adults (for studies of solely older adults, see Viard et al., 2011; Viard et al., 2010; Viard et al., 2007). Consistent with previous findings on autobiographical memory, older adults show reduced activation during the construction of events for both past and future events (Addis et al., 2011). The affected network includes the medial temporal (including the hippocampus and parahippocampal gyrus) and precuneus regions, which are thought to support contextualized and detailed memory content. As younger adults rated their memories as having more detail, activity increased in these regions. This was not the case for older adults. Older adults increased activity in the latter parts of the trial, when they elaborated events. These increases occurred in both the medial (including the hippocampus, consistent with the finding of Maguire and Frith (2003)) and lateral temporal cortices. The engagement of lateral temporal regions may reflect greater reliance on semantic content when older adults elaborate their past or future autobiographical events, consistent with their preserved semantic autobiographical memory. In fact, older adults' detail ratings correlated with the activity in lateral temporal regions, suggesting that when older adults reported detailed memories, they relied on semantic details.

4.3.10 Reactivation

One interesting finding in younger adults is the degree to which retrieval relies on **reactivation** of the same neural regions that were used to first encode an item. For example, encoding pictures engages some of the same visual regions at study and test, and encoding sounds relies on some of the same auditory processing regions at study and test (Wheeler et al., 2000). This overlap between neural regions suggests that retrieving information relies on recapitulating some of the same processes engaged during encoding. Results thus far with aging have been mixed. Although there is some evidence that older adults reactivate regions involved in processing visual scenes and objects (e.g., precuneus, posterior parahippocampal gyrus, and fusiform) less than younger adults (McDonough et al., 2014), there is some evidence of similar reinstatement of cortical regions across age groups when study conditions are manipulated (T. H. Wang et al., 2016). Reactivation for younger and older adults primarily occurred in posterior regions including the posterior cingulate and posterior parietal cortex, although word stimuli also elicited lateral prefrontal activity in this study (T. H. Wang et al., 2016). A particularly interesting study examined reactivation of memories during retrieval with videos. Younger and older adults repeatedly viewed and mentally replayed several short videos (St-Laurent et al., 2014). Results indicated that age differences were minimal in the engagement of regions during the initial perception of the videos, but were pronounced when participants mentally replayed the videos. Memory performance was also related to the specificity of the pattern of reactivation. Taken together, the results from this study suggest that older adults' difficulty with reactivation, rather than perceptual impairment, affects the vividness and distinctiveness of their memories.

4.3.11 Controlled Processes in Long-Term Memory

Complementing the role of reactivation in memory retrieval are other more effortful processes that help to distinguish "old" from "new" information. As seen for many of the studies reviewed throughout this chapter, older adults sometimes recruit more prefrontal regions during retrieval than young adults. One study demonstrated that this pattern characterized "high-control" conditions (Velanova et al., 2007). By manipulating how strongly items had been encoded (e.g., more presentations of items reduced the control needed to make memory decisions), Velanova and colleagues compared the neural activity in younger and older adults, finding that older adults engaged more prefrontal regions during high-control trials than low-. This was not the case for younger adults. Furthermore, control effects emerged late in the trial for older adults; this was considered to reflect a later, less effective control strategy than younger adults, who engaged control processes earlier and more effectively (as discussed in Section 3.3).

Irrelevant background contexts also interfere with older adults' memory more than younger adults' (Gutchess, Hebrank, et al., 2007). Greater activation of cognitive control regions, including the bilateral DLPFC, occurs alongside memory disruptions when the context is familiar. Younger adults engage these regions more than older adults, regardless of whether the older adults are high or low performers. High-performing older adults, however, engage additional regions in the prefrontal and temporal cortex, possibly reflecting compensatory processes to bolster memory performance.

Older adults' deficits in inhibition, or ignoring irrelevant information (as reviewed in Section 4.2.1), are often discussed in terms of their negative effects on cognitive processes. However, inhibition failures also may have unexpected effects on long-term memory in that they may actually *improve* older adults' memory of some information. In a study task, participants are asked to attend to one stream of information (e.g., a string of letters) and ignore another (e.g., a line drawing behind the letters). Both younger and older adults show **priming** for attended items (e.g., the strings of letters), in that they make faster responses for these items when they are presented with them again (Campbell et al., 2012). Older adults, but not younger adults, show a priming benefit for items that were supposed to be ignored. This finding is consistent with the idea that older adults did not successfully ignore those items. Neuroimaging data show that younger adults activate frontoparietal control regions more than older adults during the "ignore" condition. Furthermore, the more activity in these regions, the less priming occurs; this pattern suggests more successful ignoring of irrelevant information. Even during rest, the coupling of frontoparietal regions differs with age such that functional connectivity is higher for younger than older adults, indicating a more intact network (see Figure 4.8).

4.3.12 Pattern Separation

One emerging theory of long-term memory draws on ideas about inter-ference with aging. In order to differentiate memories from each other, the hippocampus must be able to achieve **pattern separation**, through which distinct neural patterns of activity (perhaps corresponding to two unique memories or two exemplars of "bikes") can be distinguished from each other. Pattern separation is important so that similar memor-ies do not interfere with each other, leading to forgetting; a subfield of the hippocampus seems to support this process (Yassa & Stark, 2011).

Aging may affect this process such that older adults are more attuned to **pattern completion**, reinstating an "old" pattern of activation from partial information rather than distinguishing the neural pattern as a new, distinct pattern. For example, seeing a mug that looks similar to a mug studied previously could induce pattern completion, such that the pattern of neural activity in response to the new mug matches the pattern for the original mug. The bias towards pattern completion may come at the expense of pattern separation, such that older adults need a new memory or exemplar to be more distinct from extant ones to be treated as a "new" item, compared to younger adults (Yassa, Lacy, et al., 2011). The impair-ment may be even more exaggerated for older adults with impaired memory performance (Stark et al., 2013; Stark et al., 2010). An emphasis on pattern completion may lead older adults to commit more memory errors for similar, related items than young adults. A region of the hippo-campus (right CA3/dentate gyrus) was the only region that exhibited a greater increase in the response to "similar" items compared to "new" items for older compared to younger adults (Yassa, Lacy, et al., 2011). High-resolution fMRI and DTI data further revealed disruptions with age

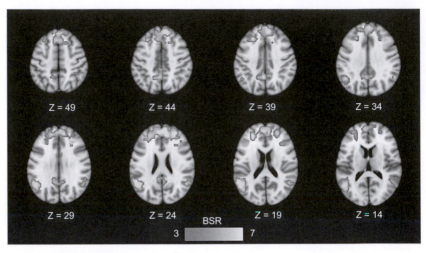

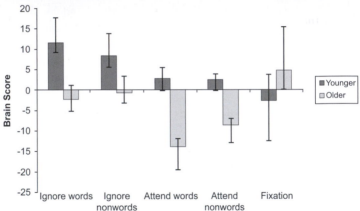

Figure 4.8 Younger adults engaged a control network (displayed in the top panel; the location of the axial slice in the z-direction is in MNI space) more than older adults. Activity is plotted as a bootstrap ratio (BSR). The bar graph in the bottom panel shows that the network is strongly engaged by young, but not older adults, when attempting to ignore words.

From Campbell et al. (2012), *Neuropsychologia*, Figure 5.

in the functional and structural integrity of the dentate gyrus and CA3, and in the pathway leading to these fields of the hippocampus (Yassa, Mattfeld, Stark, & Stark, 2011; Yassa et al., 2010). This research approach probes age differences in memory at a much finer scale than other work, proposing precise neural mechanisms informed by research on rodents.

4.4 Implicit Long-Term Memory

Implicit memory is the behavioral expression of prior learning or experience that does not rely on conscious knowledge of the prior episode. The brain regions typically involved in implicit memory are shown in Box 4.3. This type of memory can be expressed through motor or speeded responses, which show improvement with experience (e.g., riding a bike; reading text backwards in a mirror). Even if a person does not remember learning to read words backwards in a mirror, her performance could nonetheless improve through higher accuracy and faster reaction time. Implicit memory also can be measured through verbal tasks. For example, participants may make faster judgments for words encountered recently compared to words that were not encountered. When completing word stems (e.g., "star_") with the first word that comes to mind, participants are far more likely to generate a word that they encountered recently as part of a different task, an example of priming. For example, if participants read the word "stare" as part of a previous task, they would be more likely to later complete the word stem with that word than with

---

Box 4.3 Neural Regions Associated with Implicit Memory

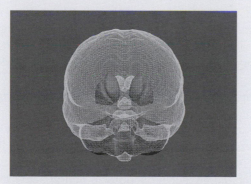

A black-and-white version of this figure will appear in some formats. For the color version, please refer to the plate section.

The cerebellum (in green) and the striatum (in yellow), consisting of the putamen and caudate, are involved in implicit memory.

Figure created with software from Madan (2015), Creating 3D visualizations of MRI data: a brief guide, *F1000Research*, *4*, 466.

other solutions (e.g., "start," "stars"), in contrast to participants who had not encountered the word "stare" recently.

Behaviorally, implicit memory is often spared with aging (Gabrieli et al., 1999; Light & Singh, 1987). In a study of repetition priming, participants made judgments for words that were repeated versus presented for the first time in the task. Both younger and older adults exhibited the typical behavioral priming benefit whereby reaction times were faster for the repeated words (Lustig & Buckner, 2004). Repetition priming impacted left inferior prefrontal activity for both younger and older adults. Priming reduces activation of these regions with repetition, and the reduction was of a similar magnitude for younger and older adults. Lustig and Buckner (2004) focused on age differences in a priori regions of interest, although a later study compared age differences across the whole brain. In this study, younger and older adults made judgments about words that were either repeated or new (Bergerbest et al., 2009). The later study converged with prior work to implicate left inferior prefrontal regions in priming, but also identified additional left prefrontal regions in which young adults demonstrated larger reductions with repetition than older adults. Older adults, in contrast, evidenced greater repetition effects in right prefrontal regions. The responsivity of the right prefrontal cortex was considered to be a beneficial pattern with age because older adults with higher vocabulary scores, a proxy for intelligence, activated these regions more than those with lower vocabulary scores.

Even though some of the core regions implicated in priming are preserved with age, there is still evidence of age-related change. Age-related changes in implicit memory may be more modest than those identified for explicit memory (as reviewed in Section 4.3), but there has been less research on this topic. There are a number of tests that may rely on distinct subtypes of implicit memory, and the effects of aging may be more pronounced for some than others. For example, a study of word stem priming revealed behavioral as well as neural differences with age. Older adults who exhibited less reduction in the activity in semantic and visual regions benefited less from priming (i.e., their reaction times were slower) than those who exhibited greater reductions in neural activity due to priming (Daselaar et al., 2005). Thus, it is necessary to directly compare the effects of aging on neural activation patterns for different implicit memory tasks.

Implicit and explicit memory rely on largely distinct neural regions. Whereas explicit memory relies on the hippocampus, implicit memory draws on the striatum and cerebellum (Knowlton et al., 1996). This dissociation is what allows patients with **amnesia**, who lack explicit memory as a result of medial temporal lobe damage, to exhibit preserved skill learning even when they have no conscious memory of having performed a task before.

Dennis and Cabeza (2011) directly compared the effects of aging on implicit and explicit learning. Despite the preserved implicit learning that can occur with age, neural systems show age-related changes under some conditions. When learning a motor sequence, such as finger taps to different keys, people often are not consciously aware that they are learning repeating patterns. This implicit task was compared to an explicit task whereby participants learned to quickly categorize words into different categories (e.g., animal, place). Younger adults displayed the expected effects, with explicit memory supported by medial temporal (including the hippocampal and parahippocampal gyrus), ventrolateral prefrontal, parietal, and visual regions, and implicit memory supported by striatal and cerebellar regions. Older adults showed a pattern of dedifferentiation such that the explicit and implicit tasks did not differ in their engagement of regions including the bilateral medial temporal lobes and right striatum. Other studies also report changes to these regions with age. Striatum activations were disrupted with age during implicit learning (Aizenstein et al., 2006) and medial temporal activity supported performance on an implicit memory task for older, but not younger, adults (Rieckmann et al., 2010).

Chapter Summary

- There are many subtypes of memory. Working memory and long-term memory differ in terms of the time scale. Within long-term memory, subtypes include explicit (episodic and semantic) and implicit memory.
- Age differences are more pronounced behaviorally in explicit memory than implicit memory, although neural differences can emerge for both types of memory.
- Recollection is often considered to be more impaired with aging than familiarity, although there are exceptions to this finding.
- Older adults are more prone to false memories than younger adults. Although a variety of neural regions contribute to false memories, temporal lobe regions linked to semantic processes may exhibit some of the largest age differences.
- Autobiographical memory is less detailed with age. Regions including the medial temporal lobe may be less engaged during the elaboration of autobiographical memories, and patterns of neural activity may be less distinct across different subtypes of memory with age.

- Prefrontal control processes contribute to a number of memory processes with age, including recollection, post-retrieval monitoring, and interference. Several studies indicate disruptions to activation of these regions with age.
- Current research on the effects of aging on future thinking, reactivation, and pattern separation/completion indicates some evidence of impairments with age in these new domains.

Discussion Questions

1. What are some of the different subtypes of memory? What neural regions support these different types of memory?
2. Does aging equivalently affect all types of memory? How does the answer depend on whether behavioral or neural measures are used?
3. What is the CRUNCH model? What pattern of data is considered consistent with it?
4. What stage of memory does a subsequent memory design allow one to compare? How is this an advance over behavioral methods?
5. What are recollection and familiarity? How does aging affect these, based on neural and behavioral data?
6. How are false memories distinct from forgetting? What types of neural regions and processes lead to these errors in younger and older adults?

For Further Reading

Dennis, N. A., Hayes, S. M., Prince, S. E., Madden, D. J., Huettel, S. A., & Cabeza, R. (2008). Effects of aging on the neural correlates of successful item and source memory encoding. *Journal of Experimental Psychology: Learning, Memory, and Cognition, 34*(4), 791–808.

Gutchess, A. H., Ieuji, Y., & Federmeier, K. D. (2007). Event-related potentials reveal age differences in the encoding and recognition of scenes. *Journal of Cognitive Neuroscience, 19*(7), 1089–1103.

Lustig, C., & Buckner, R. L. (2004). Preserved neural correlates of priming in old age and dementia. *Neuron, 42*(5), 865–875.

Reuter-Lorenz, P. A., & Cappell, K. A. (2008). Neurocognitive aging and the compensation hypothesis. *Current Directions in Psychological Science, 17*(3), 177–182.

St-Laurent, M., Abdi, H., Bondad, A., & Buchsbaum, B. R. (2014). Memory reactivation in healthy aging: evidence of stimulus-specific dedifferentiation. *Journal of Neuroscience, 34*(12), 4175–4186.

Key Terms

amnesia
associative memory
autobiographical memory
binding
encoding
explicit memory
false memories
familiarity
implicit memory
incidental encoding
intentional encoding
levels of processing
pattern completion
pattern separation
post-retrieval monitoring
priming
reactivation
recollection
refreshing
semantic memory
source memory
subsequent memory

CHAPTER FIVE

Emotion and Aging

Learning Objectives

- Which brain regions are implicated in emotion, and how does aging affect them?
- What is the behavioral and neural evidence for emotion recognition impairments with age?
- How might aging benefit emotion regulation, and what neural regions are associated with particular strategies?
- What are socioemotional selectivity theory and positivity effects? How might these relate to memory changes with age?
- What neural regions respond differently to emotionally valenced memories with age? How do these neural differences inform our understanding of how younger and older adults may differ in their processing of emotional information?

5.1 Introduction

Are our emotional reactions to stressors and pleasures the same throughout our lives? Emotion is one of the most interesting topics in the study of aging, because of both the rich possibilities for change in emotional priorities across the life span and the preserved, and perhaps even enhanced, ability to regulate emotion with age. The paradox of preserved emotional processing alongside impaired cognitive abilities has been noted multiple times (e.g., Mather et al., 2012; Samanez-Larkin et al., 2011). This chapter will review the evidence for enhanced emotion regulation and well-being in older adults, and discuss some of the neural changes that may support these abilities. In contrast, some research focuses on impairments with age, such as in the ability to recognize emotion from faces and in the patterns of amygdala response. Other work suggests that older adults' awareness of the limited time remaining in their lives can shape priorities, potentially biasing them to prioritize positive over negative information. These motivational shifts, as well as other changes, can differently impact memory of emotional information across the age groups. Although this chapter could encompass broader considerations of motivation, including response to reward and economic decisions, these topics will be discussed as future directions in Chapter 8.

5.2 Neural Regions Involved in Emotion

The **amygdala** is the brain region most strongly associated with emotion. This almond-shaped structure is located deep in the temporal lobes, with one on each side of the midline (see Box 5.1). Its location adjacent to the hippocampus (see Chapter 4) may contribute to some of the enhancements in memory for emotional information. Much of the research on aging indicates relative preservation of the amygdala, in terms of its structural integrity (e.g., Mather, 2016; Nashiro et al., 2012) as well as its functional activity. Many fMRI studies report similar levels of amygdala engagement across age groups (e.g., Kensinger & Schacter, 2008; Wedig et al., 2005; Wright et al., 2006). However, this finding is not

---

Box 5.1 Neural Regions Associated with Emotion

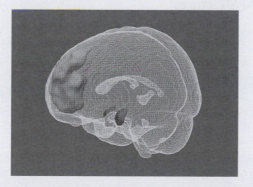

A black-and-white version of this figure will appear in some formats. For the color version, please refer to the plate section.

The amygdala (in red, one in each hemisphere) and medial prefrontal cortex (in purple) are some of the primary regions involved in emotion.

Figure created with software from Madan (2015), Creating 3D visualizations of MRI data: a brief guide, *F1000Research, 4*, 466.

universal; other studies report reduced (e.g., Fischer et al., 2005; Gunning-Dixon et al., 2003; Iidaka et al., 2002; Tessitore et al., 2005) or enhanced (e.g., Leclerc & Kensinger, 2010; Mather et al., 2004) activity with age under some conditions. (Ritchey, Bessette-Symons, Hayes, & Cabeza, 2011) propose that one reason for some of the discrepancy across studies may be that older adults often rate stimuli as less arousing than younger adults. When stimuli are not well equated on this dimension, it could trigger age differences in amygdala activity. Regions of the prefrontal cortex can also contribute to emotion, particularly in the service of **emotion regulation** (see Section 5.4). Age differences in these regions vary with task demands, as will be reviewed throughout this chapter.

Studies initially compared basic neural responses, such as how the repetition versus novelty of stimuli affects activity in a region. Aging does not seem to affect the response of the amygdala to novel fearful faces, compared to familiar neutral ones (Wright et al., 2006), nor does it affect the overall amygdala response to emotional pictures (Moriguchi et al., 2011). See Box 5.2 for a description of a set of pictures commonly used in emotion research. Although aging has a limited effect on the response to novelty, it does impact the response to repeated faces.

Box 5.2 IAPS Pictures

One of the most common sets of stimuli used in emotion research is the International Affective Picture System (IAPS) (Lang et al., 1997). The IAPS consists of 956 pictures of complex scenes, including images such as a baby with a facial deformity, a person holding a gun, puppies, and an electrical outlet. These stimuli have been well validated, normed on participants of varying ages and backgrounds (e.g., different cultures and languages). Participants rated the pictures on **valence**, the extent to which a picture is positive (pleasant) or negative (unpleasant). This dimension is distinct from **arousal**, which is how physiologically and psychologically excited or calm a picture makes one feel. Together, the dimensions of valence and arousal account for the variety of emotions (Russell, 1980). Although arousal and valence are both important concepts in psychological research, most of the research thus far investigating age differences in neural activity manipulates valence, and you will read less about arousal in this chapter.

The IAPS pictures and other emotional stimuli are freely available to researchers (http://csea.phhp.ufl.edu/Media.html).

Habituation describes the tendency for a region to respond less on subsequent presentations of a stimulus, meaning that novel stimuli tend to elicit the strongest neural responses (for a review, see Grill-Spector et al., 2006). Both younger and older adults show habituation of the response of the amygdala to repeated neutral faces, but there are slight differences across age groups in which hemisphere exhibits more habituation (Wedig et al., 2005). Other work has focused on the prefrontal cortex, finding that older adults exhibit more habituation to highly arousing negative stimuli in that cortex (Roalf et al., 2011). This alteration in prefrontal response may reflect a more controlled response to negative emotion with age. However, it is possible that older adults cannot maintain a heightened response throughout the task. In terms of connections between the amygdala and prefrontal cortex regions, connectivity with the orbitofrontal gyrus decreases with age (Moriguchi et al., 2011), indicating further changes to the system with aging.

ERP methods also have been applied to study basic responses to emotional stimuli. Both younger and older adults exhibited an early posterior negativity (EPN), which is thought to index early discrimination of emotionally relevant information. This component was delayed slightly for older adults within an early time window, but not in a later one. However, this delay was unrelated to ratings of valence or arousal of pictures, making it uncertain whether it affects the processing of emotional information in older adults (Wieser et al., 2006).

5.3 Emotion Identification

Several studies have investigated age differences in the response to facial expressions of emotion. A meta-analysis incorporating different modalities (e.g., faces, voices) concluded that older adults have more difficulty than younger adults in recognizing **basic emotions** (anger, sadness, fear, disgust, surprise, and happiness), particularly anger and sadness (Ruffman et al., 2008). One exception is in identifying disgust from facial expressions, for which older adults have an advantage over young. Consistent with these behavioral findings, initial neuroimaging studies found impaired activation of the amygdala with age. For example, older adults engaged the amygdala less than younger adults when viewing emotional faces, regardless of whether the judgments focused on emotion (Gunning-Dixon et al., 2003) or not (Iidaka et al., 2002). In contrast to the reduced amygdala activity with age, older adults may activate frontal regions *more* than young (Gunning-Dixon et al., 2003; Tessitore et al., 2005). Fischer and colleagues (2005) reported similar findings: younger adults engaged

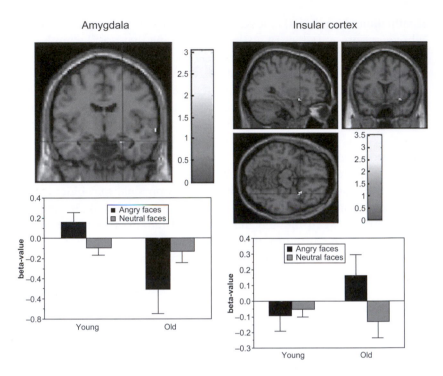

Figure 5.1 Younger adults engaged the amygdala (left) more when processing angry faces than neutral faces. In contrast, older adults engaged the insular cortex (right) in response to angry faces more than to neutral faces. This pattern suggested a subcortical (amygdala) to cortical (insular cortex) shift with age. The graphs depict estimates of neural activity. Adapted from Fischer et al. (2005), *Neuroscience Letters*, Figures 1 and 2.

an amygdala/hippocampal region more than older adults, whereas older adults recruited a region of the insula more than young adults, a pattern that also occurred during the successful encoding of fearful faces into memory (Fischer et al., 2010; see Figure 5.1). These results (Fischer et al., 2005) were particularly influential in that they identified a subcortical to cortical shift with aging, mirroring similar patterns for other abilities such as nonemotional memory (Gutchess et al., 2005). These findings were later integrated into frameworks emphasizing posterior-to-anterior shifts in activity with age (e.g., S. W. Davis et al., 2008; St Jacques, Bessette-Symons, & Cabeza, 2009) (see Section 5.6.1).

Later research has investigated how more complex patterns of neural activity underlie the ability to label specific emotions. By using a **partial least squares (PLS)** analysis approach, which identifies patterns of regions working together across the brain, Keightley et al. (2007) found a set of regions that differentiated happy faces from the other six types of faces. For younger adults, these regions included several frontal regions (ventromedial and middle frontal; anterior cingulate), as well as the posterior cingulate and lingual gyrus. Although the ventromedial prefrontal cortex (VMPFC) and lingual gyrus also emerged for older adults for happy faces, overall the regions differed with age (although neither group showed a strong amygdala response). With age, the response of these regions was not as selective, as they responded to disgusted as well as happy faces. Furthermore, older adults engaged more regions for negative expressions than younger adults. These results suggest striking changes with age in the regions that respond to emotional faces. In contrast, Ebner and colleagues (Ebner et al., 2012) largely report convergence with age. They focused on prefrontal and amygdala regions that respond to emotion identification. They found that both younger and older adults activated medial prefrontal (MPFC) regions in response to specific emotional expressions (VMPFC (ventral) for happy; DMPFC (dorsal) for neutral or angry), and that no age differences emerged in the amygdala. Notably, older adults showed a greater difference across emotions in the DMPFC response, perhaps reflecting their greater difficulty in recognizing anger.

Perceiving emotional expressions, and the underlying neural response, may be linked to measures of emotional well-being. A particularly interesting study explored neural responses to different emotional expressions over a large life-span sample of individuals aged 12–79, integrating fMRI and ERP methods (Williams et al., 2006). fMRI data showed that with age, the MPFC response decreases for happy faces while increasing for fearful faces. ERP data showed an age-related decline in the early frontal components to happy faces, but an increase in the later frontal components for fearful faces. How the MPFC responded to fear and happiness with age was associated with emotional stability. Decreased MPFC response to happiness and increased MPFC response to fear, a pattern thought to reflect better control over negative emotion, predicted emotional stability.

5.4 Emotion Regulation

In contrast to the many cognitive declines with aging, the ability to regulate one's emotions seems to improve with age. Older adults report fewer negative experiences than younger adults, and have better emotional control (Gross et al., 1997; Phillips et al., 2006). This is surprising because aging impairs controlled cognitive processes, and cognitive abilities, such as selecting information to attend to or changing one's outlook, aid in emotion regulation (Ochsner & Gross, 2005). This paradox between the cognitive demands of emotion regulation and older adults' dwindling resources may be resolved by optimizing one's selection of particular strategies based on what resources are available. This is the basis of the SOC-ER model of aging (Urry & Gross, 2010), which purports that older adults use *S*election, *O*ptimization, and *C*ompensation with *E*motion *R*egulation (Baltes & Baltes, 1990). Younger adults may use more **cognitive reappraisal** – that is, changing the meaning of a situation in order to make it less emotionally upsetting. For example, one's initial negative reaction to a picture of a sickly patient in a hospital bed could be reappraised by focusing on the ways in which treatment will help the patient to get better. Older adults, however, may rely more on **situation selection** – that is, changing the situation one is in, such as removing oneself from an upsetting situation, or even simply looking away from negative information (Isaacowitz et al., 2006b).

These counterintuitive findings with aging have made emotion regulation of keen interest in neuroimaging research. In one study, naturally experiencing emotion while viewing positive, negative, or neutral pictures engaged the amygdala bilaterally. However, reappraising pictures in order to detach oneself activated prefrontal regions in both younger and older adults (Winecoff et al., 2011). Reappraising negative pictures, compared to experiencing them naturally, engaged the left inferior frontal gyrus less for older than younger adults. Age differences during cognitive reappraisal also emerged in Opitz et al. (2012), who reported less activity in prefrontal activity regions in older than younger adults. Moreover, cognitive ability, above and beyond the influence of age, predicted greater decreases in amygdala activity as a function of regulating emotion (Winecoff et al., 2011). This suggests a role of cognitive ability in the regulation of emotion, perhaps through its effects on the functional network between the inferior frontal gyrus and the amygdala. Research using behavioral and physiological measures (e.g., heart rate) also suggests that cognition contributes to emotion regulation (Opitz et al., 2014).

Other studies have contrasted reappraisal with other emotion regulation strategies. For both younger and older adults, reappraisal induces stronger connectivity between the anterior cingulate cortex and regions of the prefrontal cortex than does **selective attention**, a strategy that relies on attending to parts of an image in order to feel better (Allard & Kensinger, 2014a). These results indicate that older adults can engage prefrontal networks in response to emotion regulation demands.

However, the specific prefrontal regions recruited with the anterior cingulate cortex vary across younger and older adults. In another study using either reappraisal or selective attention to investigate regulation, younger adults were found to recruit expansive lateral and medial prefrontal regions compared to older adults (Allard & Kensinger, 2014b). Interestingly, age differences were prominent in the timing of the activity, with younger adults engaging the VLPFC at the onset of the film clip but older adults recruiting the region later, at the emotional peak. These differences were thought to suggest that, compared to younger adults, older adults employ cognitively demanding emotion regulation strategies more selectively, and these require more time to be engaged.

Another study adopted multivoxel pattern analysis (MVPA) (see Chapter 2) to assess age differences in the neural correlates of distraction versus reappraisal (Martins et al., 2015). In the distraction conditions, participants imagined themselves in a pleasant scene (e.g., relaxing on a beach). The patterns of activity for the two emotion regulation strategies were more distinct for younger than older adults. Results were interpreted as evidence of dedifferentiation with age in emotional processing strategies, in that older adults' neural activity was less distinct.

Age differences also are thought to reflect spontaneous differences in how younger and older adults process information. During a task in which participants experienced emotions elicited by pictures and then rated them for pleasantness, the right amygdala was similarly engaged across the age groups (St Jacques et al., 2010). However, the functional connectivity with the amygdala varied with age. Older adults showed more connectivity with frontal regions (ventral anterior cingulate), whereas younger adults exhibited more connectivity with posterior brain regions, including the visual cortex (see Figure 5.2). These patterns were thought to reflect less processing of perceptual information by older adults, perhaps in the service of increased emotion regulation.

In addition to changes in the regions and connectivity that underlie emotional responses with age, younger and older adults may differ in their sensitivity to different levels of arousal. Low arousal negative stimuli spontaneously activate emotional control regions in the prefrontal cortex for older adults (Dolcos et al., 2014). Prefrontal activity made the experience less emotional, based on participants' ratings. Thus, Dolcos and colleagues (2014) suggested that older adults may chronically activate emotion regulation networks in response to low arousal stimuli. Their study converged with prior work (e.g., St Jacques et al., 2010) in revealing activation of the right amygdala by both younger and older adults, although their results indicated that the common amygdala

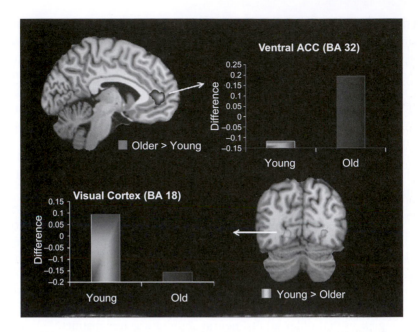

Figure 5.2 The connectivity of brain regions during the processing of emotion varies with age. Whereas the amygdala shows more connectivity with the ventral anterior cingulate (ACC) in older adults (top panel), the amygdala is more connected with the visual cortex in younger adults (bottom panel). The "Difference" measure (y-axis) reflects the difference in correlations for negative/neutral conditions. BA: Brodmann's areas.
From St Jacques et al. (2010), *Neurobiology of Aging*, Figure 3.

activity primarily occurred for high arousal negative stimuli. However, additional research is needed on the effects of emotional arousal with age, as another study found a *decreased* response to emotional arousal with age (Kehoe et al., 2013).

In summary, emotion regulation differences with age may reflect the operation of several processes, including selection of strategies, dedifferentiation, attention to distinct aspects of information, and sensitivity to varying levels of arousal. With age, prefrontal activation can be reduced during emotional processing, though older adults may recruit different regions or do so at a later time point than younger adults. In addition, changes in the network connectivity of the amygdala occur with age, with older adults exhibiting heightened connectivity with prefrontal regions as opposed to younger adults' greater connectivity with posterior visual regions.

5.4.1 Life Satisfaction and Neural Activity with Age

Emotion regulation and older adults' skill at it have been linked to life satisfaction. Older adults report higher levels of life satisfaction than younger adults (Cacioppo et al., 2008). Neural activity appears to differ in complex ways between older adults reporting higher versus lower levels of life satisfaction (Waldinger et al., 2011). For positive images, older adults with higher levels of life satisfaction engaged prefrontal regions less than older adults with lower levels of life satisfaction. This reduced neural engagement was thought to reflect efficient processing because it occurred during the successful encoding of information into memory. Furthermore, high-satisfaction older adults show weaker connectivity between emotion regions, including the prefrontal cortex and the amygdala, for negative images, but stronger connectivity for positive images. In contrast, the networks of low-satisfaction older adults do not vary much as a function of valence. In another study, older adults with higher self-reported life satisfaction displayed a stronger integration of the dorsal medial thalamus and the red nucleus, compared to those with lower levels of life satisfaction (Voss, Wong, et al., 2013). This finding reflects the stronger coordination of a network that overlaps with the frontoexecutive system and has been implicated in emotion processing, perhaps helping to regulate emotional experiences in late life.

5.5 Socioemotional Selectivity Theory and Age

With aging comes an increasing awareness of the limited time remaining in one's life. This heightened awareness shifts older adults' motivational goals, leading them to seek out time with friends and family. This pattern contrasts younger adults' goals of exploration and knowledge-seeking. These different goals across the life span lead people to allocate their time differently. This framework, **socioemotional selectivity theory**, has played a dominant role in shaping research on emotion with aging (Carstensen et al., 1999). Whereas laypeople may tend to think of aging as a time associated with sad emotions and negativity, Carstensen's work has helped to draw attention to the many positive experiences occurring in late life.

These different motivations could impact cognition, by shifting one's orientation from negative to positive with age. Young adults tend to be biased to attend to negative information, which is thought to be evolutionarily advantageous for detecting threats in one's environment. This prioritization of negative information can be tempered with age. In some cases, older adults even show enhanced processing of positive information, over the levels for negative information or even compared to young adults. This **positivity effect** has been found in a range of tasks, including attention (Mather & Carstensen, 2003), memory (Charles et al., 2003; Q. Kennedy et al., 2004; Mather & Carstensen, 2005), and even gaze (e.g., older adults looking away from negative information; Isaacowitz et al., 2006a). Although a meta-analysis shows that a positivity effect does not always emerge in cognitive tasks (N. A. Murphy & Isaacowitz, 2008), recent analyses (Reed et al., 2014) suggest that this pattern is more likely to occur when task processing is unconstrained (i.e., when participants make absolutely no judgments regarding stimuli, thoughts, or feelings).

Socioemotional selectivity theory has been difficult to study with cognitive neuroscience methods, as many of the behavioral tasks employed do not lend themselves well to cognitive neuroscience methods. For example, the tasks may contain few trials or judgments that are temporally unconstrained, making it difficult to assess neural responses to a specific event. However, several studies have applied neural measures to investigate positivity effects with age. In the first such study using fMRI, Mather and colleagues (Mather et al., 2004) showed that older adults engaged the amygdala more when viewing positive pictures than negative ones. In contrast, younger adults tended to engage the amygdala more for negative pictures compared to positive ones (although the difference did not reach significance in young adults). In the initial study, participants rated their level of arousal while viewing each picture.

Other studies have identified age differences in the neural response to positive versus negative stimuli, regardless of whether participants are consciously attending to the emotional nature of the task. In one fMRI study, younger and older adults viewed pictures of objects (e.g., grenade, ice cream sundae) determined to be positive, negative, or neutral based on ratings of other participants. Participants simply decided whether each item would fit into a shoebox, and did not attend to the emotional aspects of the information. Results indicated that the VMPFC exhibited a reversal in its response to valence across the age groups, such that young adults engaged the region more for negative than positive pictures whereas older adults engaged the region more for positive than negative pictures (Leclerc & Kensinger, 2008). This pattern of results is consistent with a positivity effect, such that the increased engagement of the VMPFC was in line with the types of stimuli that are prioritized by younger and older adults. A similar pattern emerged in a study using a visual search task, with the VMPFC again responding more for negative images in younger adults and for more positive images for older adults (Leclerc & Kensinger, 2010). In addition, the amygdala exhibited the same pattern of reversal with age in its response to negative versus positive information. This finding was unexpected, as positivity effects do not always emerge for rapid tasks relying on automatic processing, but occur more commonly on sustained tasks. Similar effects in the VMPFC were also found for a study of impression formation, in which participants learned about behaviors reflecting positive (e.g., honest) or negative (e.g., rude) traits of an individual (Cassidy et al., 2013). A study of autobiographical memory revealed a similar pattern of reversals with age in amygdala activity, with the region engaged more when retrieving negative events for young and positive events for older adults (Ge et al., 2014). However, the pattern of VMPFC/ACC activity in the autobiographical memory study was the opposite of prior studies (Cassidy et al., 2013; Leclerc & Kensinger, 2008, 2010), such that older adults engaged the region more for *negative* events but younger adults for positive. The authors speculated that these divergent findings could reflect task differences; perhaps autobiographical memory places different demands on the VMPFC/ACC than the previous studies that took place during encoding or visual search. The difference could also reflect the engagement of the VMPFC as part of a network along with the amygdala, perhaps contributing to emotion regulation during the rich retrieval and re-experiencing of autobiographical memories in the Ge et al. (2014) study.

The range of tasks and conditions under which younger and older adults show reversals in the response of the VMPFC to negative versus positive stimuli indicate that these results are robust, although more work is needed to directly link the pattern to enhancements in memory for positive information with age. The cognitive and emotional processes that differ across these age groups in response to positive and negative valence need to be better elucidated, and neural data could provide useful insights. For example, the location of many of these reversals in the VMPFC is consistent with a neural region activated when people think about the self. Studies (Kensinger & LeClerc, 2009; Leclerc & Kensinger, 2011) have suggested that perhaps younger and older adults spontaneously relate different types of information to the self, or devote additional resources to process information that is self-relevant (positive for older adults, negative for younger adults). Though this idea has not been tested directly, see Chapter 6 for discussion of **self-referencing**.

Two other models have been proposed to account for the positivity effect with age. The **aging-brain model** (Cacioppo et al., 2011) purports that changes to the amygdala underlie this effect. The **cognitive control**

hypothesis (Mather & Carstensen, 2005) asserts that emotion regulation is the cause (Nashiro et al., 2012). According to the cognitive control hypothesis, positivity effects do not occur automatically with age. Rather, they require the exertion of controlled processing, such that older adults with higher levels of cognitive resources should be able to achieve larger positivity effects than those with lower levels of cognitive resources. For example, older adults with higher scores on cognitive control measures evidence more of a positivity bias in picture recall than those with lower scores, or in comparison with younger adults. Further support for the idea comes from adding a distracting task. This manipulation reduced the positivity bias, illustrating the need for cognitive resources to achieve a positivity effect (Mather & Knight, 2005). Both the cognitive control and default mode networks may be important for achieving cognitive control of emotional information with age (Lantrip & Huang, 2017).

The cognitive control model predicts that the prefrontal cortex will play an important role in enacting positivity effects, via the region's contribution to cognitive control (Nashiro et al., 2012). Accordingly, the prefrontal cortex may help to upregulate positive emotion as well as to dampen negative emotion. A review of the literature was consistent with these ideas. Nashiro and colleagues (2012) concluded that for negative stimuli, older adults show enhanced prefrontal activity and decreased amygdala activity, and that the prefrontal cortex can also be recruited by older adults in response to positive stimuli. To more directly test the cognitive control hypothesis, future studies could directly incorporate features of behavioral studies, such as manipulating the difficulty or cognitive load of a task, the cognitive resources of the research participants, and implementing distraction. One study thus far has used this approach. When participants were able to attend to faces, the anterior cingulate responded more for older than younger adults for happy faces compared to neutral faces (Brassen et al., 2012). This paralleled a behavioral finding in the same participants in which older adults were more distracted by happy faces when they had more attentional resources available, compared to a condition in which they were distracted with limited resources available.

5.6 Emotion and Memory

5.6.1 fMRI Research

One of the first reviews of the emotional memory literature that drew on a neuroimaging and aging approach was by St Jacques and colleagues (St

Jacques, Bessette-Symons, et al., 2009), who noted a pattern of **fronto-amygdalar age-related differences in emotion (FADE)**. FADE suggested that amygdala activity is altered with age and that older adults tend to recruit regions of the prefrontal cortex more than younger adults during emotion perception and memory tasks. Note that FADE is similar to the pattern expected for PASA, of posterior-to-anterior shifts with age. Even in the earliest literature, disparate patterns of findings emerged for the amygdala such that some studies reported reduced engagement in response to negative faces with age (e.g., Iidaka et al., 2002), while others reported a shift in preferential engagement for positive stimuli with age (e.g., Mather et al., 2004). Findings of enhanced frontal activity with age were more consistently observed in the literature. However, St Jacques and colleagues emphasize the importance of considering methodological differences, including the conditions under which patterns of activation converge or diverge with age, as well as issues regarding valence, strategies, and the potential for emotion regulation.

Subsequent memory effects, the brain activity when first encountering a stimulus that is related to successfully forming a memory (for a review, see Chapter 4), can have a unique signature for emotional memories, compared to nonemotional ones. For both younger and older adults, amygdala activity at encoding predicted successful memory for negatively valenced pictures, compared to neutral pictures (St Jacques, Dolcos, & Cabeza, 2009). Interestingly, the engagement of the left amygdala marked successful encoding for young adults, but engagement of the right amygdala did so for older adults. Other neural regions showed a pattern consistent with PASA, with younger adults activating more posterior regions (visual cortex) for negative pictures than older adults, but older adults activating more frontal regions than young. In terms of the functional connectivity for negative pictures, older adults evinced decreased connectivity with typical memory regions, including the hippocampus. However, they showed *increased* connectivity with cognitive control regions, such as the DLPFC. This pattern of amygdala activity was similar across the age groups, consistent with some earlier reports (Kensinger & Schacter, 2008; Wedig et al., 2005; Wright et al., 2006). This pattern indicates that the amygdala response may be relatively preserved with age, although younger and older adults may differ in the connected regions that support the formation of memories for negatively valenced information. Whereas younger adults can rely on traditional memory regions (e.g., hippocampus) and regions associated with encoding of perceptual details of the images (e.g., the visual cortex), older adults seem to engage in more emotion regulation (via the prefrontal cortex) in response to negative information.

Murty and colleagues (2010) also identified a pattern in line with FADE or PASA. The amygdala and hippocampus were activated more for aversive than neutral stimuli. Although older adults evidenced an overall decrease in their engagement of these regions, they showed enhanced activation of prefrontal regions. This pattern also emerged for memory, such that older adults engaged a region of the left DLPFC more than young adults during the encoding and retrieval of negative pictures. In contrast, young adults showed a greater increase than older adults of activity in the amygdala and a trend in the hippocampus during the retrieval of negative pictures compared to neutral ones. Measures of functional connectivity largely converged with the patterns of activation during the task, with older adults having stronger connectivity between the amygdala and the DLPFC during encoding and retrieval. Younger adults showed stronger connectivity between the amygdala and hippocampus during retrieval, with a trend during encoding. Stronger connections between the amygdala and the hippocampus were related to better memory performance. Amygdala–DLPFC connectivity also was linked to memory performance, though the relationship tended to be stronger for older than younger adults.

One possible explanation for age differences in amygdala and frontal activity could be semantic elaboration. That is, focusing on the meaning of information supports better encoding of information into memory (Tulving & Thomson, 1973). Age differences in the encoding of emotional information could reflect discrepancies in how much younger and older adults elaborate positive versus negative stimuli. To evaluate this possibility, younger and older adults viewed positive, negative, or neutral scenes in an fMRI study (Ritchey, LaBar, & Cabeza, 2011). Participants elaborated on some trials, focusing on the meaning and interpretation of the depicted scene, and engaged in shallow processing on other trials, focusing on perceptual details irrelevant to the meaning of the scene, such as the colors and lines. Although semantic elaboration did not affect amygdala activity, it did affect the engagement of the prefrontal cortex (medial and ventrolateral regions). For the elaboration condition, older adults engaged the regions more for positive stimuli than negative compared to the shallow condition, although this pattern did not emerge for younger adults. This finding may be in line with positivity effects, reflecting the cognitive control processes deployed with age (Mather & Knight, 2005). Correspondingly, older adults with higher scores on executive function measures exhibit more of a positivity effect in the medial prefrontal cortex. In connectivity measures, the ventral striatum, implicated in reward processing, emerged as a region that had stronger

associations with medial prefrontal activity for older adults during positive trials compared to negative trials. Younger adults exhibited the
opposite pattern.

Other research considered the amount of detail with which information was encoded. Kensinger and Schacter (2008) found overlap across
younger and older adults, with subsequently remembered pictures of
positive or negative objects engaging the amygdala, orbitofrontal cortex,
and lateral parietal cortex more than positive or negative items later
forgotten. Neutral objects did not show this pattern in these regions.
Additionally, the right fusiform gyrus was selectively active for negative
items that were subsequently remembered. The activity was particularly
strong for items that were later recognized with highly specific visual
details (e.g., distinguishing a picture of one grenade from another similar
grenade), consistent with a model suggesting that negative emotion
enhances memory for sensory details (Bowen et al., 2017). For positive
objects, a large frontotemporal network emerged for items subsequently
remembered. Because this network did not vary with the amount of
detail remembered, the activity was interpreted as reflecting general
and semantic encoding processes. One age difference emerged in the
study, with older adults engaging the medial prefrontal cortex and anterior cingulate more than young adults during the successful encoding of
positive objects. This finding was suggested to reflect age differences in
self-referencing for positive information, as discussed in Section 5.5
(Kensinger & Leclerc, 2009; Leclerc & Kensinger, 2011).

Age differences in connectivity during encoding of valenced information have been investigated in multiple studies. For positively or negatively valenced objects, age differences only emerged for subsequently
remembered positive images (Addis et al., 2010). The age difference
limited to positive objects was consistent with the fMRI study using these
stimuli (Kensinger & Schacter, 2008). Both the VMPFC and the amygdala influenced hippocampal activity in older more than younger adults
during the encoding of positive objects. This pattern was again suggest-
ive of a potential role of self-relevant processing during the encoding of
positive information into memory for older adults, although it is also
possible that emotion regulation strategies, subserved by the orbitofrontal cortex, contributed. Stronger connectivity for older adults than for
young between frontal and medial temporal regions also emerged in a
study of emotional scene encoding (Waring et al., 2013). In this study,
encoding of both positive and negative items enhanced connectivity
between these regions (i.e., orbitofrontal cortex and amygdala), as well
as within prefrontal regions (i.e., orbitofrontal cortex and DLPFC), for

older adults. Although this finding is in line with the FADE and PASA models, this pattern of age differences only occurred when both the emotional item and its background were remembered. Thus, the increased connectivity was interpreted as potentially reflecting broadened attention, allowing older adults to successfully encode information into memory.

Much of the research has focused on comparisons of extreme age groups, (e.g., college-aged students versus adults aged 60–70 years), but one study (Ford et al., 2014) underscores the promise of adopting a life-span perspective (ages 19–85). Participants studied positive, negative, or neutral pictures paired with a neutral descriptive verbal label. Based on the verbal label presented at recognition, participants elaborated the studied images for the items they deemed "old." Across positive and negative correctly recognized old events, multiple prefrontal regions, as well as some temporal and parietal regions, showed enhanced activity with age. In contrast, activation of posterior visual regions declined with age. In terms of age differences as an effect of valence, no effects emerged for positive events, though several frontal and parietal regions showed increases with age for negative events. Activations in one region, the medial prefrontal cortex, were broken down across five age groups. Only the oldest group, aged 70–85, showed an enhanced response for negative over positive events, compared to the younger age groups. This pattern indicates that the age-related change in the medial prefrontal cortex only occurs in the oldest group, rather than emerging gradually over the life span. In terms of connectivity across brain regions, aging was generally associated with decreased connectivity with the hippocampus in a wide set of regions for retrieval of positive and negative events. For negative events more than positive events, there was decreased connectivity between the hippocampus and lateral prefrontal regions as age increased. This pattern was especially prominent in the oldest group, but not the younger age groups. Although results generally converged with prior work in showing enhanced prefrontal and reduced visual cortex activity with age for negative memories, Ford et al. (2014) were novel in employing a life-span sample to reveal that neural changes as an effect of valence might only occur for their most extreme age groups (i.e., oldest versus youngest).

Although much of the aging literature investigating emotion thus far has focused on functional measures, some research is beginning to probe structural measures. A fractional anisotropy (FA) measure was used in DTI to assess structural integrity of the **uncinate fasciculus** white matter tract (Ford & Kensinger, 2014), which is a structural connection between the amygdala and the VMPFC. The structural integrity of this tract was then related to measures of regions functionally connected to the amygdala. This approach allowed for a combination of measures of white matter "hardware," the pathways that physically connect gray matter regions together, with information about which cortical regions coactivate. Although age did not have an overall effect on FA in the uncinate fasciculus, age did impact the *relationship* between functional and structural connectivity differently for the retrieval of positive versus negative events. During positive event retrieval, but not for negative or neutral events, structural and functional connectivity were more tightly linked with age. These results were interpreted as indicating that older adults enhance their recruitment of the amygdala–VMPFC pathway, in line with FADE and PASA, when the structural integrity of the uncinate fasciculus allows them to do so.

Measuring the brain at rest also reveals age differences in the communication between regions related to emotion. Younger and older adults completed resting state scans before viewing videos of positive, negative, and neutral faces; memory was later tested (Sakaki et al., 2013). This design allowed comparison of brain activity at rest as well as during encoding. Participants were split into groups to distinguish those exhibiting the strongest positivity effect (i.e., better memory for positive than negative faces) from those exhibiting weaker positivity, or even negativity, effects. In a subsequent memory analysis, the positive memory older group engaged the MPFC more than the negative memory group, a pattern that was the reverse of younger adults. For the resting state scan, the older adult positive memory group exhibited stronger functional connectivity between the right amygdala and inferior/middle frontal gyrus, as well as between the right amygdala and MPFC, compared to the older adult negative memory group. These patterns did not emerge for the younger adults. Relating the neural measures collected at the time of rest with those from encoding revealed an association between the MPFC connectivity with the amygdala at rest and the MPFC activity during the successful encoding of emotional faces, such that participants with higher connectivity at rest also had higher encoding-related activity. The authors suggested that these relationships may reflect chronic goals, such that older adults who exhibit larger positivity effects have strong emotion regulation goals. These goals may enhance the coupling of emotion and control regions at rest, and allow for the efficient recruitment of brain regions during the encoding of positive information. Moreover, recent work suggests that resting state networks associated with emotion may be less impaired with age than those associated with cognition, identifying an intriguing direction for future work (Nashiro et al., 2017).

Even though most of the research has focused on long-term memory, findings are similar for emotional working memory. Working memory for emotional information seemed to be spared from the typical age-related impairment in working memory, as compared with a visual task (Mikels et al., 2005). Moreover, older adults showed a positivity effect, whereby their performance was better on positive than negative trials. Younger adults showed the opposite pattern.

In summary, there is substantial evidence for shifts with age to better remember positive than negative information. Several studies report patterns consistent with the FADE model, such that older adults recruit prefrontal regions more than young, or exhibit greater connectivity between prefrontal regions and the amygdala. Other studies also more broadly support the PASA model, with more posterior activation (e.g., fusiform or visual regions) or connectivity in younger adults, as opposed to more frontal activity or connectivity in older adults. However, none of these findings are universal in the literature on emotional memory and aging, and the role of individual differences, including how age-related differences emerge across the life span, will be important to further explore in future work.

5.6.2 ERP Research

Research investigating age differences in emotional memory with ERP also tends to focus on the positivity effect. An initial study (Wood & Kisley, 2006) employed an oddball task, in which an emotionally positive or negative picture follows a stream of neutral ones. In response to negative images compared to positive ones, younger adults exhibited a larger **late positive potential (LPP)** than older adults; (see Figure 5.3). The LPP occurs approximately 400–900 ms after the presentation of a stimulus and primarily occurs over the parietal part of the scalp. The LPP may reflect age differences in evaluative characterization. Because only the negative stimuli elicited age differences, the authors suggested that changes in the processing of negative information are what contribute to the emergence of positivity biases with age. A follow-up study (Kisley et al., 2007) extended these results across the life span, 18–81 years of age. Results indicated that the magnitude of the LPP to negative images declined across the life span, although this was not true for the positive or neutral trials. This implies that the negativity bias evident in younger adults gradually declines as one ages. It may be that the changes reflect greater attempts to regulate the response to negative information with age, an interpretation consistent with other studies.

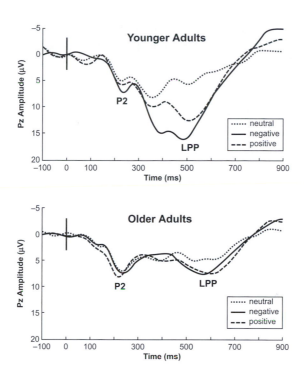

Figure 5.3 Younger adults' ERPs (top panel) show a pronounced difference in the LPP (late positive potential) response to negative stimuli (black line) compared to positive stimuli (dashed line). Older adults (bottom graph) do not. In contrast to the age differences in LPP, the P2 component does not differ with age.

From Wood and Kisley (2006), *Psychology and Aging*, Figure 1.

Another study connected findings of age-related changes in the LPP to behavioral memory outcomes (Langeslag & Van Strien, 2009). A reduced LPP with age again emerged in this study, although it occurred in a later time window (700–1,000 ms). The age difference reflected a negativity bias in young, whereas there was no bias in older adults. A similar pattern emerged in free recall, with younger adults remembering more negative than positive pictures, although older adults' recall of positive versus negative did not differ. In relating the magnitude of the LPP to memory, there was some evidence that older adults had a stronger relationship between these measures, such that those who exhibited a larger difference in the LPP for unpleasant versus pleasant pictures also recalled more positive than negative pictures. However, this tendency in older adults did not reach traditional levels of statistical significance.

ERP methods have also been employed to study the old/new effect for remembering emotional information. This recognition effect occurs over parietal regions and at around 500 ms after the stimulus onset. This has been used as a marker of recollection, the vivid re-experiencing of the encoded stimulus, as opposed to familiarity, a more general sense of having encountered a stimulus before (see Section 4.3.3). Langeslag and Van Strien (2008) found that younger adults showed a parietal old/new effect for both emotional and neutral stimuli, the effect being more pronounced for emotion. In contrast, older adults did not demonstrate an old/new effect for any condition in the 400–700 ms window. This result was interpreted as reflecting impairments with age for recollection, particularly for emotional stimuli, which likely enhance recollection in younger adults. Familiarity is thought to be marked by an early (200–400 ms) frontal old/new effect. Younger adults showed this component for both emotional and neutral stimuli, whereas older adults only exhibited it for emotional pictures. Overall, the results suggest that emotion may enhance recollection in younger adults but only benefit familiarity for older adults.

The effects of emotion also have been extended to source memory (see Section 4.3.4). Source memory was better for negative pictures than for positive or neutral ones, and this pattern was true for both younger and older adults Langeslag and Van Strien (2008). The ERP effects were expected to index recollection, which should enhance source memory. However, the pattern for the parietal old/new effect did not converge with source memory performance. An early (150–250 ms) parietal old/ new effect emerged for negative stimuli in younger adults but for positive stimuli in older adults. This effect was interpreted as consistent with prior ERP findings on the positivity effect, perhaps implicating an effect of emotion on familiarity or other more automatic retrieval processes.

In summary, some ERP data reflect differences in prioritization of positive over negative information in memory with age. Studies most consistently demonstrate a reduction in the negativity bias with age, reflected in the LPP component. The effects of emotion on recollection and familiarity have also been probed, with some evidence for age-related impairments in both processes.

Chapter Summary

- A number of emotional functions are supported by the amygdala and regions of the prefrontal cortex.

- Identifying emotion from faces or other cues can be impacted by aging, although the recognition of disgust seems to be preserved. Some of these changes may be supported by subcortical to cortical shifts with aging in the neural regions recruited.
- Emotion regulation may improve with age. This effect of age may be partly supported by strategy changes that allow older adults to adopt strategies that do not rely as strongly on compromised prefrontal regions.
- Relative to younger adults, older adults sometimes prioritize the processing of positive information over negative. Older adults may recruit frontal regions in tandem with altered patterns of amygdala activation in order to achieve positivity effects. Patterns of activity in frontal and visual cortices, as well as functional connectivity, may differ with emotion for younger versus older adults.

Discussion Questions

1. What brain regions are involved in emotion? How are these affected by aging?
2. How does aging affect the identification of emotional cues in faces? Which emotions are most impacted by aging? What consensus is there about the neural correlates of these changes?
3. Give examples of some emotion regulation strategies. How do these differently engage the brain with age?
4. Explain socioemotional selectivity theory and the positivity effect. What neural evidence is there in line with these ideas?
5. What types of changes to emotional memory have been documented with age? What theories might explain these age differences, and how does the available evidence support these notions?

For Further Reading

Kisley, M. A., Wood, S., & Burrows, C. L. (2007). Looking at the sunny side of life: age-related change in an event-related potential measure of the negativity bias. *Psychological Science, 18*(9), 838–843.

Leclerc, C. M., & Kensinger, E. A. (2008). Age-related differences in medial prefrontal activation in response to emotional images. *Cognitive, Affective, and Behavioral Neuroscience, 8*(2), 153–164.

Mather, M. (2016). The affective neuroscience of aging. *Annual Review of Psychology, 67*, 213–238.

St Jacques, P. L., Dolcos, F., & Cabeza, R. (2010). Effects of aging on functional connectivity of the amygdala during negative evaluation: a network analysis of fMRI data. *Neurobiology of Aging, 31*(2), 315–327.

Williams, L. M., Brown, K. J., Palmer, D., Liddell, B. J., Kemp, A. H., Olivieri, G., . . . Gordon, E. (2006). The mellow years?: neural basis of improving emotional stability over age. *Journal of Neuroscience, 26*(24), 6422–6430.

Key Terms

aging-brain model
amygdala
arousal
basic emotions
cognitive control hypothesis
cognitive reappraisal
emotion regulation
frontoamygdalar age-related differences in emotion (FADE)
habituation
late positive potential (LPP)
partial least squares (PLS)
positivity effect
selective attention
self-referencing
situation selection
socioemotional selectivity theory
uncinate fasciculus
valence

CHAPTER SIX

Social Cognition and Aging

Learning Objectives

- How does social neuroscience differ from the study of cognitive processes?
- In the social domain, what abilities seem preserved with age? Affected by aging?
- Which neural systems show age-related changes versus preservation?
- Why might qualitative differences in patterns of activity potentially occur more for social than cognitive processes?
- What future directions might be promising for study with neuroimaging?

6.1 Introduction

Behavioral evidence suggests that older adults may prioritize information with social and emotional meaning more than other types of tasks (Kensinger & Gutchess, 2017). Are the brain regions supporting social processes more preserved with age, or subject to the same types of declines and reorganization with age as cognitive systems? This chapter will discuss the emerging literature, covering topics ranging from the self to other people. Within these topics, we will consider research on empathy, theory of mind, impression formation, social interactions, bias, and stereotypes of age. How memory systems contribute to encoding and retrieval of socially relevant information also will be reviewed. These topics are relevant to everyday problems such as vulnerability to fraud and the effect of stereotypes on cognitive performance. Abilities studied by social neuroscience, as opposed to cognitive neuroscience, often are marked by the engagement of **cortical midline structures**, such as the medial prefrontal cortex (MPFC) and posterior cingulate cortex (PCC). Whereas these regions are *deactivated* during cognitive tasks that require external focus (as discussed as the default mode in Section 2.5), the same regions are *engaged* for tasks regarding thinking about others or the self (Heatherton et al., 2007; Lieberman, 2007). Because social tasks engage a distinct set of neural regions, compared to those that have been the focus of cognitive research, it is possible that aging will have distinguishable effects on social and cognitive abilities. There is some evidence supporting this possibility, with many findings of preservation with age in the patterns of neural activity for many social tasks. Some other tasks, though, seem highly influenced by strategy differences across the age groups. Younger and older adults may approach social tasks differently, particularly those with complex stimuli, resulting in distinct patterns of neural activity. Although there is relatively little neural data on some of these topics, behavioral research will be discussed in order to highlight some of the potential future directions.

6.2 Self-Focused Processes

Of abilities related to social processes and aging, one of the topics most studied with cognitive neuroscience methods is that of the self. Research in young adults establishes that thinking about the self activates a set of neural regions separable from regions implicated in thinking about other people, or other meaningful semantic decisions about information (Craik et al., 1999; Heatherton et al., 2006; Kelley et al., 2002; Northoff et al., 2006; Qin & Northoff, 2011). These regions lie along the midline of the cortex, in the medial prefrontal cortex and posterior cingulate cortex (displayed in Box 6.1), overlapping with networks engaged for other socially relevant information and the default mode network (discussed in Section 2.5).

When thinking about the self, older adults generally activate these regions robustly, much like younger adults. For example, in making judgments regarding the self-descriptiveness of adjectives (e.g., am I spontaneous?) compared to making judgments of how well adjectives describe another individual (e.g., is Albert Einstein reliable?), younger and older adults activated a ventral region of the VMPFC to a similar extent (Gutchess, Kensinger, & Schacter, 2007). The perspective from which younger and older adults make trait judgments may also matter (Ruby et al., 2009). In this study, participants not only made judgments about themselves and another person but they also made those judgments from a first-person perspective (e.g., am I spontaneous? Is my friend spontaneous?) or a third-person perspective (e.g., according to Dave, am I reliable? According to Dave, is he reliable?). Regardless of the perspective taken, findings for self-descriptiveness converged with prior studies (Gutchess, Kensinger, & Schacter, 2007), with similar engagement of the VMPFC in younger and older adults. Younger adults,

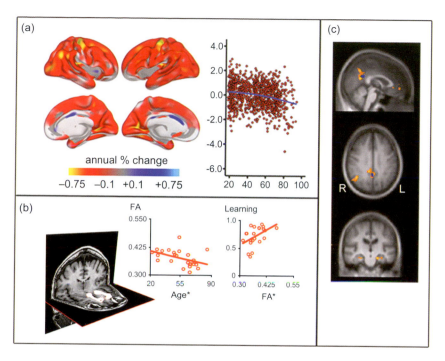

Figure 1.2 The panels display data resulting from recent methodological advances in cognitive neuroscience. The colored regions in the left side of panel A illustrate the widespread cortical thinning that occurs across the cortex with age. The hot colors (red and yellow) denote loss of volume, with the yellow regions showing the largest loss per year. The right side of panel A displays the loss of volume in the entorhinal cortex, which is exaggerated in later years (age is plotted on the x-axis) (from Fjell, Westlye, et al., 2014, *Cerebral Cortex*, Figures 5 and 2f). The left side of panel B highlights corticostriatal tracts. The graphs to the right show that the integrity of the tract (fractional anisotropy (FA)) declines with age and that greater integrity (FA, x-axis) is related to higher levels of reward learning (from Samanez-Larkin et al., 2012, *Journal of Neuroscience*, Figure 1d). Panel C shows that the default network (orange regions) is disrupted for participants with high beta-amyloid load, compared to those without (from Hedden et al., 2009, *Journal of Neuroscience*, Figure 4).

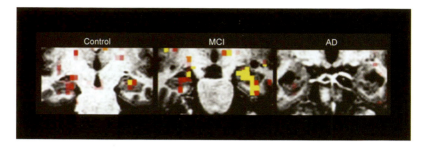

Figure 7.1 Compared with older adult controls (left panel), hyperactivation of the hippocampus may occur during associative memory tasks in early stages of MCI (middle panel), before hippocampal hypoactivation occurs in the later stages of AD (right panel). From Dickerson & Sperling (2008), *Neuropsychologia*, Figure 2.

Box 6.1 Neural Regions Associated with Social Cognition

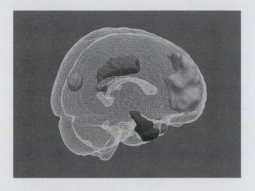

A black-and-white version of this figure will appear in some formats. For the color version, please refer to the plate section.

Regions involved in social cognition include midline regions, such as the medial prefrontal cortex (dorsal and ventral portions depicted in purple) and posterior cingulate cortex (in medium blue), as well as more lateral regions, such as the bilateral temporoparietal junction (in light blue) and bilateral temporal pole (in dark blue).

Figure created with software from Madan (2015), Creating 3D visualizations of MRI data: a brief guide, *F1000Research*, *4*, 466.

however, were more impacted by the perspective taken, with a trend in the DMFPC for the third-person perspective to drive neural activity more than the first-person perspective.

Although this initial research suggested that younger and older adults similarly engage neural regions when thinking about the self as opposed to another person, later work revealed potential differences in the network connected to the VMPFC. In making judgments of self-descriptiveness from one's own perspective, the VMPFC is coactivated with parahippocampal and precuneus regions in a common network across age groups (Feyers et al., 2010). These regions have been implicated in memory, particularly autobiographical or contextually rich varieties. In terms of age differences, the lingual gyrus is coactivated with the VMPFC for younger adults, perhaps reflecting detailed visual imagery in the service of memory. In contrast, older adults coactivated premotor regions, which are thought to reflect imagining actions, with the VMPFC more than younger adults. Interestingly, older adults exhibited more coactivation between the VMPFC and the orbitofrontal cortex, a region associated with emotion, particularly in terms of social interactions. These results may indicate that younger and older adults differ in the ways that they approach judgments of self-descriptiveness, but it may be necessary to probe networks to unearth these differences.

The research by Feyers and colleagues (2010) was not alone in suggesting emotion differently impacts self-referencing with age. In the first study of age differences in self-referencing, (Gutchess, Kensinger, & Schacter, 2007) assessed age differences as an effect of the valence of adjectives (e.g., friendly versus rude). Although the regions responding to self versus other judgments largely differed from the neural regions responding to positive versus negative adjectives, the DMPFC responded differently across the age groups. For older adults, positive words increased activity in this region more than negative words, but younger adults did not exhibit this pattern. This finding was interpreted as reflecting an increase in controlled processing of positive information for older adults, as would be consistent with prior findings in the emotion literature (e.g., Mather & Knight, 2005). This finding also contributed to Kensinger and Leclerc's (2009) suggestion that age differences in emotion processing could actually reflect spontaneous differences across the age groups in self-referencing of information (see Section 5.5).

Age differences in the positivity of self-relevant processing have been linked to the default network, during tasks as well as at rest. The default network, as well as the reward network, was engaged more for self- than non-self tasks, although this pattern was more pronounced for younger than older adults (Grady et al., 2012). In terms of the coordinated activity between regions, aging reduced the functional connectivity of the networks during tasks. During rest, this pattern of reduced functional connectivity occurred only for the default network, but not the reward network. Grady and colleagues speculated that greater engagement of these networks could be related to a more negative perspective, because younger adults endorsed more negative traits and had lower agreeableness scores than older adults. Thus, reduced engagement of these networks, or reduced connectivity between them, could be related to the more positive perspective often seen with age (Mather & Carstensen, 2005; see Chapter 5).

The self-referencing network has been implicated in age differences in broader motivational goals. When reflecting on personal agendas, midline cortical regions are engaged. Anterior regions, including the MPFC and anterior cingulate cortex, respond more when thinking about hopes and aspirations, whereas posterior regions, such as the posterior cingulate cortex, respond more to thinking about duties and obligations (K. J. Mitchell et al.,

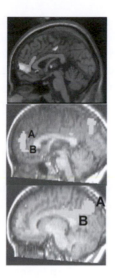

Figure 6.1 Cortical midline regions, including the medial prefrontal cortex (MPFC) and posterior cingulate cortex (PCC), respond under different social and self-relevant conditions. The top panel displays medial prefrontal activations, as well as a mid-cingulate activation, a region that is more anterior than the PCC. These activations emerge when younger and older adults make self-reference judgments, compared to judgments about another person. Panel adapted with permission from (Gutchess, Kensinger, & Schacter, 2007), Taylor & Francis. The middle panel highlights MPFC activations and the bottom panel depicts PCC activation (regions denoted by letters). These regions responded to thinking about duties and obligations, as well as hopes and aspirations, more than a control task, although some age differences emerged. Panels adapted with permission from K. J. Mitchell et al. (2009), American Psychological Association. *A black-and-white version of this figure will appear in some formats. For the color version, please refer to the plate section.*

2009). Although older adults evince less engagement of midline cortical regions than younger adults, this is most pronounced for the anterior regions that respond to promotion-focused goals (see Figure 6.1). Behavioral reports also indicate that younger and older adults may focus on different information. These findings are consistent with the interpretation that age differences in the engagement of subregions of the self-referential network may reflect shifts in motivational goals with age.

6.3 Self-Referencing and Memory

How self-referencing contributes to memory has been a popular research question. Relating information to the self is an effective encoding strategy, dubbed the **self-reference effect**, in younger adults (Rogers et al., 1977; Symons & Johnson, 1997) as well as in older adults (Glisky & Marquine, 2009; (Gutchess, Kensinger, & Schacter, 2007); Mueller et al., 1986). The MPFC, the same region implicated in making judgments about the self as opposed to another person, supports effective encoding of self-relevant information into memory for young adults (Macrae et al., 2004). This finding has emerged less consistently in aging research. In an fMRI study comparing the encoding of information related to oneself and another person, younger and older adults differently engaged neural regions in the service of memory formation. Regions, including the DMPFC, anterior and posterior cingulate, and left inferior prefrontal cortex, supported memory for information related to other people for older adults. Surprisingly, these same regions contributed to *forgetting* of information related to the self for younger adults (Gutchess et al., 2010). Later work, however, identified more convergence in the engagement of regions across younger and older adults. Although age groups exhibited focal differences in neural regions linked to emotion and cognitive control during encoding of self-relevant information, the overall pattern was similar across age groups, as shown in Figure 6.2 (Gutchess et al., 2015). In making judgments only about the self (without also judging another person), the MPFC was engaged by both younger and older adults for those words that were successfully remembered later on a test. These different patterns across studies suggest that younger and older adults may differ in the ways that they think about themselves depending on whether they are also thinking about other people. Additional behavioral data support this argument. Older adults' memory performance is affected by whether they are making judgments only about the self (as opposed to also making judgments about another person), and whether judgments are absolute (rather than relative to others). In contrast, younger adults' memory performance is unaffected by these manipulations (Gutchess et al., 2015). Thus, it seems that younger and older adults may consider different information when thinking about the self and others, potentially recruiting different strategies. Future work could probe the ways in which changes over the life span in social and self-identities affect recruitment of the self-reference network.

The studies reviewed thus far generally examine the encoding of items, such as adjectives, into memory. In terms of the encoding of details of information (e.g., perceptual features of objects; the source of who performed an action), both younger and older adults similarly benefit from a self-referential strategy (Hamami et al., 2011; Rosa & Gutchess, 2011).

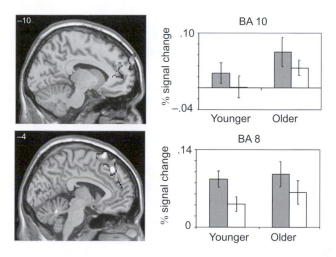

Figure 6.2 Younger and older adults exhibit similar engagement of the medial prefrontal cortex when successfully encoding items into memory (remembered items (gray bars) higher than for forgotten items (white bars), as assessed with recall (top panel) and recognition (bottom panel). BA: Brodmann's area.

From Gutchess et al. (2015), *Brain Research*, Figure 1.

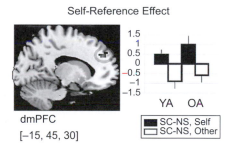

Figure 6.3 Younger adults (YA) and older adults (OA) activate the DMPFC more when source information is correctly encoded (SC, compared to the no source, NS trials) in the self condition, compared to another person condition.

From Leshikar & Duarte (2014), *Cognitive, Affective, and Behavioral Neuroscience*, Figure 4.

Across both age groups, the DMPFC supports the encoding of source details into memory for information judged relative to the self, as opposed to another person (Leshikar & Duarte, 2014; see Figure 6.3).

Effects of self-referencing on memory have also been investigated with ERPs. The ERP research thus far focuses on neural activity when information is retrieved from memory, contrasting the encoding focus of the fMRI work. For both younger and older adults, the old/new effect occurred earlier when retrieving self-relevant details, compared to other conditions (Dulas et al., 2011).

In summary, evidence from behavioral, fMRI, and ERP studies indicates much preservation of self-referential processing with age. Research thus far, however, has largely occurred at a foundational level, extending basic effects established in young adults to older adults. Future work can extend these findings to domains more likely to differ with age, such as age differences in self-concept (Gutchess et al., 2015), motivational goals (K. J. Mitchell et al., 2009), the intersection of emotion and self-referencing (Kensinger & Leclerc, 2009), and false memory (Rosa & Gutchess, 2013). Incorporating the study of the functional connectivity of different regions and subnetworks related to self-referencing is also an important direction for additional research, as some work (Feyers et al., 2010; Grady et al., 2012) reveals more robust age differences in networks, as opposed to individual regions.

6.4 Own-Age Bias

Thinking about others starts with the perception of another person's face. Age cues are salient when processing faces; as with other "own group" (e.g., race) biases, people exhibit a bias to remember faces from their own age group better than those from other age groups (He et al., 2011; Rhodes & Anastasi, 2012). **Own-age biases** in face processing have been proposed to reflect greater familiarity or motivational relevance for in-group faces. The same-age bias is stronger for younger adults; older adults do not exhibit the same-age bias as consistently (e.g., Wolff et al., 2012).

In terms of ERP measures, The N170, a negative-going component peaking around 170 ms, reflects face processing. In one study of the same-age effect during a face recognition task, both younger and older adults had a greater N170 peak amplitude when viewing older compared to younger adult faces (Wiese et al., 2008). The P2 component was also impacted for older adult faces, leading to the interpretation that age effects reflect differences in the difficulty of early perceptual processes. Old/new effects, in the later 400–600 ms window, also differed as a function of face age. Whereas younger adults exhibited a stronger old/new effect for own-age faces, this was not the case for older adults. This effect mirrored the behavioral data in reflecting better memory for same-age faces for younger, but not older, adults.

An ambitious ERP study (Wolff et al., 2012) of four age groups, from young adulthood (age 19) to older adulthood (age 80), examined the own-age bias in face memory. Younger and younger middle-aged adults had the most pronounced same-age bias in memory, whereas the same-age bias was absent in the older middle-aged and older adults. In terms of the ERP components, the N170 was delayed and enhanced as age increased across the groups of participants. An old/new effect, reflecting memory processes at 400–600 ms, emerged for the younger two groups of participants, but not the older two groups, consistent with the absence of an own-age bias in memory for the older adults. Replicating other studies, the P2 response was reduced for older faces compared to younger. Face age, however, did not interact with the age of the participant, suggesting that effects largely reflected general changes in cognitive processes with age or visual properties of the older faces.

Beyond early perceptual and attentional processes that differ for same- versus other-aged faces, relatively little is known about how faces from different age groups are processed. One fMRI study explored the identification and neural response to seeing emotional expressions (e.g., happy, neutral, or angry) on same- versus other-age individuals. Same-age faces recruited regions of the MPFC, insula, and amygdala more than other-age faces, and this was true while both younger and older adults identified all of the emotional expressions (Ebner, Johnson, et al., 2013). For angry facial expressions, the own-age effect was reduced in the response of the VMPFC and the insula, such that the response was more similar for same- and other-age faces. This may be because anger was more difficult to identify than the other expressions; emotion identification may have recruited more attentional processes, thereby reducing the processing of same- versus other-age information. Overall, the results indicate that threat information, such as angry facial expressions, may be prioritized in cognitive processing for both younger and older adults.

Another study investigated same-age effects by probing judgments of personality characteristics for younger or older target faces (e.g., is the depicted woman easily frightened?). Younger and older adults engaged a ventral region of the MPFC, overlapping with the anterior cingulate, more when rating own-age than other-age individuals (Ebner et al., 2011). This was interpreted as perhaps reflecting the similarity between same-aged others and the self, or the ambiguity of making judgments about unknown others from a different age group. However, it is also possible that the pattern of neural activity reflected greater **mentalizing**, or attempting to infer the thoughts of another person, for same-aged peers.

In summary, although relatively little research has investigated the response of the brain to same- versus other-aged individuals, studies thus far are fairly consistent in identifying differences in early perceptual processes and neural regions. Some work has moved beyond studying the simple perception of same- versus other-aged faces to investigate the influence of face age on personality judgments (Ebner et al., 2011) and emotion identification (Ebner, Johnson, et al., 2013). Future work could include further investigation of the cognitive and affective processes invoked by encounters with own-age and different-aged peers, including considering the effects on the perceived individual.

6.5 Stereotype Threat and Stigma

Negative stereotypes about aging are pervasive, with both younger and older adults expressing negative views about older adults (e.g., Bodur-oglu et al., 2006; Fiske, 2017; Mueller et al., 1986). These stereotypes can contribute to **ageism** – that is, prejudice against older adults (North & Fiske, 2012). Such negative views of aging can be internalized by older adults, impacting their performance on tasks. The original studies of **stereotype threat** investigated this as a function of race, finding that reporting one's minority racial group membership impaired performance on tests of aptitude and intelligence (Steele & Aronson, 1995). Later research extended these findings to aging. Older adults may exhibit poorer performance, including on memory tests, when the cognitive declines that occur with age are made salient (Barber, 2017; Hess et al., 2003; Levy, 2003).

There has been a dearth of research investigating the neural regions that are affected by stereotype threat in older adults. An EEG study found that under stereotype threat conditions older adults had stronger reponses (P300 and theta band oscillations) to negative self-concept words than to positive or neutral words (Zhang et al., 2017). These conditions did not differ in the control condition. Future fMRI work with older adults might be expected to converge with prior research that investigated the effects of stereotype threat on neural activity in other stigmatized groups. For example, invoking stereotype threat by mentioning gender differences in math ability increased activity in the anterior cingulate cortex, reflecting heightened emotional and social processing when under threat, compared to a control condition (Krendl et al., 2008). Similarly, older adults might be expected to show heightened emotional and social processing when under threat.

One extension of steretotype threat research intersected with self-referencing research, to investigate the neural response to making judgments about age-stereotyped versus neutral words. Older adults exhibit a larger difference than younger adults in the engagement of posterior midline regions during judgments about stereotype words compared to neutral words (Colton et al., 2013). This pattern was thought to reflect the processing of steretotyped words in a more self-referential fashion for older adults than younger adults. Additional research is needed to assess whether stereotype threat reduces cognitive resources in older adults or whether stereotypes simply induce different strategies and modes of processing information, without decreasing cognitive capacity.

Rather than probing older adults as the target of stereotypes, the study of stereotypes and stigma can also examine how older adults view people from stigmatized groups. When viewing pictures of stigmatized individuals, such as individuals who are homeless or have facial deformities, both younger and older adults tend to activate regions associated with automatic (e.g., amygdala, fusiform gyrus) and controlled processing (e.g., inferior prefrontal cortex) (Krendl et al., 2009). Group differences emerged, however, when examining prefrontal regions involved in regulation and inhibition of emotion. Levels of executive function capacity contributed to older adults' neural activation patterns. Older adults with higher levels of executive function engaged these regions more than those with lower levels of executive function, as well as younger adults. Comparing across individuals' scores rather than simply high and low groups, the older adults with the highest levels of executive function activated these regions the most (see Figure 6.4). Because younger adults and high-functioning older adults expressed similar explicit attitudes towards stigmatized individuals, the neural results may suggest that older adults need to engage more of an emotion regulation response than younger adults in order to regulate their reaction to stigmatized individuals. Perhaps only older adults with higher levels of executive function are able to successfully engage prefrontal regions in response to this demand; older adults with lower levels of executive function may lack the necessary cognitive resources to mitigate the effects of stigma. Subsequent research supported that interpretation (Krendl, in press). Furthermore, reducing cognitive capacity in young adults through a divided attention manipulation also impaired their ability to regulate negative emotions in response to stigma, providing additional evidence that cognitive capacity plays an important role in reducing negative bias towards stigmatized individuals.

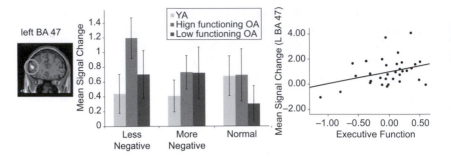

Figure 6.4 Older adults (OA) with higher levels of executive functioning engage a region of the prefrontal cortex (Brodmann's area (BA) 47) in response to pictures of stigmatized individuals (people with facial deformities or amputations). This condition is labeled in the graph as "less negative," which contrasts to the "more negative" condition of stigmatized individuals (people who are substance abusers or homeless), which people do not view as warmly. The OA high executive function group exhibits the response more than younger adults (YA) or OA with lower levels of executive functioning. The right panel displays the positive correlation between the level of engagement of BA 47 and executive function scores.

Adapted from Krendl et al. (2009), American Psychological Association, Figures 2 and 3.

6.6 Empathy and Theory of Mind

On the flip side of feeling bias towards stigmatized individuals is **empathy**. Empathy consists of an emotional component that allows one to feel what it must be like to walk in another person's shoes and a cognitive component, closely related to **theory of mind**, that allows one to understand another person's experiences. Although results are mixed, most evidence suggests that there is reduced cognitive (e.g., Maylor et al., 2002), but not affective (e.g., Phillips et al., 2002), empathy with age. Furthermore, the age-related deficits in theory of mind, the cognitive component, seem to extend across a wide variety of scenarios and tasks, based on a meta-analysis (Henry et al., 2013). Although some studies have demonstrated associations between theory of mind and cognitive abilities such as inhibition (P. E. Bailey & Henry, 2008), executive function (Duval et al., 2011), updating of information in memory (Phillips et al., 2011), intelligence (Charlton et al., 2009), or speed of processing (Charlton et al., 2009), the overall consensus of the literature seems to be that theory of mind deficits emerge with age regardless of the overall level of cognitive functioning (e.g., Henry et al., 2013; Maylor et al., 2002; Moran, 2013; Sullivan & Ruffman, 2004).

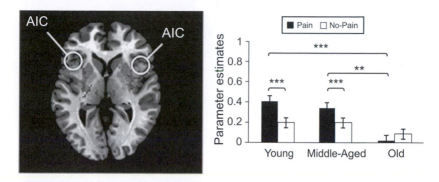

Figure 6.5 The anterior insular cortex (AIC) responds more during the perception of others' pain, compared to the no-pain condition, in younger and middle-aged adults, but this is not true for older adults.

Adapted from Chen et al. (2014), *Neurobiology of Aging*, Figure 2.

One study adopted a life-span approach to examine neural responses to affective empathy. Younger (20–35 years old), middle-aged (40–55), and older (65–80) adults viewed pictures of body parts in pain or no pain (e.g., a hand closed in a door or resting on a counter), predicated on the idea that pictures of pain would induce empathy (Chen et al., 2014). The response of the insula changed across the life span, with younger and middle-aged, but not older, adults activating an anterior region for the empathy-inducing painful scenes compared to the control scenes (see Figure 6.5). A contribution from the posterior region of the insula emerged only in midlife, with the middle-aged group exhibiting a pain effect in the region. Connectivity between regions involved in the perception of pain did not change with age. When pain was intentionally caused by another person in the scenarios, the regions that were related to ratings of unpleasantness varied across age groups, with the posterior superior temporal sulcus (pSTS) tracking unpleasantness ratings in younger adults but a mid-cingulate region tracking ratings in older adults. The results indicated some shifts in the types of processes induced across the life span, and were interpreted as indicating some loss in the neural response to emotional empathy with age. As the passive viewing task did not address potential differences in attention and mindset across the age groups, future tasks constraining the strategies employed by participants will be important to probe the effects of aging on empathy.

A handful of neuroimaging studies have investigated the relationship between aging and theory of mind. The first such study employed structural measures, including diffusion tensor imaging (DTI), white matter hyperintensities, and whole-brain volumes, in a sample of participants aged 50–90 (Charlton et al., 2009). Performance on theory of mind tasks declined with age. Those participants who performed the best had the highest levels of white matter integrity, as assessed with DTI; none of the other neural measures related to performance. Other studies have used functional measures to probe the connection between theory of mind ability and the brain. One study investigated age differences during the Reading the Mind in the Eyes Test (Baron-Cohen et al., 1997; Baron-Cohen et al., 2001), in which individuals select the word that corresponds to the mental state depicted in a picture cropped to show only the eye region. Core hubs of the mentalizing network, pSTS and the temporal pole, were engaged by both younger and older adults for the theory of mind condition (Castelli et al., 2010). Only younger adults, however, activated the anterior cingulate cortex. This region is also considered to play a role in mentalizing, perhaps reflecting monitoring of self and other in preparation for future action. In contrast, older adults engaged prefrontal regions associated with language more than young adults. The authors suggested that both groups were responding empathically during the task, but that older adults required additional engagement of verbal processing regions to do so.

More general age deficits in neural activity during mentalizing were identified in a study by Moran and colleagues (Moran et al., 2012). The fMRI study incorporated a variety of social cognitive tasks, compared to nonsocial control conditions. Results implicated a region of the DMPFC that older adults engaged less than younger adults across all of the social tasks; this region was thought to reflect the fact that older adults thought less about others' mental states when making judgments, compared to younger adults.

Although the two extant fMRI studies relevant to theory of mind focus on different brain regions and employ different tasks, the studies converge to identify age-related disruption in the neural activity thought to support thinking about the mental states of others. Research addressing the effects of aging on neural regions supporting theory of mind is in its infancy. Some of the inconsistencies across studies may reflect small sample sizes and different neuropsychological measures of ability. Future work should address these problems, including using multiple measures to assess cognitive abilities (e.g., multiple tests of inhibition) as well as attempting to assess the contributions of different strategies. Because these tasks typically involve complex scenarios (e.g., moral judgment tasks involve a story in which an individual is harmed either knowingly or unknowingly by another party), participants may differ in their comprehension of the content, how they weigh different parts of the scenario, or the reasoning that they employ. Neural changes with age could reflect differences in any of these aspects, and links with cognitive ability could be inconsistent because some problem-solving strategies draw on cognitive resources more than others.

6.7 Social Interactions

Aside from mentalizing, social interactions involve a number of cues that must be decoded and interpreted correctly in order to facilitate appropriate exchanges with others. Very little research has been conducted in this domain, but a number of interesting and complex social behaviors are beginning to be investigated behaviorally in the laboratory. For example, aging may be associated with failing to identify *faux pas* (Halberstadt et al., 2011) or finding gaffes less funny (Stanley et al., 2014) compared to younger adults. Processing of humor appears to differ with age, with older adults selecting fewer correct endings for jokes and finding those jokes less funny than younger and middle-aged adults (Uekermann et al., 2006). In this study, both mentalizing ability and executive function were related to the selection of joke completions. Studies of humor processing implicate the frontal lobes, a region that undergoes pronounced age-related change (Shammi & Stuss, 1999, 2003).

Although the effect of aging on *complex* social interactions has yet to be studied with cognitive neuroscience methods, two studies emphasize potential differences in the orientation that young and old bring to tasks. One study purports that motivational differences may invoke distinct processes in younger and older adults in response to different types of cues. The right temporal pole was engaged by different types of socially relevant pictures across younger and older adults (Beadle et al., 2012). Whereas older adults engaged the region more in response to isolation images, younger adults engaged it more to affiliation images (see Figure 6.6). The results were interpreted in terms of age differences in the qualities of social information that are most salient to different age groups, based on motivational goals (e.g., avoiding loneliness, or seeking out social groups). Age differences emerged in a study investigating the successful encoding of socially relevant source information into memory. Participants encoded statements that were true or false, and were either noted as such at the time of encoding by a label or inferred through the identity of the source (either an honest or dishonest individual). Although younger adults recruited regions of the left DMPFC more than older adults, older adults had corresponding increases in the left VMPFC and

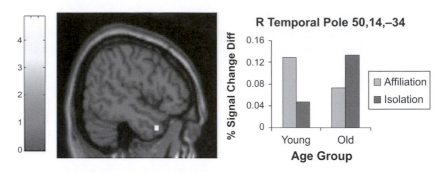

Figure 6.6 With age, the right temporal pole responded to different motivational content in pictures. Younger adults engaged the region more for affiliation (the left bar in each group) and older adults engaged it more for isolation (the right bar in each group), a finding interpreted to reflect the saliency of information based on motivational goals.
From Beadle et al. (2012), *Cognitive, Affective, and Behavioral Neuroscience*, Figure 3.

right insula activity compared to younger adults (Cassidy et al., 2014). Results were interpreted as potentially revealing age differences in orientation to information, with younger adults focused on knowledge acquisition (subserved by the DMPFC) and older adults attuned to emotional relevance (subserved by the VMPFC). Thus, these studies suggest that the neural response to complex social interactions may be marked by qualitative differences in the processes evoked by younger and older adults.

Based on a review of some of the literature, Freund and Isaacowitz (2014) suggest that the age of the perceiver may contribute little to the type of social judgments made about others. Whether this overall similarity in the social judgments of younger and older adults extends to similar neural activity across age groups is a question to be addressed by future studies. Although some extant work is consistent with this suggestion, with similar neural activity in younger and older adults during self-relevant judgments (Gutchess, Kensinger, & Schacter, 2007) and mentalizing (Castelli et al., 2010), other work highlights the age differences in neural responses to mentalizing (Moran et al., 2012) and forming impressions (Cassidy et al., 2012), all processes that could be invoked during complex social judgments.

6.8 Impression Formation

Although rich social interactions have yet to be probed with neural measures, there is a growing body of research on the effects of aging on impression formation, including some work employing neural correlates. Ratings of first impressions based on facial appearance show a high level of convergence across individuals, and this is true for both younger and older adults. For example, younger and older individuals showed high levels of agreement in their ratings of impressions of competence, health, hostility, and trustworthiness (Zebrowitz et al., 2013). The **attractiveness halo effect**, by which attractive people are rated and perceived positively across a number of different abilities (e.g., kindness, intelligence), extends to older adults (Zebrowitz & Franklin, 2014). In terms of the accuracy of judgments, in which strangers' ratings of faces are compared with objective measures (e.g., self-reports, medical records, evaluations), younger and older adults do not differ in the accuracy of their judgments of health and competence (Zebrowitz et al., 2014) or aggression (Boshyan et al., 2014). Using different methods to assess accuracy, such as associating strangers' leadership judgments of CEOs with information about the profitability of their companies, Krendl and colleagues (2014) also concluded that younger and older adults are similarly accurate in their judgments of others. Furthermore, they assessed how emotion recognition accuracy and level of cognitive function, both known to be disrupted with aging, contribute to first impression accuracy. Results suggested that neither of these abilities affect judgment accuracy. Despite the overall similarity in first impressions and level of accuracy for younger and older adults, some shifts can occur in ratings with age. Older adults tend to rate faces more positively than younger adults, particularly for the most negatively valenced faces (Zebrowitz et al., 2013). This shift in the magnitude of ratings was driven by older adults with lower levels of cognitive ability, suggesting a contribution of cognition to the positivity bias in ratings (Zebrowitz et al., 2013). The findings also imply that cognitive function may contribute some role in impression formation with age.

Forming impressions of others draws not only on facial features but also on information gleaned from behaviors. Measures of memory indicate that younger and older adults generally form similar impressions based on behavioral information provided alongside a face (J. M. Park et al., 2017). When integrating multiple streams of information about the behavior of others, older adults can emphasize different information than younger adults. Younger adults attend to the consistency of information and proficiently integrate newly acquired information with previous knowledge. Older adults, however, attend more to the *diagnosticity* of information, or whether the behavior (e.g., lying) is likely to predict a certain trait (e.g., dishonesty) (Hess et al., 1999; Hess & Pullen, 1994). In addition to diagnosticity, congruence of facial appearance and behaviors may be important. Faces and behaviors can be congruent with one another but they can also conflict (e.g., a trustworthy-looking fellow has a reputation for being a swindler). Although congruency similarly impacts memory for younger and older adults, such that people better remember congruent pairings, younger adults exhibit more extreme ratings of individuals whose appearance and behaviors are congruent, compared to older adults (Cassidy & Gutchess, 2015).

In terms of the neural underpinnings for impressions of others, research thus far with younger adults has highlighted the contribution of the amygdala, which is particularly responsive to facial cues such as trustworthiness, thought to largely reflect the valence of these cues (Engell et al., 2007; Todorov & Engell, 2008). The amygdala, as well as the DMPFC, is also engaged when faces are paired with sentences reflecting behaviors (Baron et al., 2011). When receiving diagnostic information about behaviors or traits, the mentalizing network, including the DMPFC, VMPFC, temporoparietal junction, and precuneus, is engaged by both younger (J. P. Mitchell, 2008) and older (Cassidy et al., 2012) adults. Orienting individuals to make social judgments about an individual, compared to nonsocial control judgments, robustly engages these regions (Cassidy et al., 2012; see Figure 6.7). The age groups differ in the recruitment of the right temporal pole, which may reflect age differences in strategies such as emphasizing stored social knowledge for older adults, given the role of the region in social knowledge (Zahn et al., 2007). Younger adults engaged the posterior cingulate cortex more than older adults for social judgments that were personally irrelevant compared to personally meaningful (Cassidy et al., 2012). This pattern could reflect the value younger adults place on ambiguous information (Schiller et al., 2009), consistent with their knowledge acquisition goals (Carstensen et al., 1999).

The positivity bias seen with age extends to the neural regions recruited during impression formation. Younger adults engaged the DMPFC and VMPFC for negative more than positive impressions of face–behavior pairs. Interestingly, the pattern reverses for older adults, with the regions more engaged for positive than negative impressions (Cassidy et al., 2013; see Figure 6.8). See Section 5.5 for further discussion of these patterns in terms of the emotion literature.

6.9 Impression Formation and Memory

Until recently, there had been little research examining how aging affects memory for impressions of others. This is surprising in that being able to

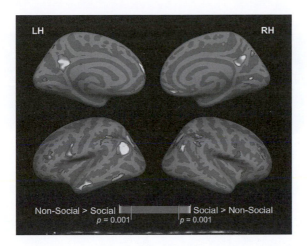

Figure 6.7 A network of regions (including the DMPFC, VMPFC, temporoparietal junction, and precuneus) that responded more for social than nonsocial information in both younger and older adults. The top row displays a medial view of the brain, including DMPFC activations shown on the left hemisphere (LH) and VMPFC on the right hemisphere (RH), with the precuneus on both hemispheres. The bottom row displays a lateral view, with temporoparietal junction activation more pronounced on the LH.
From Cassidy et al. (2012), *Social Neuroscience*, Figure 2.

act on impressions at a future point in time requires that the information gleaned about others be successfully encoded and retrieved from memory. Initial research established that the consistency of behaviors differently affects memory with age such that younger, but not older, adults remember inconsistent behaviors more than consistent ones (Hess & Tate, 1991). Later work demonstrated that older adults can successfully remember impressions of others (Todorov & Olson, 2008). The conditions in which information is learned affects the extent to which age differences occur. When older adults are attuned to the personal meaningfulness of others' behaviors, they can remember impressions as well as younger adults (Cassidy & Gutchess, 2012a). The specificity of the information that must be remembered may also influence the success of older adults. Younger and older adults can similarly remember general (e.g., good/bad) impressions of others, although younger adults are advantaged at remembering the specific details of behaviors (Limbert et al., 2018).

How similar a person is to oneself also affects how well impressions are remembered with age. Younger and older adults better remember

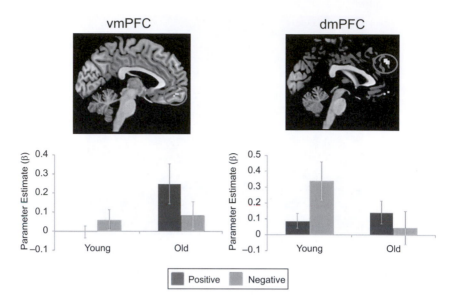

Figure 6.8 When forming impressions of others, younger and older adults differ in their engagement of MPFC regions. Younger adults engage regions more during negative impression trials, whereas older adults engage regions more during positive impression trials, consistent with shifts in focus on negative versus positive affect with age.
Adapted from Cassidy et al. (2013), *Social Neuroscience*, Figure 2. *A black-and-white version of this figure will appear in some formats. For the color version, please refer to the plate section.*

their impressions when the other person exhibits a positive trait that is true of themselves (Leshikar & Gutchess, 2015; Leshikar, Park, & Gutchess, 2015). In contrast, negative impressions of others are remembered more poorly when the trait characterizes oneself. The overall effects of valence on memory differ somewhat with age, as younger adults tend to better remember negative impressions of others whereas older adults exhibit a slight benefit for positive impressions (Leshikar, Park, et al., 2015), consistent with the positivity bias literature (Carstensen et al., 1999; Mather & Carstensen, 2005).

These behavioral studies set the stage for neuroimaging research. However, so far, there is no fMRI research with older adults examining the neural correlates of memory for impressions of others. One study (Cassidy & Gutchess, 2012b) did use structural MRI measures to relate the integrity of neural regions to memory performance. Results suggested that overall memory for impressions was related to the volume of the left amygdala across age groups. The role of the VMPFC differed across the age groups. Older, but not younger, adults with thicker VMPFC better remembered impressions of others when those impressions had been learned via socially meaningful judgments.

Functional neuroimaging research with older adults will likely implicate the amygdala and medial prefrontal cortex in the encoding of impressions. Research examining young adults by fMRI methods reveals that successful memory formation for impressions relies on the DMPFC (J. P. Mitchell et al., 2004) as well as the amygdala (Leshikar, Cassidy, & Gutchess, 2015). Studies of patients with lesions converge with these findings. Damage to the amygdala or temporal poles impairs memory of impressions (Todorov & Olson, 2008), whereas damage to the hippocampus and other typical memory structures does not (M. K. Johnson et al., 1985; Todorov & Olson, 2008). These findings may suggest that memory of impressions relies on a system distinct from the one that underlies other types of explicit memory. Thus, it will be important to assess the effects of aging on memory of impressions and the corresponding engagement of neural systems, given that what is known thus far about the effects of aging on memory (see Chapter 4) may not extend to memory of social information, such as impressions.

6.10 Trust

Trust is a powerful social interaction that may gain even more importance with age. Some accounts argue that older adults are particularly vulnerable to fraud, with half of the targets of scams over the age of 50 (AARP Foundation, 2003). Notably, a recent account (M. Ross et al., 2014) suggests that these claims, and the declines reported in the literature from laboratories, do not reflect the reality. The authors suggest that older adults are not more prone to be victims of consumer fraud than other age groups, and they consider the factors that may protect against the threat (M. Ross et al., 2014). The potential for victimization and finding ways to safeguard against this threat make it important to investigate the ways in which older adults can detect deceit and trustworthiness in their interactions with others. Older adults are poorer than younger adults at determining whether statements are truths or lies (Ruffman et al., 2012). Interestingly, although it is easier to tell when older, compared to younger, adults are lying (despite overall higher ratings of truthfulness for older adult targets), there is no same-age benefit in detecting deception. Some research suggests that age differences emerge in deception detection when the task is visual (Stanley & Blanchard-Fields, 2008). This finding led to research that adopted a reverse correlation technique to substantiate the finding. Using this method, participants discriminated faces covered with noise patterns by selecting the one they would most trust with their money (Ethier-Majcher et al., 2013). Although the results suggest a largely similar representation of trust across younger and older adults, with trustworthiness related to the judgment of happiness for both age groups, some age differences emerged. The representation of trustworthy faces is not as distinct from angry faces for older adults as it is for young adults. This result suggests some changes with age in the way that trustworthiness is assessed in others' faces.

Neuroimaging research indicates some ways in which trustworthiness judgments may vary with age. Although trustworthy faces were rated similarly by younger and older adults, older adults rated untrustworthy faces as less so (i.e., more trustworthy) than younger adults (Castle et al., 2012; see also Zebrowitz et al., 2013). Similarly, younger adults' anterior insula activated differentially to trustworthiness, with a larger response for untrustworthy than trustworthy faces, but older adults' response differentiated these faces to a lesser extent (Castle et al., 2012). Interestingly, younger adults showed an exaggerated anterior insula response when they made trust judgments, compared to a control tasks, whereas older adults' anterior insula were insensitive to the task. This difference in insula activity could suggest that younger adults' bodily reactions, or "gut feelings," are sensitive to cues of untrustworthiness, while older adults' are not. A diminished response to cues of untrustworthiness could contribute to older adults' vulnerability to scams and fraud, though research thus far has not consistently identified a diminished response with age. A more recent study did not replicate the insula finding from the Castle et al. (2012) study, and instead found that older adults' reward network is sensitive to variation in trustworthiness and some evidence of an age difference in the amygdala response (Zebrowitz et al., 2018).

Research on the neuropeptide **oxytocin** is also a promising future direction for research on the cognitive neuroscience of aging. Oxytocin impacts socioemotional processes, such as trust and pair bonding, perhaps through its effect on the amygdala. Despite a growing body of research on this topic in young adults, very little research has been conducted with aging, and of that, even less with humans (for review, see Ebner et al., 2013). Ebner, Maura, et al. (2013) proposes a model by which it is important to consider the complex potential contributions of oxytocin with age, given older adults' mixed profile of improved socioemotional function (e.g., emotion regulation) in some contexts but their increased vulnerability in other contexts (e.g., determining trust). Levels of oxytocin are potentially reduced with age, although levels can be increased by administering oxytocin intranasally (see Ebner et al., 2016). It will be important to consider the potential effects with aging on different abilities, particularly considering the number of levels at which oxytocin can exert effects (e.g., genes, brain, behavior).

6.11 Conclusions

The application of a cognitive neuroscience perspective to the study of social cognition promises to diverge from the study of age-related changes to strictly cognitive processes (for further discussion, see Gutchess, 2014). The patterns of underactivation and recruitment of additional neural regions by older adults, as reviewed in other chapters, generally do not characterize the age differences that emerge for social processes. As illustrated in Box 6.2, studies thus far seem to underscore *qualitative* differences and changes with aging in the conditions under which neural regions are engaged. Additional work is needed to understand the extent to which these changes reflect strategy differences, motivational goals that vary across the life span, or attention to different aspects of complex social information. The nature of these qualitative differences need to be better characterized and manipulated in future work, in order to distinguish processing *preferences,* which should be malleable with age, from processing *capacities,* which may be limited with age. Given the difficulties of inferring a unique process from a region of brain activation, as each region contributes to many processes (Poldrack, 2006), it will be important to use behavioral studies alongside neuroimaging in order to understand the nature of age-related differences in strategy or approach.

The potential for qualitative differences with age also begs for the direct comparison of multiple tasks against each other. While this approach was admirably adopted by Moran and colleagues (2012) in a study incorporating three different mentalizing tasks, their finding of decline in DMPFC activation with age differs from other findings in the literature of intact or enhanced activation of the same region with age (e.g., Cassidy et al., 2012; Gutchess et al., 2010). Although motivational differences have been suggested to contribute to these disparate patterns of findings (Cassidy et al., 2013; Gutchess, 2014), the potential differences across studies in participants and task parameters vary widely. This underscores the need for direct comparisons to conclusively determine under which conditions these age differences appear and disappear. As the literature on the social neuroscience of aging grows,

Box 6.2 Qualitative Differences with Age

This box details some of the qualitative differences that have been proposed to occur across age groups. Rather than undergoing declines in processing ability with age, social domains may reveal strategy shifts with age, such that younger and older adults engage the same neural region under different conditions or engage different networks for the same condition. The table contains examples of these types of patterns from the literature (OA = older adults; YA = younger adults).

Changes in prefrontal response to positive versus negative information with age.	e.g., OA > YA for positive > negative information; YA > OA for negative > positive information.	*Cassidy et al., 2013; Leclerc & Kensinger, 2008*
Theory of mind judgments engage different networks with age.	e.g., YA > OA for mentalizing regions (anterior cingulate cortex); OA > YA for language regions.	*Castelli et al., 2010*
Stigmatized individuals elicit a larger executive function response in older adults with high ability compared to those with low ability or younger adults. This could indicate that OA need to regulate emotion more than YA.	e.g., Activity in prefrontal regions tracks with OAs' executive function scores.	*Krendl et al., 2009*
Own-age biases in face recognition are stronger for YA than OA.	e.g., YA show a larger old/new ERP response in the 400–600 ms time window to own-age faces.	*Wiese et al., 2008; Wolff et al., 2012*
Regions responding to encoding of self versus other information reverse with age. This could reflect that OA think about others more when making judgments of the self.	e.g., Encoding memories for other-relevant information engaged regions in OA that responded to forgetting of self-relevant information in YA.	*Gutchess et al., 2010, 2014*
The neural response to goal motivations changes with age, perhaps reflecting focus on different information with age.	e.g., OA show reduced activity in anterior medial prefrontal regions when thinking about promotion-related goals.	*K. J. Mitchell et al., 2009*

meta-analyses will also help to identify the truisms and qualifying conditions for various patterns of brain activity with age.

Chapter Summary

- The extension of neuroscience methods to social processes has resulted in a diversity of patterns of findings, including loss, preservation, and strategic shifts.
- An overall pattern of losses with age does not seem to characterize the social domain to the same extent as other abilities.
- Research applying neuroscience tools to social questions is in its infancy, and there is much to learn.
- Context, motivations, and task orientations will be important to consider when comparing performance and neural activity between younger and older adults on complex social tasks.

Discussion Questions

1. What are the cortical midline regions? How do the patterns of age differences presented in this chapter compare to those findings presented in other chapters?
2. How do the first impressions of others formed by older adults compare with those formed by younger adults? How does age affect the underlying neural regions?
3. How pervasive are memory problems with age for information relevant to self and other? What neural regions support memory for socially relevant information?
4. What types of neuroscience tools have been applied to the study of social cognition thus far? What opportunities do you see for new research approaches in the future?

For Further Reading

Cassidy, B. S., Leshikar, E. D., Shih, J. Y., Aizenman, A., & Gutchess, A. H. (2013). Valence-based age differences in medial prefrontal activity during impression formation. *Social Neuroscience, 8*(5), 462–473. doi: 10.1080/ 17470919.2013.832373

Castle, E., Eisenberger, N. I., Seeman, T. E., Moons, W. G., Boggero, I. A., Grinblatt, M. S., & Taylor, S. E. (2012). Neural and behavioral bases of age differences in perceptions of trust. *Proceedings of the National Academy of*

Sciences of the United States of America, 109(51), 20848–20852. doi: 10.1073/pnas.1218518109

Gutchess, A. H., Kensinger, E. A., & Schacter, D. L. (2007). Aging, self-referencing, and medial prefrontal cortex. *Social Neuroscience, 2*(2), 117–133.

Krendl, A. C., Heatherton, T. F., & Kensinger, E. A. (2009). Aging minds and twisting attitudes: an fMRI investigation of age differences in inhibiting prejudice. *Psychology and Aging, 24*(3), 530–541.

Moran, J. M., Jolly, E., & Mitchell, J. P. (2012). Social-cognitive deficits in normal aging. *Journal of Neuroscience, 32*(16), 5553–5561.

Key Terms

ageism
attractiveness halo effect
cortical midline structures
empathy
mentalizing
own-age biases
oxytocin
self-reference effect
stereotype threat
theory of mind

CHAPTER SEVEN

Alzheimer's Disease and Other Age-Related Disorders

Learning Objectives

- What are the symptoms of Alzheimer's disease (AD)? How does it progress from earlier stages of diagnoses, including amnestic mild cognitive impairment (aMCI)?
- How do AD and aMCI affect brain structure, function, and connectivity?
- How can AD be distinguished from other neurodegenerative diseases, as well as the typical aging process?
- How are social cognitive abilities affected by different disorders?
- Why is depression important to consider in late life, alongside other disorders or in the context of typical aging?

7.1 Introduction

Discussion of aging inevitably brings **Alzheimer's disease (AD)** to mind. Although advanced age is a risk factor for AD (Alzheimer's Association, 2017), the terms are not synonymous. Many aspects of cognitive and other functions are affected by normal aging processes to some degree, as you have learned throughout this book. This chapter will discuss the specific behavioral and neural changes associated with AD and related disorders, such as **mild cognitive impairment**. Readers interested in learning more about distinguishing normal from abnormal changes in memory with age are referred to books such as that by Budson and O'Connor (2017). AD is likely the most commonly known type of dementia or neurodegenerative disease, but this chapter will briefly discuss other disorders associated with aging, such as Parkinson's disease.

Neurodegenerative diseases are progressive in nature, meaning that patterns of deficits and corresponding neural changes continue as the disease advances. Although some treatments can slow the progression of deficits, at present there are no cures for these diseases. Finally, the chapter will briefly discuss neural changes resulting from late-life depression. Despite the fact that the peak onset of depression occurs early in the life span during adolescence and young adulthood, depression may have some unique features when it emerges late in life. It is also important to consider as it can emerge alongside other disorders discussed in this chapter.

7.2 AD

AD is the most common form of dementia and the sixth leading cause of death in the United States. About 5.5 million Americans are living with the disease and its associated impairments of memory and other functions (Alzheimer's Association, 2017). By 2050, it is projected that 12 million Americans will be living with the disease (Brookmeyer et al., 2011). Worldwide, current estimates indicate that 9.9 million new cases of AD occur each year, with a total of over 46 million people living with the disease (Alzheimer's Disease International, 2015). **Dementias** refer to changes to intellectual functioning that impair an individual's daily functioning. AD is but one subtype of dementia, associated with a specific pattern of behavioral impairments and corresponding neural changes. The impact is most notable for memory but the disease also impacts cognitive orientation, personality, and even perception. The research reviewed in this section typically involves patient groups that have mild or moderate AD, as the ability to complete tasks declines as the disease progresses. The risk of developing AD increases with age. Thus, as the population ages, the public health burden of AD is predicted to increase dramatically. This is particularly true for countries with disproportionately fewer younger adults, such as China.

Historically, AD could be definitively diagnosed only at autopsy, by confirming the presence of the neurofibrillary **plaques** and **tangles** that are hallmarks of the disease (Braak & Braak, 1991). Plaques are deposits of **beta-amyloid** that are found outside neurons, whereas tangles are **tau** deposits that occur inside neurons. Although neuroimaging findings will be reviewed extensively in this chapter, the methods are not specific enough to allow a conclusive diagnosis of AD. Imaging methods such as MRI or fMRI can be used to assess atrophy or changes in functional activation in regions and networks commonly affected by AD, but they are not sensitive to the specific molecular changes that indicate AD, such as deposits of amyloid (K. A. Johnson et al., 2012). Nevertheless, neural markers such as pronounced atrophy of the medial temporal lobes are a strong predictor of who will receive a diagnosis of AD down the road (as discussed by K. A. Johnson et al., 2012).

In the past 20 years, much research has focused on identifying precursors to AD. **Amnestic mild cognitive impairment (aMCI)** represents the earliest stage in the AD pathophysiological process when symptoms are present and cognitive tests are abnormal. However, patients are not demented and are able to live independently. The amnestic subtype is the most common presentation of MCI due to AD. Diagnostic focus has shifted to emphasizing that this diagnosis must reflect early changes in memory function as well as the pathophysiological processes (e.g., changes to the medial temporal lobes) that underlie AD, as cognitive impairments can occur for a number of reasons unrelated to AD pathology (e.g., medications that impair cognitive orientation) (M. S. Albert et al., 2011).

Research on AD increasingly emphasizes the importance of early detection, as treatments are likely to be most promising if they can prevent, rather than reverse, AD. Thus, some research reviewed in this section concerns **subjective cognitive decline (SCD)**, when individuals report awareness of memory or cognitive declines but lack the neurobiological markers necessary to receive a diagnosis of AD or MCI. Thus, subjective cognitive complaints may not be specific to AD pathology *per se*, but are important to consider as the scientific and medical communities seek to expand the time frame in which they can investigate and treat AD.

7.2.1 Structural Changes in AD and aMCI

The brain shrinks dramatically with AD, as can be seen in Box 7.1. The vast majority (estimates of around 80–90%) of AD patients exhibit medial temporal lobe atrophy (compared to only 5–10% of healthy controls, as reviewed by Schröder & Pantel, 2016). Increased blood flow has been identified in aMCI patients in the medial temporal lobes even before the appearance of gray matter atrophy in the hippocampus (e.g., Westerberg et al., 2013). Loss of hippocampal volume seems to correspond to postmortem measures of dementia severity, such as the reduced density of neurofibrillary tangles in the hippocampus (Csernansky et al., 2004). Despite the consistent findings of group differences in hippocampal volume and the relationship between the extent of volume loss and behavioral impairments in memory performance, thus far hippocampal volume has not been useful diagnostically. Although some research suggests that hippocampal atrophy can be useful in predicting who is at risk of conversion to AD, the results are also variable across studies and specific methodological choices. In particular, individual difference

Box 7.1 Brain with Alzheimer's Disease

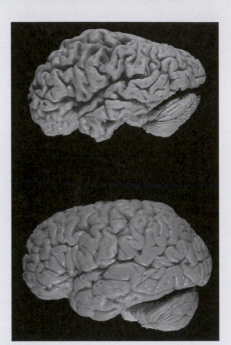

The top brain is from a donor with Alzheimer's disease and the bottom brain is from a healthy donor.

Source: Hersenbank (own work) [GFDL (www.gnu.org/copyleft/fdl.html) or CC BY-SA 3.0 (http://creativecommons.org/licenses/by-sa/3.0)], via Wikimedia Commons.

factors that could contribute to having higher levels of cognitive reserve may play a protective factor in helping individuals with substantial atrophy in the medial temporal lobe compensate to the point of staving off a diagnosis of AD for some period of time (as discussed by Schröder & Pantel, 2016).

Some have suggested that aging and AD differ in the regions that are most vulnerable, with normal aging affecting frontal regions mediating executive function and AD largely affecting posterior regions implicated in memory, including the medial temporal lobes and posterior cingulate/precuneus (Buckner, 2004). A different organizing schema draws on the principle of "last-in, first-out" (Fjell, McEvoy, et al., 2014). This idea is that the last regions to develop are the most prone to age- or disease-related decline. Another take on this idea emphasizes the evolutionary processes, such that the regions that have expanded the most in recent times (e.g., are disproportionately larger in humans than in other primates) are most vulnerable. In contrast to these organizing principles, Fjell, McEvoy, and colleagues (2014) suggest that the regions most affected by AD can be best characterized by referencing the default mode network. They also highlight the exceptional plasticity of these regions, suggesting that plasticity is a critical property of regions that support learning and memory. Moreover, perhaps plasticity makes regions particularly vulnerable to disruption and dysfunction (however, see Mufson et al., 2015 for arguments that the plasticity of the hippocampus makes it a promising target for therapeutic intervention).

Memory is not the only function affected in the early stages of AD, with recent work increasingly identifying the roles of medial temporal lobe structures in vision and perceptual processing (e.g., Graham et al., 2010). For example, AD patients with the expected pattern of hippocampal damage were impaired in identifying which scene was the odd-ball that did not match the others in a task that did not rely on memory (A. C. Lee et al., 2006). Another study of aMCI patients and older adults at risk of aMCI revealed heightened vulnerability to perceptual interference, compared to healthy older controls, presumably as a result of damage to the perirhinal cortex (Newsome, Duarte, & Barense, 2012). Indeed, enhancing visual contrast improves task performance for AD patients (Cronin-Golomb et al., 2007).

Although pathological changes begin in the medial temporal lobes, it is important to note that as the disease progresses, gray matter atrophy is pronounced throughout much of the cortex. This pattern can account for the widespread functions that are impacted by advanced AD. After early atrophy in the entorhinal cortex, the hippocampus, parahippocampal gyrus, amygdala, and limbic regions such as the posterior cingulate are impacted, with more of the temporal cortex to follow. There is eventually widespread deterioration across the cortex (for a review, see K. A. Johnson et al., 2012).

White matter pathways are also affected by AD; some even argue that these pathways are affected to a greater extent than gray matter (for discussion, see Oishi & Lyketsos, 2014). A higher load of white matter hyperintensities was related to poorer cognitive performance, as well as greater cognitive decline over a 1-year period (Carmichael et al., 2010). Some research links white matter hyperintensities specifically to

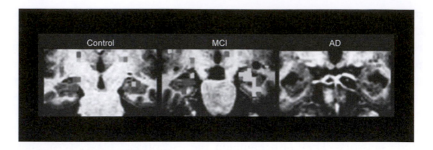

Figure 7.1 Compared with older adult controls (left panel), hyperactivation of the hippocampus may occur during associative memory tasks in early stages of MCI (middle panel), before hippocampal hypoactivation occurs in the later stages of AD (right panel). From Dickerson & Sperling (2008), *Neuropsychologia*, Figure 2. *A black-and-white version of this figure will appear in some formats. For the color version, please refer to the plate section.*

impairments in executive function, but not memory (Hedden et al., 2012). In terms of white matter pathways, the corpus callosum, fornix, and other pathways in limbic regions are affected by AD (Acosta-Cabronero & Nestor, 2014). The fornix is a white matter bundle located in the limbic-diencephalic network, which includes the hippocampus. Methods such as DTI have been employed to show that reduced fractional anisotropy (FA) of the fornix can predict the cognitive decline and atrophy of the hippo-campus that occur with AD (Oishi & Lyketsos, 2014).

7.2.2 Functional Changes in AD and aMCI

Much as the medial temporal lobes are subject to structural changes with aMCI and AD, functional changes also occur in the region. Research employing fMRI to study changes as an effect of AD largely investigates the brain response during associative memory tasks, such as learning which names are paired with particular faces. This type of memory relies on the hippocampus. The pattern of functional changes throughout the course of the disease differs from that for structural changes. Early stages of aMCI may be marked by increased activation of the hippocampus and medial temporal regions during learning and memory tasks, even when there is little atrophy (Dickerson et al., 2005). Hyperactivation of the medial temporal lobes, depicted in Figure 7.1, is thought to reflect ineffi-cient engagement of the region, possibly in an attempt to compensate for memory declines (as reviewed by Chhatwal & Sperling, 2012). Such a finding, however, is not universal, with reports of hyper- as well as hypoactivation in MCI patients compared to controls. The heterogeneity of findings may reflect differences across studies in the severity of the memory impairments in participants, a problem that could be exacerbated when they attempt to perform a task in the scanner (Dickerson & Sperling, 2008). At later stages of AD, patients generally underactivate the region compared to healthy controls. Longitudinal studies have established that this progression from overactivation to underactivation of the hippocampus occurs as the disease progresses, with those MCI patients who show the sharpest cognitive decline over 2 years exhibiting both higher hippocampal activation at baseline and greater decline in activation over this time window (O'Brien et al., 2010). Although the structural changes are well recognized as moving from rostral to caudal areas (see Box 1.1) of the medial temporal lobes, Dickerson and Sperling (2008) note the dearth of studies that have investigated this same gradient with functional methods.

In terms of changes to regions outside the medial temporal lobes, some studies (e.g., Sperling et al., 2003) identify increased activation in patients with mild AD. This occurred in parietal, precuneus, and frontal regions, perhaps akin to the recruitment of additional prefrontal regions in healthy older adults in other literatures, and as a response to neural insult. AD patients also seem to engage the cognitive control network, a frontoparietal network, less than healthy controls (see review by Chhatwal & Sperling, 2012). Regions in the default network also undergo alterations in functional activity, with some evidence of exaggerated deactivation of the precuneus occurring alongside increased activation of the hippocampus (Celone et al., 2006).

Research has increasingly adopted a network approach to probe the effects of AD on the default mode network, including the study of connectivity between regions during tasks as well as during rest. The medial temporal lobe network, including the hippocampus, sometimes couples with the default mode network, such as during rest, but the networks may uncouple during tasks such as associative encoding. In these instances, the medial temporal lobe system is activated during the task while the default mode network is deactivated. This relationship between networks may be disrupted for individuals at risk of AD (reviewed by Chhatwal & Sperling, 2012). The researchers speculate that the emergence of changes in connectivity early could be useful in early identification of people at risk of memory decline, before substantial atrophy occurs. See further discussion of changes to these networks in Section 7.2.3.

Implicit memory, memory that does not require conscious access to prior experiences (see Section 4.4), may be less affected by AD. In one

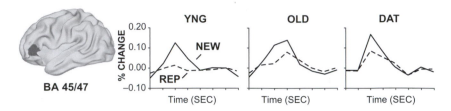

Figure 7.2 The left inferior frontal cortex shows priming-related reductions, with reduced activity for repeated than novel trials for younger and older adults, and participants with early-stage dementia of Alzheimer's type (DAT).
From Lustig & Buckner (2004), *Neuron*, Figure 2.

study, patients with AD exhibited intact behavioral priming, a form of implicit memory (Lustig & Buckner, 2004). Priming was measured by the extent to which judgments of animacy (e.g., is a cat living or nonliving?) are made faster for trials that are repeated compared to novel. Activation of the inferior frontal gyrus is linked to priming benefits, such that novel trials engage the region more than repeated trials; this is true for younger adults, healthy older adults, and patients with AD (see Figure 7.2). Despite the number of cognitive and corresponding neural changes that occur with AD, this study illustrates one preserved domain of processing for which neural activity is consistent across groups.

Although much of the research has focused on changes to memory and related systems, functional measures also have been used to probe other processes affected by AD. Attentional abilities decline in early stages of AD, and performance on measures of attention may be useful in predicting which healthy participants will later develop AD (Balota et al., 2010). These deficits are consistent with the fact that cholinesterase inhibitors are prescribed early in AD. This class of drugs prevents breakdown of acetylcholine, a neurotransmitter that contributes to attentional control (discussed by Gordon et al., 2015). One measure of attention is the mismatch negativity (MMN) (see Section 3.2), an event-related potential (ERP) component that can be reduced in normal aging as well as in AD. The component reflects monitoring in the environment and detection of unusual events, even when participants are not consciously monitoring their environments. The MMN is reduced at a site over the right temporal pole for patients with MCI, compared to controls (Mowszowski et al., 2012). This finding was true for patient groups with memory-focused impairments (aMCI) as well as those whose cognitive impairments were not specific to memory. Moreover, reductions in the

MMN were greater for MCI patients with more impaired cognition, assessed through self-reported disability and verbal learning scores. These findings suggest that MCI may impair the efficiency of information processing at an early stage, even before information reaches conscious awareness. Individuals with subjective cognitive decline (SCD) exhibit impairment of another ERP marker, the P3, which indexes allocation of attention (see Section 7.2) (Smart et al., 2014). SCD characterizes individuals who complain of changes in cognition but who are not at the point where neuropsychological measures can detect these impairments. Many, but not all, individuals with SCD go on to eventually develop MCI or AD. Changes to these attentional markers with early-stage cognitive changes or MCI suggest that ERP components have the potential to serve as biomarkers useful in detecting precursors to AD with more sensitivity than traditional neuropsychological tests.

Another study identified heightened activation for attentional control tasks in a cognitively normal population of middle-aged and older adults whose family history put them at heightened risk of AD. In a fMRI study, participants completed animacy judgments of whether items were living or nonliving as well as the Stroop Task (see Box 3.1), and provided other biological markers, including samples of cerebrospinal fluid (CSF) to assay tau, a marker related to neurofibrillary tangles in the brain. Participants with higher CSF levels of tau exhibited higher levels of activation during the animacy and Stroop Task in several regions, including the frontoparietal network (Gordon et al., 2015; see Figure 7.3). This pattern was interpreted as reflecting greater attentional demand in participants more susceptible to cognitive impairment. This research illustrates ways in which neural measures may be more sensitive to

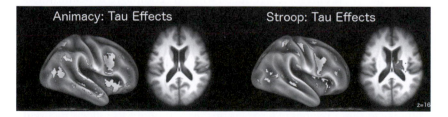

Figure 7.3 The panels show the relationship between levels of tau, measured in cerebrospinal fluid, with levels of brain activity on the animacy and Stroop attentional tasks. The highlighted regions depict where higher levels of neural activation are related to participants' levels of tau.

From Gordon et al. (2015), *Neurobiology of Aging*, Figure 4.

detecting risk of AD than behavioral measures, which were unrelated to levels of biomarkers such as tau.

Neurological disorders can impact one's awareness of deficits, possibly because some of the same brain regions responsible for the function itself also contribute to conscious awareness. Patients with AD may lack some awareness of their disorder, with changes to personality reported less commonly by patients than by their caregivers. One study employed fMRI to assess the effects of mild AD on making self-judgments and taking the perspectives of others. Results indicated some disruption to these systems. Patients with AD activated the intraparietal sulcus when judging the self-relevance of adjectives (see Section 6.2 for a discussion of neural regions implicated during self-referencing in healthy aging), perhaps indicating reliance on familiarity rather than recollection of one's personality (Ruby et al., 2009). Patients also differed in the neural regions engaged when taking the perspective of another person. Whereas younger adults engaged frontal regions, which are thought to reflect reasoning processes, and visual association areas, which are thought to reflect imagery during autobiographical memories, aging and AD seemed to differently affect recruitment of these processes. Patients with AD engaged frontal regions more than older adults, who engaged visual regions more. These patterns of findings indicate emphasis on different processes, with patients with AD reasoning rather than using imagery to adopt another person's perspective.

Some research has also addressed the effects of AD on emotion, with one study reporting that patients with AD show increased amygdala activity while viewing faces with emotional or neutral expressions, compared to fixation baseline (Wright, Feczko, Dickerson, & Williams, 2007). Healthy younger and older adults did not differ in amygdala activation. Although the volume of the amygdala is reduced with AD compared to healthy aging, this atrophy did not account for the functional changes in amygdala activity. Emotional contagion, the process through which an individual is influenced affectively, behaviorally, and physiologically by the emotional state of another individual, increases with MCI and the progression to AD (Sturm et al., 2013). Temporal lobe volumes are implicated, such that individuals exhibiting the highest levels of emotional contagion have the smallest volumes in these regions. This relationship is thought to reflect the break-down of inhibitory processes related to emotion, leading to greater suscep-tibility to being influenced by the emotional states of others.

The interactions between emotion and working memory have also been of interest. During an emotional working memory task, patients with aMCI exhibited a stronger negativity bias, with the precuneus engaged more for negative than neutral stimuli (Döhnel et al., 2008). In contrast, this pattern did not characterize older adult controls. The authors interpreted the results as suggesting that healthy older adults disengage self-referential processing during the emotional task, consistent with the deactivation of the precuneus. The increased activity in patients might reflect compensation, perhaps through self-referential processes, at early stages of memory disorder. A recent review of the literature converges to suggest complex shifts in processes with AD. Although emotion tends to enhance working memory performance in younger and older adults, results are mixed in terms of whether emotion benefits working memory performance in patients with AD (Fairfield et al., 2015). When an enhancement does occur with emotion, it does not consistently favor negative or positive information. The authors suggest that emotion regulation is impaired in AD, perhaps reflecting declines in the prefrontal cortex. Their review further suggests that despite atrophy of both the amygdala and hippocampus in AD, patients largely recruit the same prefrontal–medial temporal (amygdala and hippocampus) network as healthy older adults to support performance on emotional long-term memory tasks. Other work indicates stronger connectivity between the amygdala and prefrontal cortex for patients with AD compared to controls, perhaps reflecting compensation through incidental processing of emotion rather than engaging memory-specific processes (Rosenbaum et al., 2010). Taken together, the literature on the effects of AD on emotional processing may indicate overlap with the networks engaged in healthy older adults, but there are suggestions of shifts in strategies that could engage, or differentially weight, different processes across the groups. Given the paucity of research in this area, additional research is needed to clarify the interplay of these processes and the potential effects of AD.

In summary, studying the effects of AD on the activation of the hippocampal and medial temporal lobes has long been a focus. Early studies identified hyperactivation of the region in early stages of the disease, but the region is underactivated by patients in later stages of the disease. In terms of other regions, the default mode network shows declines in its integrity and its ability to couple with the medial temporal lobe network in AD. Attentional markers may be helpful in early diagnosis of the disease, with changes occurring in individuals before evidence of the disease emerges (e.g., subjective cognitive decline or heightened familial risk of AD).

7.2.3 Amyloid and Tau Imaging

The development of compounds that bind to amyloid was an important advance in the ability to image lesions related to AD *in vivo*. One of these, Pittsburgh compound B (PiB), is used in PET scanning to detect the deposition of amyloid-β (Aβ) (as discussed by K. A. Johnson et al., 2012). Scans of patients with aMCI or AD reveal deposition of PiB throughout the association cortex, particularly in the default mode network.

Buckner and colleagues (2005) observed substantial overlap among the regions implicated in the default mode network in younger adults and those regions that evidenced the highest concentrations of amyloid deposition, atrophy, and metabolic disruption in patients with AD. These regions are implicated in younger adults in memory processes such as retrieval success, coinciding with the profile of abilities that are impaired early in AD. The authors suggested that default state activity and metabolism might make regions more prone to the disruptions associated with AD. In later work, they noted that amyloid deposits were at their highest concentrations in cortical hubs, regions that are interconnected with disproportionately more networks than are other regions (Buckner et al., 2009). Furthermore, individuals with mild cognitive impairment who had high amyloid burdens exhibited more whole-brain disruption in these cortical hubs than individuals with low amyloid burdens (Drzezga et al., 2011).

Research thus far has shown associations between the default mode network and portions of the memory network. In terms of structural changes, amyloid deposition in the default mode network has been linked to the rate of atrophy in the hippocampus (Nosheny et al., 2015). In terms of activation patterns, older adults with higher levels of Aβ deactivated the default network (Sperling et al., 2009) and entorhinal cortex (Huijbers et al., 2014) during memory tasks less than those participants without Aβ deposition. In contrast, Aβ deposition was unrelated to how older adults modulated hippocampal activity during the memory task (Huijbers et al., 2014). This pattern may emerge because the entorhinal cortex, but not the hippocampus, is functionally connected to regions of the default network. Disruptions even appear for basic processes. When stimuli are presented repeatedly, people typically habituate to them, exhibiting less neural response across repetitions. This pattern does not characterize older adults with a high amyloid burden, who show greater responses in the hippocampus and posterior regions in the default mode across repetitions, compared to younger adults or older adults with a low amyloid burden (Vannini et al., 2012). These results begin to illustrate the relationships between the medial temporal lobes and default mode, but much more work is needed to understand how the changes to these systems together contribute to AD.

Amyloid is particularly implicated in disruptions of the functional connectivity within the default mode network. In a study of cognitively normal older adults, amyloid burden was related to the coupling of the default mode network, with those individuals with more accumulation of amyloid exhibiting weaker correlations among regions in the network (Hedden et al., 2009). The relationship between the posterior cingulate cortices and the hippocampus was also disrupted in those individuals with high levels of amyloid (as shown in Figure 7.4), indicating the early emergence of a disconnection between these networks. These results suggest that the communication of networks is altered as a result of amyloid even before individuals exhibit any symptoms of AD. Functional connectivity between other regions, such as between medial temporal and prefrontal regions, is also impaired in individuals with amyloid deposition (Oh & Jagust, 2013). Moreover, whereas older adults without amyloid change their patterns of connectivity based on task demands, older adults with amyloid do not. These results highlight the importance of engaging coordinated networks in a task-specific manner. This ability may be impaired in individuals with high levels of amyloid, perhaps indicating precursors of pathological aging.

Amyloid burden also relates to cognitive abilities, with those individuals with higher levels of amyloid showing greater impairments in performance on memory tasks (Hedden et al., 2012) as well as expressing less confidence in their memory abilities (Perrotin et al., 2012). Although the amount of white matter hyperintensities also relates to cognitive performance (as discussed in Section 7.2.1), the effects are separate from those of amyloid burden (Hedden et al., 2012). The authors caution, however, that this finding is based on a cognitively normal sample, and it is possible that these effects co-occur or have broader implications in cognitively impaired samples.

Although there is some evidence of associations between amyloid levels and cognitive performance, the overall profile is mixed. This is because both cognitively normal and cognitively impaired older adults can exhibit high levels of amyloid, with PiB appearing in about 30% of older adults who do not exhibit cognitive impairment (Jagust, 2009). This makes it difficult to appreciate the causal role that amyloid may play in cognitive decline. Jagust (2009) argues that amyloid may be an important precursor that leads to additional neural changes that cause cognitive

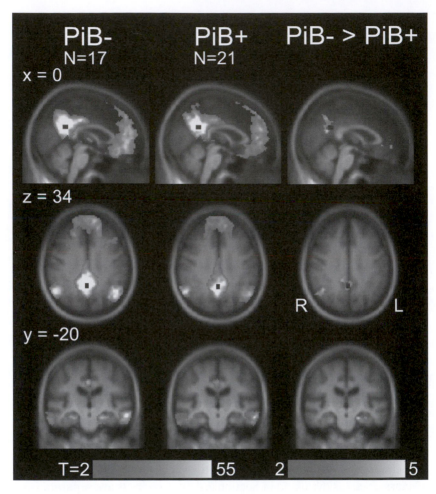

Figure 7.4 Connectivity between the default network (top and middle panels) and the hippocampus (bottom panel) is disrupted in older adults with a high amyloid burden (PiB+), compared to those without amyloid (PiB-). N denotes sample size. The small square denotes the seed region in the posterior cingulate cortex, which was used to test connectivity between this region and others. X, z, and y denote the position of the brain slices in MNI space in the sagittal, axial, and coronal planes, respectively. The bars at the bottom denote the strength of the effects, with higher values as brighter (here, more white).
From Hedden et al. (2009), *Journal of Neuroscience*, Figure 4.

changes down the road. Although many share this view, it is not held universally. For example, Fjell, McEvoy, and colleagues (2014) proposes that changes in the default mode, including amyloid deposition, may reflect normal aging processes rather than representing hallmarks of

AD *per se*. Thus, these regions and changes may contribute only *indirectly* to AD, as the high plasticity of these regions may make them vulnerable throughout the aging process. Another aspect to consider is that amyloid level is related to reduced levels of activation and deactivation across the adult life span, even for younger adults (K. M. Kennedy et al., 2012). Thus, the connections among these processes, normal aging, and pathological changes appear to be complex and require substantially more research to clarify the nature of the relationships.

The concerns about what amyloid represents if it emerges even in individuals with normal cognition have been exacerbated by recent failures of clinical trials that attempted to target amyloid in order to treat AD. It is possible that treatment will only be effective at early stages of the disease rather than once damage has been done, spurring work to identify early biomarkers of the disease. Some have argued that the mechanisms through which some of the drugs treat amyloid may be problematic, and other approaches could be more effective (Abbott & Dolgin, 2016). Others are far more doubtful, declaring it time to move on from the amyloid hypothesis of AD and investigate other mechanisms that could serve as therapeutic targets (Herrup et al., 2013; Le Couteur et al., 2016).

An approach based on PET tracers to measure tau is just now emerging in the literature. Histopathological changes associated with levels of tau contribute to the tangles found predominantly in the medial temporal lobes in AD, and levels of tau relate to the extent of hippocampal atrophy (De Souza et al., 2012). Levels of tau, as measured through CSF or PET, can distinguish individuals with AD from those who do not have it (La Joie et al., 2017) Moreover, tau levels in regions associated with cognitive processes, particularly the entorhinal cortex (Maass et al., 2018), have been linked to cognitive impairments, and these effects are largely separable from levels of amyloid (Bejanin et al., 2017). Thus, even as enthusiasm wanes for treatments focused on amyloid, early evidence indicates the potential of tau as a therapeutic target.

7.2.4 Genes

AD has a strong genetic risk factor. The Ɛ4 variant of the **apolipoprotein E (*APOE*) gene** is the polymorphism most commonly associated with late-onset AD. The gene is implicated in the production of amyloid and tau, which are elevated in patients with AD. The *APOE* gene operates in a dose-dependent manner such that having one copy of the Ɛ4 variant is associated with an approximately 20% risk of developing AD, but having a second copy of the Ɛ4 variant further increases the risk

(Bookheimer & Burggren, 2009). The *APOE* ε3 polymorphism occurs most commonly, with the rare ε2 polymorphism possibly offering a protective effect against AD. Although additional genes are implicated in AD, the effect of different *APOE* alleles is the best understood genetic component, with the most research to date. Structurally, possessing the *APOE* ε4 polymorphism is linked to higher rates of cortical atrophy over time as well as decreased thickness in the entorhinal cortex in children as well as older adults, indicating that the ε4 polymorphism may be a lifetime risk factor for AD (as reviewed by Bookheimer & Burggren, 2009). Functionally, fMRI measures reveal heightened activation while PET measures find exaggerated hypometabolism in ε4 carriers (as reviewed by Bookheimer & Burggren, 2009). A recent review, however, highlights the inconsistent nature of the fMRI findings, with some reporting increased BOLD activity for ε4 carriers and others reporting increased BOLD activity for noncarriers (Trachtenberg et al., 2012). Thus, fMRI measures do not seem to distinguish individuals with the ε4 polymorphism from those without it in a consistent manner.

Recent work has turned to investigating the effect of *APOE* polymorphisms on levels of amyloid. Although *APOE* ε4 is directly linked to the production of amyloid, *APOE* status and amyloid load seem to exert separate effects on cognition. In a sample of clinically normal older adults, both having higher levels of amyloid and the *APOE* ε4 polymorphisms were associated with greater cognitive decline over a short-term follow-up (Lim et al., 2015; Mormino et al., 2014).

Additional work has examined the effects of *APOE* status on network connectivity. Interestingly, cognitively normal *APOE* ε4 carriers had two patterns that differed from noncarriers. Connectivity was reduced in the posterior regions of the default mode network, in regions connected to a posterior cingulate seed region. But connectivity was *increased* in the anterior "salience" network, connected to an anterior cingulate region, implicated in cognitively demanding tasks requiring external attention (Machulda et al., 2011). These disruptions may reflect difficulty in regulating functional networks that contribute widely to cognition.

7.2.5 Concluding Thoughts on AD

Research has exploded into the neural changes associated with AD and risk of developing it. However, it is still unclear which of these measures have the potential to serve as biomarkers to predict the development of AD. Many of these measures, such as rate of atrophy of entorhinal cortex or amyloid burden, differentiate normal from abnormal aging at the group level. However, they may lack the sensitivity to detect one individual who will progress to AD from another individual who will not. Currently, there is considerable enthusiasm about tau. Research has begun to probe the relationship between a number of biomarkers in predicting age-related decline in cognition and memory in clinically normal samples (e.g., Hedden et al., 2014; Ward et al., 2015; Wirth et al., 2013), but more work is needed to extend this into samples with MCI and AD. Furthermore, the risk factors and development of AD need to be considered in a wider environmental context, particularly given suggestions that the immune system contributes to the development of AD through the detrimental effects of neuroinflammation (e.g., Heneka et al., 2015).

Further complicating the study of neural markers associated with AD are individual differences and lifestyle factors. For example, years of formal education may offer some protective benefits against the effects of AD. The amount of plaques in the brain predicts cognitive function, but those older adults with higher levels of education evidenced higher levels of cognitive ability than would be predicted on the basis of their brain autopsy (D. A. Bennett et al., 2003). Some research suggests that bilingualism may protect against cognitive decline or delay the onset of AD symptoms for approximately 3–4 years compared to controls (Bialystok et al., 2012; Perani & Abutalebi, 2015). However, interpretation of the effects of bilingualism as protective may be premature (e.g., Zahodne et al., 2014). See Section 2.8.6 for further discussion of bilingualism. Other individual difference factors, such as loneliness and race, may multiply the impact of amyloid. Higher levels of loneliness relate to higher levels of amyloid burden in older adults (Donovan et al., 2016). African Americans who were amyloid-positive exhibited exacerbated cortical thinning compared to a matched group of non-Hispanic White Americans (McDonough, 2017). Thus, the relationship of biomarkers to AD may vary across individuals based on a number of factors that can improve cognitive outcomes or exaggerate impairments in the face of aging or dementia.

7.3 Other Age-Related Neurodegenerative Diseases

Although far more research has investigated the effects of AD by using cognitive neuroscience methods, other diseases have received some attention. **Parkinson's disease** results from the loss of neurons that produce dopamine, and the primary clinical symptoms involve motor changes, including tremor, rigidity, slowing of movement, and impaired balance and coordination. The basal ganglia are primarily affected by

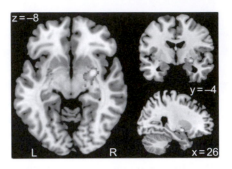

Figure 7.5 Activation of the right posterior putamen was reduced for patients with Parkinson's disease, compared to control participants, in a meta-analysis of tasks. The region is shown in different planes, with z, y, and x denoting the position of the brain slices in MNI space in the axial, coronal, and sagittal planes, respectively.
From Herz et al. (2014), *Human Brain Mapping*, Figure 1B.

Parkinson's disease. A meta-analysis revealed that the posterior region of the putamen showed reduced activity in Parkinson's disease patients during motor tasks, and administering dopaminergic medication increased activation of this region (Herz et al., 2014; see Figure 7.5). The meta-analysis of motor control studies further revealed the contributions of the frontal-parietal network, including motor and parietal regions. The engagement of this network differed in recruitment between controls and patients with Parkinson's disease, depending on task demands and performance (Herz et al., 2014). The connectivity between the striatum and other regions is also affected by Parkinson's disease, with more pronounced motor deficits related to weaker coupling between anterior regions of the putamen and midbrain regions including the substantia nigra (Manza et al., 2015). **Huntington's disease**, a genetic disorder that emerges in midlife and primarily affects the motor system, also impacts connectivity of the basal ganglia. Structural connectivity was altered between the basal ganglia and cortical structures for patients in the early stages of the disease, although individuals with the genetic marker who had not yet manifested the disease looked like healthy controls (Novak et al., 2015). Thus, connectivity changes with Huntington's disease emerge as the disease progresses.

Although motor symptoms are the most prevalent in Parkinson's disease, cognitive, reward, and social (see Section 7.4) functions are also impaired. In terms of cognitive changes, the learning of motor sequences is impaired, with the supporting neural networks differing across patient and control groups (Nakamura et al., 2001). Whereas a network of regions encompassing the DLPFC, supplementary motor cortex, anterior cingulate, and striatum predicts learning in controls, patients relied on a network encompassing frontal and premotor regions, but not the striatum. The authors suggested that patients with Parkinson's disease may recruit a broader cortical network to compensate for the failing basal ganglia function. This interpretation is in line with another study of automatically performing learned motor sequences (Wu & Hallett, 2005a). Even individuals presymptomatic for Huntington's disease showed disruptions in the neural substrates subserving motor sequence learning in a PET study (Feigin et al., 2006). Functional connectivity changes related to Parkinson's disease can differ depending on the extent to which patients show cognitive versus motor deficits. Patients with greater cognitive decline exhibit stronger coupling of dorsal portions of the caudate and rostral anterior cingulate cortex (Manza et al., 2015).

7.4 Social Cognition across Neurodegenerative Disorders

Many neurodegenerative disorders affect social and interpersonal functioning. Much of this research explores neural changes linked to dysfunction across disorders, rather than in a disease-specific manner. This approach reflects the difficulty of recruiting large samples of participants with different disorders, and the high level of variability across individuals with the same diagnoses, which is pronounced due to factors such as disease progression. The effects of typical aging on social and emotional processes are discussed in Chapters 5 and 6; this section will focus only on deficits resulting from various kinds of neurodegenerative disorders. In a review of the effect of different disorders on social cognition, Shany-Ur and Rankin (2011) highlight that disorders affecting frontotemporal regions impact social functioning much more than diseases such as AD, for which deficits are more limited to the cognitive components of tasks until the later stages of the disease. **Aphasias**, disorders of language production or comprehension, can impair social cognition when tasks rely on linguistic elements. Furthermore, several types of disorders impact emotion recognition, related to the volume of gray matter in the orbitofrontal cortex in Parkinson's disease and the volume of the cingulate in Huntington's disease (as reviewed by Shany-Ur & Rankin, 2011).

Recall from Chapter 6 that theory of mind involves both a cognitive component, the ability to read another person's mental state, and an emotional component, the ability to feel empathy for the other person. Investigation of the effects of neurodegenerative disease on theory of mind suggests that distinct neural pathways contribute to different aspects of this ability. **Frontotemporal dementia** particularly impairs the affective component whereas AD primarily affects the cognitive component (Poletti et al., 2012). However, the cognitive deficits may, in part, reflect the cognitive demands of the tasks typically used to assess theory of mind rather than the ability itself. Diseases such as Parkinson's disease, Huntington's disease, and **amyotrophic lateral sclerosis** (see Box 7.2), which damages the frontal-subcortical circuit including the basal ganglia, have widespread effects on theory of mind ability (Poletti et al., 2012; Poletti et al., 2011; Shany-Ur & Rankin, 2011). Overall, the review of the literature implicated both cortical (primarily supporting cognitive components) and subcortical (primarily supporting affective components) pathways in theory of mind ability. The disruptions unique to different disorders are in line with the observed patterns of neural changes across various patient groups. This assessment of the processes and regions underlying theory of mind converges with another review concluding that a frontal-subcortical circuit is important in theory of mind ability, by connecting the basal ganglia to frontal lobe regions (Kemp et al., 2012).

Additional studies extended research on theory of mind to other aspects of interpersonal communication. Understanding when someone else is lying or speaking sarcastically relies on theory of mind ability to read the intentions of another person. In a study across different groups of patients, Shany-Ur and colleagues (2012) found that patients with **behavioral variant frontotemporal dementia (bvFTD)** (see Box 7.2) were particularly impaired in these abilities (see also Adenzato et al., 2010; Henry et al., 2014). This is consistent with impairments in the emotional salience network in bvFTD, due to deterioration in frontal regions involved in attending to socially relevant cues and in the temporal lobe regions that mediate social conceptual knowledge. Probing the brain regions linked to ability to detect sarcasm, Rankin and colleagues (2009) used voxel-based morphometry to analyze the volume of regions and test which regions related to behavioral performance. Patients with smaller volumes in the posterior parahippocampi, temporal poles, and right medial frontal pole performed poorer at sarcasm comprehension (see Figure 7.6). The authors interpreted these data as suggesting a role for the parahippocampal gyrus in recognizing an unusual pattern of speech, which then triggers additional interpretation relying on temporal and frontal poles. In addition, the patient group with **semantic dementia** (see Box 7.2) was most impaired at detecting sarcasm, perhaps due to failure to recognize a dissonant tone of voice.

Several degenerative diseases can impact self-awareness of deficits, particularly when the right frontal lobe is impaired. In one study, patients with neurodegenerative diseases, as well as informants who were well acquainted

Box 7.2 Description of Age-Related Neurodegenerative Diseases

Disease	Symptoms	Brain Regions Affected Initially
Alzheimer's disease (AD)	Cognitive impairrments, including memory, that interfere with daily life (including social and occupational function).	Medial temporal lobes, paralimbic, temporoparietal cortices (Sperling et al., 2011).
Amnestic mild cognitive impairment (aMCI)	Cognitive impairrments greater than expected for one's age, but individual can still live independently. "Amnestic" indicates the subtype of MCI that specifically impacts memory.	Clinician judgment that early indicators of pathology are likely to be of the AD subtype, after ruling out other possible explanations (M. S. Albert et al., 2011).
Parkinson's disease	Motor changes, including tremor, rigidity, slowing of movement, and impaired balance and coordination.	Basal ganglia (Herz et al., 2014).
Huntington's disease	Motor changes, including jerky, uncontrollable movements.	Basal ganglia (Novak et al., 2015).
Frontotemporal dementias (FTD)	This class includes several subtypes, with examples appearing in this chapter described below.	Progressive damage to frontal and temporal lobes (Association for Frontotemporal Degeneration, 2017; Ghosh & Lippa, 2015)
– Aphasia (progressive nonfluent aphasia)	Impairrments of language can result from FTD. This variant includes slow, nonfluent speech (difficulty with language production and naming).	Left frontal regions most affected.
– Semantic dementia	This aspect of language impairrment affects knowledge about objects, including identification and naming. Speech is fluent.	Temporal lobes most affected.
– Behavioral-variant FTD (bvFTD)	This type of FTD affects personality and emotion.	Medial and orbital frontal lobes and anterior temporal poles most affected.
Amyotrophic lateral sclerosis (ALS)	Motor symptoms, including stiffness, atrophy of muscles, flailing limbs, and difficulty swallowing. Cognitive symptoms can include FTD.	Upper and lower motor neurons are affected (Martin et al., 2017).

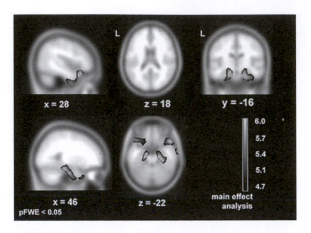

Figure 7.6 Lower scores on a test of sarcasm detection related to atrophy in brain regions depicted in the figure, including the temporal poles, posterior parahippocampal gyrus, and right medial frontal pole. Data are thresholded and presented at the significance level of $p <.05$, corrected for family-wise error (pFWE).

Adapted from Rankin et al. (2009), *NeuroImage*, Figure 3.

with the patients, rated the patients' functioning across different abilities: daily living activities, cognition, emotional control, and interpersonal behavior (Shany-Ur et al., 2014). Researchers first compared discrepancies between the patients' and informants' scores, and found that those with bvFTD were most impaired, overestimating their abilities in all domains, whereas other patient groups had more circumscribed deficits. Specifically, patients with AD overestimated their cognitive and emotional abilities whereas those with right temporal frontotemporal dementia were impaired in estimating their interpersonal abilities. Those with nonfluent aphasia misestimated both emotional and interpersonal abilities. In contrast, patients with semantic aphasia were relatively accurate. In the next stage of the experiment, discrepancy scores were related to brain volumes, assessed with voxel-based morphometry. These analyses revealed that self-awareness deficits were associated with the volume of dorsal frontal regions, which are thought to reflect the importance of domain-general attention, as well as the ability to assign reward to self-related processes, mediated by the orbitofrontal cortex and subcortical regions (see Figure 7.7).

7.5 Depression

Although depression is not a disorder of aging *per se*, it is important to consider in this chapter. One reason is that depression has a high public

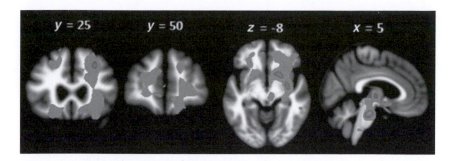

Figure 7.7 The figure displays the predominantly frontal regions associated with patients' overestimation of their abilities. Results are presented after controlling for overall severity of the disease.
Adapted from Shany-Ur et al. (2014), *Brain*, Figure 1.

health burden in older populations, with the heightened potential for functional disability and suicide in older adults (Lebowitz et al., 1997). Depression also has a high **comorbidity** rate with other disorders of aging, such as dementia or other physical disabilities, including those affecting the vascular system. Despite the potential shifts to higher ratings of life satisfaction and biases towards more positive emotional experiences with age, late-life onset depression can be a serious concern. Its profile differs from depression that emerges earlier in life, including the high incidence of white matter hyperintensities (Herrmann et al., 2008) and its resistance to treatment with antidepressant medications (for discussion, see Felice et al., 2015; Mather, 2012).

The age-related changes to frontal and striatal circuits may make older adults particularly vulnerable to cognitive deficits with late-life depression, even in the absence of dementia (as reviewed by Lamar et al., 2013). For example, depressed older adults showed reduced prefrontal activation, alongside increased activation of the striatum, during an explicit learning task, particularly for stimuli that violated expectations (Aizenstein et al., 2005). These deficits did not extend to an implicit learning task. Of considerable concern, subsequent research suggested that deficits in the activation and connectivity of frontal regions for depressed patients can persist even after treatment, indicating that changed neural functioning as a result of depression can have pervasive effects (Aizenstein et al., 2009). This is not to suggest that all effects of depression on the brain are immutable, as the same study showed evidence of increased activation of the right DLPFC as a result of pharmacological treatment.

Broader changes to gray matter occur in limbic regions as well as frontal-subcortical networks as a result of late-life depression. A meta-analysis identified several regions that had reduced volumes in older adults with late-life depression compared to healthy controls. For the frontal lobes, reductions of orbitofrontal cortex arose most often in the literature, with other volumes, such as that of the anterior cingulate, also affected (Sexton et al., 2013). The hippocampus emerged consistently, too, alongside sparse evidence for volume losses in the putamen and thalamus. The meta-analysis speculates on mechanisms, considering that white matter hyperintensities could contribute to alterations in gray matter and that the hippocampus could be impacted by the release of glucocorticoids in response to stress (for a discussion of stress, see Chapter 2).

Given that some alterations emerge even in the brains of older adults with subthreshold levels of depression, there is a substantial risk of widespread depression-related changes in the brain with aging. In older adults who report higher levels of depression symptomatology, but do not meet the criteria for a diagnosis of depression, the activity of the dorsal anterior cingulate, as well as its functional connectivity with other regions, is altered (R. Li et al., 2014). See Figure 7.8 for illustrations of these changes in connectivity.

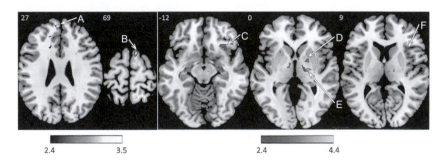

Figure 7.8 Subclinical levels of depression in older age alter functional connectivity, compared to healthy older adult control participants. The panel on the left displays regions that exhibit *increased* connectivity with the dorsal anterior cingulate, including the left dorsolateral prefrontal cortex (DLPFC) (A) and right supplementary motor cortex (B). The panel on the right displays regions that exhibit *decreased* connectivity with the dorsal anterior cingulate, including the right interior orbitofrontal cortex (C), right pallidum (D), right thalamus (E), and right anterior insula (F).

Adapted from R. Li et al. (2014), *Psychiatry Research: Neuroimaging*, Figure 4.

Chapter Summary

- AD, the most common form of dementia, is related to widespread changes in the volume, functional activation, and functional connectivity of the brain.
- Advances in imaging methods have allowed for the measurement of amyloid *in vivo*. Despite associations between amyloid burden and dysfunctional patterns of brain activation as an effect of AD, it is uncertain whether amyloid has the potential to serve as a biomarker to predict conversion to AD.
- The potential for compensation in early stages of AD, as well as the potential protective effects of lifestyle factors, makes it difficult to compare across individuals and conclusively predict the onset of the disease.
- Other degenerative diseases that occur with age have patterns of impairments and neural changes that can be distinguished from AD. Some of these particularly impact social cognitive function.
- Late-life depression can occur alongside neurodegenerative disorders and can have long-lasting effects on neural networks.

Discussion Questions

1. What is AD? How does it differ from "normal aging," as reviewed in this book?
2. What are some ways in which AD affects the brain? Which of the changes discussed in this chapter do you think have potential for early detection of AD, thus extending the window for potential treatments in the future?
3. Contrast a second neurodegenerative disease (e.g., Parkinson's disease, Huntington's disease) to AD. How do the symptoms and effects on neural systems differ?
4. Which neurodegenerative disease reviewed in the chapter is associated with the most impairment to social cognitive function? Why might this be?
5. How does depression affect brain activity? Why is it important to consider with aging?

For Further Reading

Fjell, A. M., McEvoy, L., Holland, D., Dale, A. M., Walhovd, K. B., & Alzheimer's Disease Neuroimaging Initiative. (2014). What is normal in normal aging? Effects of aging, amyloid and Alzheimer's disease on the cerebral cortex and the hippocampus. *Progress in Neurobiology, 117,* 20–40.

Hedden, T., Van Dijk, K. R., Becker, J. A., Mehta, A., Sperling, R. A., Johnson, K. A., & Buckner, R. L. (2009). Disruption of functional connectivity in clinically normal older adults harboring amyloid burden. *Journal of Neuroscience, 29*(40), 12686–12694.

Johnson, K. A., Fox, N. C., Sperling, R. A., & Klunk, W. E. (2012). Brain imaging in Alzheimer disease. *Cold Spring Harbor Perspectives in Medicine, 2*(4), a006213.

Shany-Ur, T., & Rankin, K. P. (2011). Personality and social cognition in neurodegenerative disease. *Current Opinion in Neurology, 24*(6), 550–5.

Sperling, R. A., LaViolette, P. S., O'Keefe, K., O'Brien, J., Rentz, D. M., Pihlajamaki, M., . . . Hedden, T. (2009). Amyloid deposition is associated with impaired default network function in older persons without dementia. *Neuron, 63*(2), 178–188.

Key Terms

Alzheimer's disease (AD)
amnestic mild cognitive impairment (aMCI)
amyotrophic lateral sclerosis (ALS)
aphasias
apolipoprotein E (*APOE*) gene
behavioral variant frontotemporal dementia (bvFTD)
beta-amyloid (or amyloid)
comorbidity
dementias
frontotemporal dementia (FTD)
Huntington's disease
mild cognitive impairment (MCI)
Parkinson's disease
plaques
semantic dementia
subjective cognitive decline
tangles
tau

CHAPTER EIGHT

Current and Future Directions

Learning Objectives

- How does aging affect neural activity during decision making and economic tasks?
- What types of decision and motivation tasks lack neural data? What are the challenges of applying cognitive neuroscience methods to these areas?
- How is neuromodulation, or stimulation of brain regions, being used in an attempt to improve cognition with age?
- What are promising future directions for research, and what knowledge can be gained in these areas? What are the challenges facing the application of cognitive neuroscience methods to these questions?

8.1 Introduction

Throughout this book, you have learned ways in which aging affects the brain and the ways in which neural activity underlies a number of different cognitive, emotional, and social processes. This concluding chapter presents current exciting areas of investigation, probing neural systems related to reward and decision making and exploring the effects of **neuromodulation** on aging. The chapter ends with consideration of some current themes in the field, such as the importance of studying aging longitudinally and considering how early-life factors impact the aging process, whether socioemotional and cognitive domains should be considered separately, and the importance of context.

8.2 Decision Making and Reward

One behavior highly relevant to everyday life is decision making. There are few cognitive neuroscience studies of basic decision making processes and heuristics, perhaps due to the challenges of cognitive neuroscience designs. Designs require many trials in order to compare brain activity and some decisions are not able to be meaningfully repeated so many times. The potential for variability in the time course is also a challenge. For example, for prolonged processes, it may be difficult to consistently identify, across individuals and trials, the particular decision points at which neural activity would indicate critical subprocesses. Much of the research to date has adopted a **neuroeconomics** approach, studying the effects of aging on the neural substrates underlying reward and economic tasks, rather than other types of deliberative and complex choices.

8.2.1 Reward and Economic Tasks

Early work on the effects of aging on reward and decision making primarily converged with socioemotional selectivity theory (see Chapter 5.5), with older adults displaying more sensitivity to positive than negative information (Carstensen et al., 1999). Extending this framework to the domain of reward, an initial study showed that older adults exhibit a robust response when anticipating gains, marked by intact activation with age of the striatum and insula (Samanez-Larkin et al., 2007). In contrast, the response of these regions was reduced for older adults when participants expected losses. This neural evidence substantiated older adults' self-reports of experiencing less negative emotion than young adults, and identified a neural or physiological basis for these age differences in sensitivity to gains versus losses. Reduced neural responsivity to loss could leave older adults vulnerable to biases in decision making.

Overall striatal response seems to be intact with age. Across the time course, older adults differentiate reward and punishment feedback in the caudate and ventral striatum and also exhibit a more sustained response to rewards than punishment (Cox, Aizenstein, & Fiez, 2008). These features are also true for younger adults, but age differences emerge in the early post-outcome window, which exhibits a reduced striatal response with age to punishment. In addition, the response of the striatum is more constrained spatially in older adults. This study overall emphasized the intact striatal response with age, albeit with a younger sample of older adults (ages 50–70).

Potential changes in the response of reward regions with age have major implications for older adults' financial decisions and well-being. Some have suggested that older adults are simply risk averse, but there is considerable variability in performance, perhaps reflecting brain changes (Goh et al., 2016; see also Seaman, 2017). Other research is beginning to consider the contribution of poor learning or poor discrimination of noisy value signals in trying to understand suboptimal decisions. In an

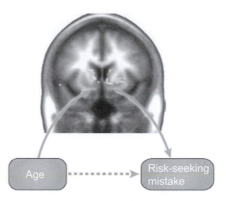

Figure 8.1 Variability in the activation of the nucleus accumbens mediates the relationship between age and risk-seeking mistakes.
From Samanez-Larkin & Knutson (2015), *Nature Reviews Neuroscience*, Figure 2b.

investment task, older adults were no more likely than younger adults to commit mistakes due to risk aversion, even though rational choices decreased with age and mistakes due to risk-seeking and confusion increased with age (Samanez-Larkin et al., 2010). No age-related differences emerged in neural regions that responded to risk-seeking mistakes, suggesting that reduced sensitivity to feedback did not account for age differences. Thus, it appears that risk aversion does not completely explain older adults' financial decision making. Instead, temporal variability in the neural response from one measurement to the next could indicate noise in the system, contributing to mistakes in risk-seeking behavior. Indeed, temporal variability in the response of the nucleus accumbens accounted for the relationship between aging and risk-seeking mistakes (see Figure 8.1). Thus, poor choices may result from variability in the nucleus accumbens signal with age, impairing predictions of risk.

In terms of the contribution of white matter pathways, diffusion tensor imaging (DTI) was employed to evaluate whether the effects of age on white matter integrity accounted for some of the age-related deficits in reward learning (Samanez-Larkin et al., 2012). Thalamocorticostriatal pathways, white matter tracts between the thalamus and medial prefrontal cortex and between the medial prefrontal cortex and ventral striatum, were impacted by aging. The integrity of these pathways predicts age differences in reward learning across the life span, indicating the importance of being able to transmit relevant information throughout this circuit (see Figure 8.2).

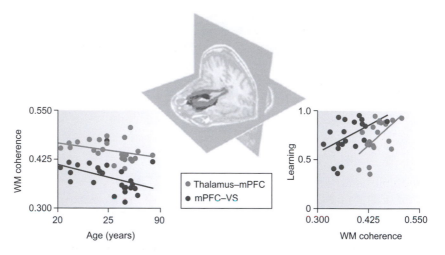

Figure 8.2 The integrity of the structural pathways (white matter (WM) coherence) connecting the thalamus to the medial prefrontal cortex (mPFC) to the ventral striatum (VS) decreases with age (graph on the left). Individuals with higher levels of WM coherence learn more effectively about reward than those with lower levels (graph on the right).
From Samanez-Larkin & Knutson (2015), *Nature Reviews Neuroscience*, Figure 3b.

Delay is another aspect of reward processing that may disrupt performance across the life span. Research in young adults illustrates that people discount rewards that will be received in the future rather than now, a phenomenon known as **delay discounting**. One study using behavioral measures found no age differences in preferences for immediate versus delayed rewards, but neural measures differed with age (Samanez-Larkin et al., 2011). Younger adults exhibited the typical pattern of heightened responsivity in the mesolimbic dopamine activity system for a reward that would be received today rather than in 2 weeks, but the temporal manipulation affected older adults' neural response less. Both immediate and delayed rewards engaged the ventral putamen in older adults, leading to the interpretation of this age difference as reflecting older adults' substantial experience with receiving delayed rewards over a lifetime, rather than as reflecting a deficit in reward responsivity with age.

The decline in cognitive abilities with age could contribute to difficulty in decision making. Some research suggests that younger and older adults perform similarly when tasks do not involve learning. This idea was supported by a meta-analysis (Mata et al., 2011) that suggested that older adults were most impaired when tasks involve **reversal learning**, or learning that the rewarded response changes. For example, if choosing the item on the left initially was rewarded, the contingencies would change such that choosing the item on the *right* would be rewarded. Samanez-Larkin and colleagues (Samanez-Larkin et al., 2014) also found that age effects depend on whether or not tasks required learning. During probabilistic learning, there was reduced frontostriatal activity with age across the life span. In contrast, no age differences emerged for a task focused on reward outcome without a learning component. These results are consistent with other findings of similar neural activity for younger and older adults when tasks do not require learning. Spaniol and colleagues (2015) analyzed fMRI data by a partial least squares approach, which identifies spatiotemporal patterns of activity varying across task conditions. Age differences occurred about 10 s after cue onset, and reflected increased engagement of cognitive control regions and reduced deactivation of the default network regions in older adults compared to younger adults. This pattern differs from prior findings of age differences in the default and cognitive control networks, as the activity varied across levels of reward, extending previous findings of general age differences to the domain of motivation.

8.2.2 Gambling Tasks

One task used to probe responses to risky situations in which the rewards and payoffs are not transparent, mimicking a gambling context, is the **Iowa Gambling Task** (see Box 8.1). The task reveals deficits in trading off immediate gains for long-term profit in patients with damage to the ventromedial prefrontal cortex (VMPFC) (Bechara et al., 1994). This work has been extended to reveal deficits in cognitively normal older adults (Denburg et al., 2007); moreover, volume reductions in gray matter in VMPFC relate to irrational economic decisions with age (Chung et al., 2017). An fMRI study assessed the response of VMPFC in older adults performing the Iowa Gambling Task, finding that VMPFC is involved bilaterally for older adults, with the left hemisphere region implicated in *successful* decision making (Rogalsky, Vidal, Li, & Damasio, 2012). Without a direct comparison with younger adults, it is not possible to draw strong conclusions about changes in strategies or activation patterns with age. However, the authors suggest that older adults may be more attuned than younger adults to signals of positivity, indicating "safe" packs of cards in this paradigm.

Subsequent research explored individual differences in older adults' performance. In one study, older adults who performed advantageously on the Iowa Gambling Task were compared with those who exhibited

Box 8.1 Iowa Gambling Task (Bechara et al., 1994)

In this task, participants select cards from one of four decks (packs). Each card either wins or loses money, and participants want to accumulate as much money as possible. Two decks are "good decks," as drawing from these decks will overall result in gains. Other decks are "bad decks," leading to overall losses. Bad decks initially are appealing as they contain some trials with larger gains than the good decks, but other trials result in much higher losses. Thus, the bad decks are risky decks. Participants initially tend to sample from all of the decks and return to the risky desks. Over time, participants learn to avoid the risky desks and draw predominantly from the good decks. However, patients with damage to the VMPFC continue to draw from the bad decks, resulting in overall loss of money.

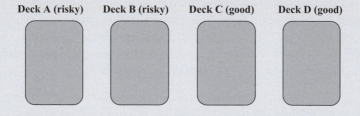

disadvantageous performance (Halfmann et al., 2014). The groups engaged different mechanisms at different stages of the task, with prefrontally based compensatory mechanisms contributing before participants made a choice (the pre-choice phase) and posterior regions reflecting differential reward sensitivity during feedback about choice. Potential differences with age in reward sensitivity were investigated further in a study linking performance on the Iowa Gambling Task with neural activity during an intertemporal choice task, which probes delay discounting (Halfmann et al., 2015). Consistent with prior findings (Halfmann et al., 2014), older adults who showed advantageous performance engaged regions associated with reward valuation more than those showing disadvantageous performance. In this task, those regions included the VMPFC and striatum. In addition, the disadvantaged group also showed more temporal variability in the striatum, possibly reflecting more noise in the neural system that contributed to poorer decision making.

Age differences were widespread with a slot-machine gambling task, which is analogous to real-world gambling. Older adults recruited prefrontal regions, including the left superior and orbitofrontal cortex, more than younger adults (McCarrey et al., 2012). This pattern was interpreted as reflecting compensatory mechanisms, such that aging necessitated recruiting additional neural regions compared to the regions required by younger adults. The increased prefrontal engagement with age could reflect deficits in executive function that make older adults more vulnerable to perseveration, thus increasing gambling losses. Indeed, individuals with gambling problems have been shown to exhibit dysfunction in prefrontal regions (reviewed by McCarrey et al., 2012). This finding is in line with others from the risk-taking literature, such as older adults' greater engagement than younger adults of the bilateral prefrontal cortex and right insula (T. M. Lee et al., 2008). Results were interpreted as reflecting age-related changes necessitating increased recruitment of regions in an attempt to regulate behavior or overcome decline in neural systems.

8.2.3 Economic Decision Making in a Social Context

Despite the frequent occurrence of fraud and scams among older populations (AARP Foundation, 2003; but see M. Ross et al., 2014), there is little research addressing the neural basis of changes in relevant processes with age. A recent study compared older adults who were victims of financial exploitation with those who avoided exploitation. Exploited older adults exhibited greater cortical thinning in regions including the insula and superior temporal cortex with reduced functional connectivity between these regions (Spreng et al., 2017). These results hint at the potential to use neural measures as markers of risk of exploitation with age.

Decision making in a social context may require a broader network of regions than the reward system reviewed above, including a role for the medial prefrontal cortex due to its contributions to social cognition and theory of mind (L. Zhu et al., 2012). Using computational modeling, Zhu and colleagues propose that the ability to update information may be what is most affected by aging. Many decision making parameters in their model appear to be intact with age, but social contracts and interactions may be most affected by dynamic changes, accounting for older adults' particular vulnerability in social domains.

Study of economic behavior in social contexts often relies on interpersonal interactions such as the Ultimatum Game. In this task, one individual proposes how to split a pool of money with a second individual. If the second party accepts the offer, both individuals may keep the proposed sum of money. If the second party declines, no one receives money. Typically, young adults playing the game will reject unfair offers, such as an $8/$2 split. However, this is less true for older adults, who will accept more unfair offers than young (Bailey, Ruffman, & Rendell, 2013). Older adults differ from younger adults in the types of offers they make. Older adults tend to make fairer offers of splits than younger adults (P. E. Bailey et al., 2013), and this finding extends to other economic games. In the Dictator Game, an individual proposes a split of money that will be received by the opponent. There is no opportunity to decline the offer and no further interaction between the proposer and the recipient. Under an empathy induction, in which participants were led to believe that the other player was experiencing a health scare, older adults made larger offers to their opponent than did young adults (Beadle et al., 2015). Both of these findings suggest that older adults exhibit more prosocial behavior than young adults, making fairer offers to opponents and more generous offers to partners in need.

One fMRI study of the Ultimatum Game compared the effects of aging on cognitive and affective systems. In this study (Harle & Sanfey, 2012), older adults actually rejected more moderately unfair offers (e.g., $7/$3 splits) than younger adults, in contrast to some of the behavioral studies. The neural data revealed age differences in the left DLPFC, with older adults engaging the region more than younger adults during unfair offers. The bilateral insula exhibited a reduction with age during unfair offers. The authors interpreted the results as indicating higher demands on executive function for older adults, reflected through DLPFC activity, during decision making. Older adults' acceptance of fewer offers in this study could reflect difficulty in integrating the competing demands of the task (e.g., norms for social interactions versus making money). The reduced insula activation in older adults was thought to indicate a reduced emotional reaction to unfair offers, in line with preserved emotion regulation in older adults. Taken together, the data reflect greater reliance on the cognitive, executive control system rather than the emotion-based system, with age. Although this interpretation might be plausible for economic games in a social context, it is uncertain why this domain would differ from others in which older adults rely on intact emotional processes (see Chapters 5 and 6) rather than more impaired cognitive processes.

8.2.4 Future Directions in Decision Making and Reward

Overall, the study of decision making and response to reward has not emphasized the widespread losses that emerge with age in some other domains, such as cognition. Older adults even evidence some potential advantages such as a reduced delay discounting effect, which could allow them to value temporally distant rewards more than younger adults. Continued work on areas of strength and vulnerability with age could ultimately lead to the development of decision aids and interventions to better support decision making and response to reward in older adults (Samanez-Larkin & Knutson, 2015). Research on interventions in decision making is particularly important given the number of decisions, such as regarding healthcare and finances, that must be made later in life. Older adults may face some of these decisions for the first time, potentially confronted with new and competing information with complex risk–benefit trade-offs. Sometimes this information is presented in social contexts or requires opaque interpersonal interactions, aspects that can pose additional challenges in making optimal decisions. Moreover, the potential for physical and cognitive declines further threatens decision quality (Nielsen & Mather, 2011).

The study of decision making merely begins to illuminate the need for further study of motivation across the life span. Thus far, research has investigated motivation largely through shifts with age in priorities, such as socioemotional selectivity theory (see Chapter 5), and the economic games and decisions reviewed in this chapter. It is helpful to keep in mind the distinct neural systems that underlie emotion, chiefly engaging the amygdala and orbitofrontal cortex, as opposed to the involvement of the mesolimbic dopamine system (e.g., the striatum including the nucleus accumbens) in motivation. The aging literature focuses largely on financial rewards thus far, without extending to other ways of studying motivation, such as through physiologically relevant rewards (e.g., appetitive or sexual stimuli) or interpersonal incentives (e.g., power, achievement) (Braver et al., 2014). In contrast to the body of work on the interactions of emotion with cognition in later life (see Chapter 5), there has been very little research on the intersection of motivation with cognition, with the studies reviewed here only beginning to speculate on the interplay between these systems. Changes in the availability of cognitive resources with age could affect the circumstances under which older adults are motivated to deploy resources. If cognitive processes are more effortful to engage with age, this may make older adults less motivated to engage cognitive resources, more selective of when to do so, or even more driven by intrinsic than extrinsic motivations (Braver et al., 2014; Hess, 2014). Although these shifts would affect when and how older adults are motivated, the focus has largely been on how this would affect *behavior*. The ways in which aging would affect the underlying neurobiological mechanisms have yet to be probed, or even speculated upon at great length (Braver et al., 2014). Age differences in situation selection allow for the possibility that the motivational system could be intact but engaged by older adults under different and more limited circumstances. Given the changes in response to financial motivations and reward with age (Samanez-Larkin & Knutson, 2015) and the effects of aging on the dopamine system (S. C. Li et al., 2013), it is likely that the neurobiology underlying motivation undergoes extensive change across the life span.

Another important consideration for research in this area is the use of age-appropriate tasks. This may be a particular concern for financial and economic decisions, in which older adults might adopt strategies and approaches in laboratory tasks that are unlike those they would use in actual decisions. Do the economic games employed in laboratory studies mimic the financial decisions made in real life? Older adults participating in laboratory studies often do not seem particularly motivated by the extrinsic financial incentives for participation. Rather, they express intrinsic motivations, such as contributing to the scientific study of aging and interest in the development of interventions and aids for future generations. Moreover, the relationship with interaction partners may be important to consider. Whereas laboratory studies often involve interactions with unknown others, older adults may be at the greatest risk of being manipulated by familiar others rather than strangers, with financial mistreatment of older adults more common than other types of abuse (Nielsen & Mather, 2011). Do the interpersonal interactions in socioeconomic games studied thus far reflect the reality of trusting known acquaintances with loans or financial decisions? Such aspects must be considered in future work.

8.3 Neuromodulation

8.3.1 Overview

One particularly exciting research development is in brain stimulation. Noninvasive techniques allow neural activity to be enhanced or suppressed by holding a coil over the scalp (**repetitive transcranial magnetic stimulation (rTMS)**) or through a weak electrical current from a battery delivered through electrodes attached to the scalp (**transcranial direct current stimulation (tDCS)**) (Freitas et al., 2013; Gutchess, 2014; Zimerman & Hummel, 2010). See an illustration of tDCS in Figure 8.3. Research can be safely conducted in humans using these methods, and there has been great interest in whether stimulating the brain can enhance cognitive function in the short term or even the long term, when paired with extended protocols and training.

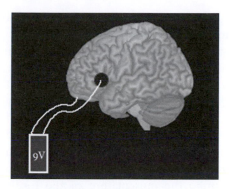

Figure 8.3 Depiction of tDCS. Electrodes are placed on the scalp, and current from a 9-V battery is administered to a region of the brain.
Figure adapted from Gutchess (2014), *Science*, Figure 2.

These techniques are also of interest due to their role in determining causality. Although methods such as fMRI can illustrate which brain regions are active during particular tasks (e.g., activity in the DLPFC increases as working memory load increases), these methods do not reveal whether the neural activity is *necessary and sufficient* for task performance. It could be that the region works in conjunction with other regions but is not on its own (or even at all) contributing to successful task performance. For example, early debates about whether or not bilateral prefrontal activation served a compensatory function considered the possibility that activating homologous regions across hemispheres with age could be the result of vascular changes or dedifferentiation that prevented regions from being activated in task-specific ways. If this is so, then disrupting activity in the additional hemisphere recruited by older adults should not impair task performance. An early rTMS study suggested that both hemispheres contribute to task performance more for older adults (Rossi et al., 2004). Young adults showed lateralized recruitment of the DLPFC during retrieval, with only right hemisphere rTMS stimulation impairing performance. By *manipulating* brain activity through rTMS and finding an effect on performance, as opposed to simply observing which regions were activated during retrieval as with fMRI, these findings established that the left DLPFC plays a critical role in retrieval processes; performance was worse when the region was inhibited. In contrast to younger adults, older adults did not exhibit lateralized effects during the administration of rTMS. This pattern of findings was interpreted as illustrating that both hemispheres contribute to task performance in older adults, because disrupting either region alone did not disproportionately impair performance during retrieval.

Despite the utility of the methods for determining causality and understanding the effects of stimulating regions, the potential of the methods is limited by the spatial resolution. It is difficult to precisely target specific regions, as the rTMS or tDCS signal may not be focal, and the regions that can be targeted are limited by how far the signal can travel (e.g., it is unlikely to permeate the cortex enough to modulate structures deep in the brain, such as the hippocampus). Some regions cannot be comfortably stimulated with rTMS, restricting where it can be applied. For example, the musculature of the forehead makes some prefrontal regions difficult to target due to the twitching and discomfort reported by participants. Despite its spatial limitations, recent work has revealed some creative uses of the methods to target regions not particularly amenable to the methods by stimulating other nodes in the networks. As the hippocampus and medial temporal lobes cannot be stimulated from the scalp, one group of researchers used resting state fMRI scans to identify a region of the left lateral parietal cortex that exhibited the strongest connectivity to a region of the left hippocampus. The experimenters then administered five sessions of rTMS to the parietal region in young adults in order to enhance activity of the entire parietal-hippocampal brain network (J. X. Wang et al., 2014). Stimulation enhanced connectivity between the regions as well as memory performance for associations between faces and words. Thus, the methods have potential for more flexible uses, which is particularly intriguing given the interest in enhancing memory.

8.3.2 Neuromodulation Studies of Normal Aging

A few studies have investigated the effects of neurostimulation on cognitive performance. Although literature on its effectiveness is somewhat mixed, there is reason to believe that the techniques may have a larger effect in older adult or cognitively impaired populations (e.g., aMCI or AD) due to structural and functional neural plasticity and the potential to benefit low levels of performance. A meta-analysis of neurostimulation studies, comprised predominantly of tDCS studies but some TMS ones, found that neurostimulation improved cognitive performance for older adults (Hsu et al., 2015). Effects were larger when stimulation was performed across multiple sessions rather than in a single session, although few studies in the meta-analysis employed multi-session designs.

Several cognitive abilities have been improved with neurostimulation in older adults, including performance on motor tasks, picture naming, and response inhibition. Neurostimulation improved motor learning in older adults, compared to a **sham simulation** group (in which stimulation is not actually administered or applied to a region uninvolved in the task), and these effects were maintained over 24 hours (Zimerman et al., 2013). Applying tDCS to the cerebellum allowed older adults to learn to adapt on a motor reaching task at a rate similar to young adults, whereas older adults performed worse under sham stimulation (Hardwick & Celnik, 2014). Naming the item depicted in a picture, as well as the time taken to do so, can be improved for older adults by administering tDCS to the left DLPFC during the naming task (Fertonani et al., 2014). However, the benefits are more constrained for older adults than for younger adults, who benefit regardless of whether tDCS is administered before or during the actual picture naming task. Administering tDCS to the anterior temporal lobe improves the ability to name famous faces and landmarks for younger and older adults, but the laterality of the effects differs some with age (L. A. Ross et al., 2011). Neurostimulation of the right DLPFC with tDCS increases older adults' awareness of committing errors on a response inhibition task, compared to sham stimulation (Harty et al., 2014). Without a young adult control group, this study cannot address whether aging affects the magnitude of this benefit.

Given its noticeable decline with age, memory has been a target of neurostimulation studies. During retrieval, tDCS improves verbal episodic memory for younger and older adults (Manenti et al., 2013). Administration over either the left or right hemisphere frontal or parietal regions benefited younger adults, whereas only left hemisphere administration improved older adults' performance. Object-location learning also benefited from tDCS administration, with older adults receiving tDCS over the right temporoparietal cortex better recalling learned information 1 week later than older adults who received sham stimulation (Floel et al., 2012). However, different subgroups of older adults may respond differently to neurostimulation. Older adults with higher levels of education benefited widely from tDCS, across different cortical sites of administration and working memory tasks, compared with those with lower levels of education (Berryhill & Jones, 2012). Likewise, the laterality of the effects of prefrontal cortex stimulation differed across high- and low-performing older adults. Low-performing older adults were more impacted by TMS administration to left DLPFC during encoding whereas high-performing older adults were more bilateral (Manenti et al., 2011).

Although there have been some suggestions that the effects of tDCS may be more constrained in older than younger adults, based on the timing or location of administration, the studies reviewed above largely emphasize the shared benefits across younger and older adults. One study, however, suggested that risk-taking behavior could be altered with tDCS in rather different ways across age groups. In this study, the laterality of the effect is entirely flipped with age. In younger adults, tDCS stimulation over the left DLPFC decreased the selection of low-risk choices on a gambling task whereas tDCS stimulation over the right DLPFC increased risk taking. For older adults, the effects of stimulating the left versus right DLPFC with tDCS had the opposite pattern of effects (Boggio et al., 2010). These results may indicate changes to the underlying neural system implicated in risk behavior, highlighting the importance of understanding the effects of aging on the underlying neural networks before administering neurostimulation. Similarly, changes in the motor system with age, such that older adults recruit motor cortex bilaterally, lead them to be disrupted more broadly by neurostimulation than young adults (Zimerman et al., 2014).

Very little work has combined neurostimulation techniques with neuroimaging methods in the study of aging. One study has found that administering tDCS over the left inferior frontal gyrus, compared to sham stimulation, improved older adults' performance on a semantic word-generation task and altered brain activity such that older adults' patterns of activation became more like young adults' (Meinzer et al., 2013). Under sham stimulation, older adults exhibited greater activity in the bilateral prefrontal cortex during task performance, and functional connectivity was greater in anterior regions but reduced in posterior regions. Administration of tDCS reduced prefrontal activation in older adults and adjusted functional connectivity patterns such that older adults appeared more like young adults. This work reveals that a single session of neurostimulation not only can improve performance but also seemingly "repair" neural networks to behave in a more young adult-like fashion. Much more work is needed to investigate whether these benefits can extend over a longer time frame.

One direction thought to hold promise is combining neurostimulation with cognitive training protocols, as this may increase the impact of either intervention on its own (Hsu et al., 2015). Recent research combining working memory training with tDCS yielded greater far transfer benefits for older adults compared to a control group (Stephens & Berryhill, 2016). Although this result is promising, more work is needed to evaluate this possibility, particularly as only some types of cognitive training programs broadly benefit cognition (as discussed in Section 3.6.3). Furthermore, it will also be important to investigate how neural networks and activation of particular regions are affected over time by neurostimulation protocols (Hsu et al., 2015). Such an approach would help to clarify the mechanisms that are affected by neurostimulation and support predictions of what types of protocols and interventions should be most effective. One study hints at the promise of these types of multisystem intervention approaches. Although it did not employ neurostimulation, it combined measures of neural network connectivity with a month of cognitive training in which the tasks were designed to engage neural regions that constitute the default mode network (De Marco et al., 2015). The cognitive training group was compared to a control group emphasizing social interactions. Functional connectivity within the default mode network increased for the cognitive training group to a greater extent than for the control group. Despite the fact that this was not a true study of aging, as it lacked a comparison with young adults, the authors were optimistic about extensions to disorders associated with aging. They suggested that such an intervention approach might improve function in patients prone to or in the early stages of AD, as the disease seems to particularly impact the default network. Combining such a training regimen with neurostimulation may have even greater benefits.

8.3.3 Neuromodulation Studies of Age-Related Disorders

The meta-analysis of neurostimulation studies of older adults also included studies of patients with AD. These analyses revealed benefits from neurostimulation, including improved performance on tasks such as picture naming and memory, and as a common screening measure to assess cognitive orientation (Hsu et al., 2015). In one study, patients with AD completed a recognition test of visual drawings. Memory performance was compared when participants received neurostimulation through tDCS with performance at another point in time without neurostimulation (Boggio et al., 2012). Patients performed better when tDCS was administered than with sham tDCS, and this benefit was maintained over a month after stimulation. High-frequency rTMS stimulation over the right followed by the left DLPFC improved performance on a screening measure of cognitive orientation in patients with AD compared to controls who received low-frequency rTMS or sham stimulation (Ahmed et al., 2012). The advantage was maintained for 3 months after neurostimulation. The benefits of neurostimulation, however, did not emerge in all studies. One study found that regardless of whether or not neurostimulation was applied with tDCS, computerized memory training improved memory performance in patients with AD compared with a control group that received tDCS with motor training (Cotelli et al., 2014).

Another interesting potential application of TMS is in predicting the likelihood of converting from aMCI status to AD. One preliminary study prospectively recruited and studied healthy older adult control participants and those with a diagnosis of MCI over a period of 4 years (Trebbastoni et al., 2015). During this time frame, many of the participants converted to a diagnosis of AD. TMS was administered at the outset of the study and subsequently in each year for those participants with aMCI who had not yet converted to AD. Patients with a diagnosis of MCI had a decreased resting motor threshold, which is thought to reflect increased cortical excitability and changes to synaptic plasticity. The extent of the change to the resting motor threshold was related to the conversion time to AD, indicating that resting motor thresholds could be used as a diagnostic marker and predict the time course of conversion to AD. Successful application of tDCS to individuals with subject memory complaints (e.g., Manenti et al., 2017) could prove useful in delaying functional impairments and diagnoses.

Other types of invasive brain stimulation techniques also have been used in patient groups. **Deep brain stimulation (DBS)** uses a surgically implanted device to electrically stimulate regions of the brain in a direct, controlled, and reversible manner. The subthalamic nucleus, a dopamine-rich region, has been targeted in advanced Parkinson's disease. In a randomized, controlled clinical trial, the reference standard for assessing the efficacy of treatments, patients receiving DBS exhibited greater improvement over a 6-month period on measures of mobility and activities of daily living (e.g., grooming and self-care), compared with patients who received medication alone (Deuschl et al., 2006). Although improvement to motor symptoms are possible, there have been concerns about whether DBS actually exacerbates impairments to cognition. A meta-analysis concluded that overall the deficits from stimulating the subthalamic nucleus were small across different cognitive abilities (Combs et al., 2015). However, the effects on semantic and phonemic fluency, tasks that require one to name as many members of a category (e.g., animals) or words beginning with a particular letter as possible in a given time limit, showed moderate levels of impairment. The fact that these tasks are often included in tests of cognitive orientation could exaggerate the apparent extent of cognitive difficulties for patients receiving DBS. Overall, the authors considered the effects on cognition modest enough to continue to recommend DBS as a treatment for Parkinson's disease, given the potential to decrease motor symptoms. The meta-analysis, however, also indicated that cognitive deficits may be less severe when stimulating the globus pallidus rather than the subthalamic nucleus, although there are relatively few studies of globus pallidus stimulation at this time. Although deep brain stimulation represents an exciting development for relieving symptoms in some clinical populations, the technique is unlikely to be extended to healthy populations in the near future. The higher instance of side effects, including serious adverse events, limits the potential for extending DBS to ameliorate cognitive declines in healthy populations.

8.4 Emerging Directions

8.4.1 Studying Aging across the Life Span

In terms of where the field is heading, more attention will be devoted to the unfolding of the effects of adult development and aging over the life span. This includes **cognitive epidemiology** (Deary & Batty, 2007), which links childhood ability to late-life outcomes. Interventions, such as training in mnemonic strategies, could be easier to implement in midlife when cognitive resources are more available and could lead to longer-term benefits than employing them late in life. Moreover, adopting a life-span perspective is important in studying disorders that emerge with age, such as AD. The ability to investigate the trajectories of cognitive performance and changes in structure or functional activation may also be fruitful in distinguishing normal from pathological aging processes (e.g., Fjell, Westlye, et al., 2014). Research increasingly underscores the need for early detection of who is at risk of developing disease in order to develop effective interventions. Neurodegeneration seems difficult to offset once brain systems undergo atrophy or disruption, but there is hope that diseases can be better addressed before the onset of the neuropathological cascade.

Longitudinal research allows for consideration of the rate of decline. By measuring ability only later in life, it is impossible to distinguish ability level from rate of decline. Research increasingly reveals the importance of considering rates of cognitive decline with age, rather than absolute levels of performance. In addition to finding that measures of current and midlife levels of performance relate to patterns of neural activity, the *rate* of change also affects activations. Each of these three factors (current levels, midlife levels, and rate of change) relate to activation of distinct yet overlapping regions in the left inferior frontal cortex and bilateral hippocampus (Pudas et al., 2014; see Figure 8.4). Midlife memory scores emerged as one of the strongest predictors of brain activity in multiple regions. This led Pudas and colleagues to

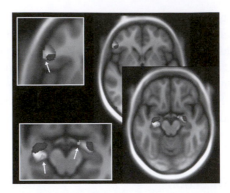

Figure 8.4 Regions of the inferior frontal cortex (top half of figure) and the hippocampus (lower half of figure) exhibit the effects of current memory performance (light gray), midlife memory performance (dark gray), and the slope of change in memory performance (medium gray; indicated by arrows).
Adapted from Pudas et al. (2014), *Neurobiology of Aging*, Figure 1C.

emphasize the importance of considering individual differences at mid-life, as well as highlighting the increased sensitivity of estimates of cognitive change from longitudinal studies.

Ultimately, longitudinal studies will be needed to uncover the links between early-life experiences and outcomes with aging. Even though data collection is underway for several large longitudinal studies, many begin collecting data at midlife rather than starting in childhood or young adult-hood. This feature of longitudinal studies limits the ability to detect the effects of early childhood adversity such as low socioeconomic status, poor access to education or nutrition, or the general effects of stress (as discussed by Nielsen & Mather, 2011). Some evidence that the level of intelligence in childhood can contribute to late-life outcomes is reviewed in Section 2.8.2. The contextually based factors of socioeconomic status and early-life adver-sity have far-reaching effects on cognitive and emotional development (Hackman et al., 2010). For example, parental levels of education predict the level of activation in the anterior cingulate and DLPFC, as well as connectivity within a network including these regions (Gianaros et al., 2011).

8.4.2 Exploring the Distinction of Socioemotional and Cognitive Domains

Another intriguing direction for future research is in delineating the dis-tinction between the effects of aging on the neural systems supporting socioemotional versus cognitive processes. As discussed in Chapter 6, social processes may dissociate from cognitive ones in a number of ways, including engaging separate networks. The effects of aging on social systems, particularly in terms of brain measures, have been little explored and require substantially more research. As outlined by Kensinger and Gutchess (2017), there are several ways in which the study of cognitive aging has informed our understanding of the effects of aging on socioaffective processes. Cognitive resource limitations can contribute to difficulty in social and affective processes, such as regulating one's response to stigma. However, cognitive resources may be allocated differently by younger and older adults for socioaffective tasks, such as prioritizing negatively versus positively valenced information. Moreover, there are some socioaffective tasks for which cognitive ability cannot entirely account for performance, including tasks on which older adults outperform younger adults. Such patterns support the notion that socioaffective abilities can be separated from cognition. The extent to which the networks for social and affective abilities are impacted by aging, and the degree to which these networks operate in tandem with cognitive ones, remain to be tested.

Approaches that have been useful for the study of cognitive aging must be extended to the study of social and affective abilities (Kensinger & Gutchess, 2017). Namely, individual differences, longitudinal approaches, and manipulation of resource availability have not been applied extensively to social and affective domains. Nor has it been delineated to what extent emotional (Chapter 5) and social (Chapter 6) processes constitute distinct domains.

8.4.3 Contribution of Context to Aging

Context can be conceptualized in a number of ways, including the way in which information is presented (e.g., the sentence or tone in which a word is used), the situation in which one encounters or applies new information (e.g., was the health tip learned from a reputable doctor or a friend?), the sociocultural context in which one lives (e.g., what are the cultural stereotypes about older adults? does one have a rich social network?), and the physical context one navigates or relies on to support routines (e.g., leaving keys in a set location). Some evidence suggests that context may impact older adults more than young. Older adults' speech perception benefits from sentence context. Even when auditory perception of a word is difficult due to age-related hearing loss, older adults can often disambiguate the word without difficulty in a sentence (Wingfield et al., 2015). Studying words in a sentence context particularly benefits memory of older adults (Matzen & Benjamin, 2013). Memory of complex and semantically meaningful pictures can be age-equivalent (Gutchess & Park, 2009; A. D. Smith et al., 1990), in contrast to many other types of memory that show robust age differences. Supporting and distracting contexts exaggerate the benefits and deficits, respectively, of memory of older adults compared with younger adults (Earles et al., 1994). Attempting to recognize novel items presented in familiar, previously studied background contexts results in increased memory errors for the items for older adults (Gutchess, Hebrank, et al., 2007). Moreover, older adults fail to engage frontal cognitive control regions as much as younger adults when attempting to recognize novel items in familiar contexts, although high-performing older adults activate the region to a greater extent than low-performing older adults (Gutchess, Hebrank, et al., 2007). These benefits and vulnerabilities suggest that context may have the potential to profoundly modulate older adults' recruitment of neural regions.

Although older adults can benefit from context in many situations, social contexts may be particularly potent in supporting performance with age. Social and affective contexts can operate as rich forms of environmental support, allowing context to be a major contributor to older adults' more preserved abilities in these domains (Kensinger & Gutchess, 2017). Social context has the potential to support cognitive performance. For example, data suggest that large social networks may be related to lower odds of developing dementia (Wilson et al., 2007). These types of studies are largely prospective and based on self-report, rather than manipulating effects in real time and measuring brain function under different social conditions. Extant studies are limited in their meaningfulness and approximation of real-world situations. Although research is growing in areas such as **collaborative cognition** (e.g., Derksen et al., 2015; Harris et al., 2011; Henkel & Rajaram, 2011), in which participants work together in groups to complete memory or other cognitive tasks, studies have only begun to investigate the importance of working with a known partner (e.g., a spouse) versus a stranger, or to consider the meaningfulness of the interactions. Naturalistic interactions pose challenges for integrating with cognitive neuroscience methods. Some studies have investigated empathy by comparing the overlap in the neural response to self and a familiar friend, as opposed to a stranger (e.g., Beckes et al., 2013) or have employed **hyperscanning** (Montague et al., 2002), in which two individuals are scanned simultaneously while interacting on a task. However, the tasks are by necessity artificial and scripted, and thus cannot capture the natural aspects of everyday interactions and challenges.

The laboratory-based research reviewed here may not even capture the most robust effects of context. For example, older adults prefer to "age in place," living in their own homes as long as feasible rather than moving to senior housing or assisted living (Cutchin, 2003). Although aging in place may not be the best option for the most vulnerable older adults (S. Park et al., 2015), advances in home healthcare and assistive technology make aging in one's home possible for more of the population. Because the vast majority of research is conducted in the laboratory or an out-of-home setting, we may be missing many of the rich ways older adults arrange their environments and employ strategies to optimize cognition. An important challenge for the field is how to study older adults in familiar contexts, particularly given the limitations of cognitive neuroscience methods, which often necessitate testing in a highly unfamiliar, controlled environment. The ability to study older adults in their homes or throughout their typical routines, using, for example, portable, head-mounted EEG systems, may one day allow better study of older adults in their everyday context and consideration of how this impacts their functioning and ability to harness appropriate strategies and compensatory mechanisms, including neural resources.

Chapter Summary

- Decision making and response to reward do not seem to be impacted by aging as much as many other domains, unless tasks involve a learning component.
- Age groups can differ in thalamus activity during decision and reward tasks. The integrity of thalamocorticostriatal white matter tracts predicts the extent of age differences in reward learning.
- Research is limited on motivation outside the domains of decision making and neuroeconomics, including study of the neural regions affected by socioeconomic tasks. This could be a rich area for future work, as behavioral data suggest there could be large shifts across the life span in what motivates people.
- Research overall suggests that neuromodulation, such as noninvasively stimulating regions of the brain with tDCS or TMS, can improve older adults' performance, as well as that of patients with aMCI or AD, on a variety of tasks. However, neurostimulation may be best used in conjunction with neuroimaging techniques, due to changes to neural networks with age.
- Two important directions for future research are to study aging across the life span and to assess the extent to which the well-understood

changes to neural systems implicated in cognition also extend to socio-affective domains.

- Although context may play a more important role for older than younger adults, there are challenges to studying rich and meaningful everyday contexts with cognitive neuroscience methods.

Discussion Questions

1. What neural system and regions support decision making? What are some of the ways that it is affected by aging?
2. What factors impact whether age differences occur in decision making and reward tasks?
3. What is the Iowa Gambling Task and why has it been a popular method for studying risky economic behavior? How does aging affect neural recruitment in this task?
4. What types of tasks have benefited from neurostimulation in older adults? In patients with AD? What are some of the ways in which effects might vary for older adults?
5. What do you think are some promising future directions for research on the cognitive neuroscience of aging? Will the technology eventually overcome some of the challenges outlined here in studying the effects of aging in contexts meaningful to everyday life?

For Further Reading

Braver, T. S., Krug, M. K., Chiew, K. S., Kool, W., Westbrook, J. A., Clement, N. J., ... MOMCAI Group. (2014). Mechanisms of motivation–cognition interaction: challenges and opportunities. *Cognitive, Affective, & Behavioral Neuroscience, 14*(2), 443–472.

Hsu, W. Y., Ku, Y., Zanto, T. P., & Gazzaley, A. (2015). Effects of noninvasive brain stimulation on cognitive function in healthy aging and Alzheimer's disease: a systematic review and meta-analysis. *Neurobiology of Aging, 36*(8), 2348–2359.

Kensinger, E. A., & Gutchess, A. H. (2017). Cognitive aging in a social and affective context: advances over the past 50 years. *Journals of Gerontology. Series B, Psychological Sciences and Social Sciences, 72*(1), 61–70.

Meinzer, M., Lindenberg, R., Antonenko, D., Flaisch, T., & Floel, A. (2013). Anodal transcranial direct current stimulation temporarily reverses age-associated cognitive decline and functional brain activity changes. *Journal of Neuroscience, 33*(30), 12470–12478.

Samanez-Larkin, G. R., & Knutson, B. (2015). Decision making in the ageing brain: changes in affective and motivational circuits. *Nature Reviews Neuroscience*, *16*(5), 278–289.

Key Terms

cognitive epidemiology
collaborative cognition
deep brain stimulation (DBS)
delay discounting
hyperscanning
Iowa Gambling Task
neuroeconomics
neuromodulation
repetitive transcranial magnetic stimulation (rTMS)
reversal learning
sham stimulation
transcranial direct current stimulation (tDCS)

Bibliography

AARP Foundation. (2003). *Off the Hook: Reducing Participation in Telemarketing Fraud.* Retrieved from https://assets.aarp.org/rgcenter/consume/d17812_fraud.pdf

Abbott, A., & Dolgin, E. (2016). Failed Alzheimer's trial does not kill leading theory of disease. *Nature, 540*(7631), 15–16. doi:10.1038/nature.2016.21045

Abutalebi, J., Canini, M., Della Rosa, P. A., Green, D. W., & Weekes, B. S. (2015). The neuroprotective effects of bilingualism upon the inferior parietal lobule: a structural neuroimaging study in aging Chinese bilinguals. *Journal of Neurolinguistics, 33,* 3–13.

Abutalebi, J., Canini, M., Della Rosa, P. A., Sheung, L. P., Green, D. W., & Weekes, B. S. (2014). Bilingualism protects anterior temporal lobe integrity in aging. *Neurobiology of Aging, 35*(9), 2126–2133.

Acosta-Cabronero, J., & Nestor, P. J. (2014). Diffusion tensor imaging in Alzheimer's disease: insights into the limbic-diencephalic network and methodological considerations. *Frontiers in Aging Neuroscience, 6.*

Addis, D. R., Giovanello, K. S., Vu, M.-A., & Schacter, D. L. (2014). Age-related changes in prefrontal and hippocampal contributions to relational encoding. *NeuroImage, 84,* 19–26.

Addis, D. R., Leclerc, C. M., Muscatell, K. A., & Kensinger, E. A. (2010). There are age-related changes in neural connectivity during the encoding of positive, but not negative, information. *Cortex, 46*(4), 425–433. doi:10.1016/j.cortex.2009.04.011

Addis, D. R., Roberts, R. P., & Schacter, D. L. (2011). Age-related neural changes in autobiographical remembering and imagining. *Neuropsychologia, 49*(13), 3656–3669. doi:10.1016/j.neuropsychologia.2011.09.021

Adenzato, M., Cavallo, M., & Enrici, I. (2010). Theory of mind ability in the behavioural variant of frontotemporal dementia: an analysis of the neural, cognitive, and social levels. *Neuropsychologia, 48*(1), 2–12.

Ahmed, M. A., Darwish, E. S., Khedr, E. M., El Serogy, Y. M., & Ali, A. M. (2012). Effects of low versus high frequencies of repetitive transcranial magnetic stimulation on cognitive function and cortical excitability in Alzheimer's dementia. *Journal of Neurology, 259*(1), 83–92. doi:10.1007/s00415-011-6128-4

Aizenstein, H. J., Butters, M. A., Clark, K. A., Figurski, J. L., Stenger, V. A., Nebes, R. D., . . . Carter, C. S. (2006). Prefrontal and striatal activation in elderly subjects during concurrent implicit and explicit sequence learning. *Neurobiology of Aging*, *27*(5), 741–751.

Aizenstein, H. J., Butters, M. A., Figurski, J. L., Stenger, V. A., Reynolds, C. F., & Carter, C. S. (2005). Prefrontal and striatal activation during sequence learning in geriatric depression. *Biological Psychiatry*, *58*(4), 290–296.

Aizenstein, H. J., Butters, M. A., Wu, M., Mazurkewicz, L. M., Stenger, V. A., Gianaros, P. J., . . . Carter, C. S. (2009). Altered functioning of the executive control circuit in late-life depression: episodic and persistent phenomena. *American Journal of Geriatric Psychiatry*, *17*(1), 30–42.

Albert, K., Hiscox, J., Boyd, B., Dumas, J., Taylor, W., & Newhouse, P. (2017). Estrogen enhances hippocampal gray-matter volume in young and older postmenopausal women: a prospective dose-response study. *Neurobiology of Aging*, *56*, 1–6. doi:10.1016/j. neurobiolaging.2017.03.033

Albert, M. S., DeKosky, S. T., Dickson, D., Dubois, B., Feldman, H. H., Fox, N. C., . . . Petersen, R. C. (2011). The diagnosis of mild cognitive impairment due to Alzheimer's disease: recommendations from the National Institute on Aging–Alzheimer's Association workgroups on diagnostic guidelines for Alzheimer's disease. *Alzheimer's & Dementia*, *7*(3), 270–279.

Alexander, A. L., Lee, J. E., Lazar, M., & Field, A. S. (2007). Diffusion tensor imaging of the brain. *Neurotherapeutics*, *4*(3), 316–329. doi:10.1016/j.nurt.2007.05.011

Allard, E. S., & Kensinger, E. A. (2014a). Age-related differences in functional connectivity during cognitive emotion regulation. *Journals of Gerontology. Series B, Psychological Sciences and Social Sciences*, *69*(6), 852–860. doi:10.1093/geronb/gbu108

(2014b). Age-related differences in neural recruitment during the use of cognitive reappraisal and selective attention as emotion regulation strategies. *Frontiers in Psychology*, *5*, Article 296. doi:10.3389/fpsyg.2014.00296

Ally, B. A., Waring, J. D., Beth, E. H., McKeever, J. D., Milberg, W. P., & Budson, A. E. (2008). Aging memory for pictures: using high-density event-related potentials to understand the effect of aging on the picture superiority effect. *Neuropsychologia*, *46*(2), 679–689.

Almela, M., Hidalgo, V., van der Meij, L., Pulopulos, M. M., Villada, C., & Salvador, A. (2014). A low cortisol response to acute stress is related to worse basal memory performance in older people. *Frontiers in Aging Neuroscience*, *6*, Article 157. doi:10.3389/fnagi.2014.00157

Alzheimer's Association. (2017). *2017 Alzheimer's Disease Facts and Figures*. Retrieved from www.alz.org/documents_custom/2017-facts-and-figures.pdf

Alzheimer's Disease International. (2015). *World Alzheimer Report.*
    Retrieved from www.worldalzreport2015.org

Andrews-Hanna, J. R., Snyder, A. Z., Vincent, J. L., Lustig, C., Head, D.,
    Raichle, M. E., & Buckner, R. L. (2007). Disruption of large-scale
    brain systems in advanced aging. *Neuron, 56*(5), 924–935.

Angel, L., Bastin, C., Genon, S., Balteau, E., Phillips, C., Luxen, A., . . .
    Collette, F. (2013). Differential effects of aging on the neural correlates
    of recollection and familiarity. *Cortex, 49*(6), 1585–1597.

Anguera, J. A., Boccanfuso, J., Rintoul, J. L., Al-Hashimi, O., Faraji, F.,
    Janowich, J., . . . Johnston, E. (2013). Video game training enhances
    cognitive control in older adults. *Nature, 501*(7465), 97–101.

Antonenko, D., Brauer, J., Meinzer, M., Fengler, A., Kerti, L., Friederici, A.
    D., & Flöel, A. (2013). Functional and structural syntax networks in
    aging. *NeuroImage, 83*, 513–523.

Association for Frontotemporal Degeneration. (2017). *Disease Overview.*
    Retrieved from www.theaftd.org/what-is-ftd/disease-overview/

Backman, L., Karlsson, S., Fischer, H., Karlsson, P., Brehmer, Y.,
    Rieckmann, A., . . . Nyberg, L. (2011). Dopamine D(1) receptors and
    age differences in brain activation during working memory.
    Neurobiology of Aging, 32(10), 1849–1856. doi:10.1016/j.
    neurobiolaging.2009.10.018

Backman, L., Lindenberger, U., Li, S. C., & Nyberg, L. (2010). Linking
    cognitive aging to alterations in dopamine neurotransmitter
    functioning: recent data and future avenues. *Neuroscience and
    Biobehavioral Reviews, 34*(5), 670–677. doi:10.1016/j.
    neubiorev.2009.12.008

Backman, L., Nyberg, L., Lindenberger, U., Li, S. C., & Farde, L. (2006).
    The correlative triad among aging, dopamine, and cognition: current
    status and future prospects. *Neuroscience and Biobehavioral Reviews,
    30*(6), 791–807. doi:10.1016/j.neubiorev.2006.06.005

Baddeley, A. D. (2000). The episodic buffer: a new component of working
    memory? *Trends in Cognitive Science, 4*(11), 417–423.
    (2003). Working memory: looking back and looking forward. *Nature
    Reviews Neuroscience, 4*(10), 829–839.

Baddeley, A. D., & Hitch, G. J. (1974). Working memory. In G. A. Bower
    (Ed.), *Recent Advances in Learning and Motivation* (vol. VIII,
    pp. 47–89). New York: Academic Press. http://dx.doi.org/10
    .1016/s0079-7421(08)60452-1

Bailey, H. R., Zacks, J. M., Hambrick, D. Z., Zacks, R. T., Head, D., Kurby,
    C. A., & Sargent, J. Q. (2013). Medial temporal lobe volume
    predicts elders' everyday memory. *Psychological Science, 24*(7),
    1113–1122.

Bailey, P. E., & Henry, J. D. (2008). Growing less empathic with age: disinhibition of the self-perspective. *Journals of Gerontology. Series B, Psychological Sciences and Social Sciences*, *63*(4), P219-P226.

Bailey, P. E., Ruffman, T., & Rendell, P. G. (2013). Age-related differences in social economic decision making: the ultimatum game. *Journals of Gerontology. Series B, Psychological Sciences and Social Sciences*, *68*(3), 356–363. doi:10.1093/geronb/gbs073

Balota, D. A., Tse, C. S., Hutchison, K. A., Spieler, D. H., Duchek, J. M., & Morris, J. C. (2010). Predicting conversion to dementia of the Alzheimer's type in a healthy control sample: the power of errors in Stroop color naming. *Psychology and Aging*, *25*(1), 208–218.

Baltes, P. B. (1993). The aging mind: potential and limits. *Gerontologist*, *33*(5), 580–594.

    (1997). On the incomplete architecture of human ontogeny: selection, optimization, and compensation as foundation of developmental theory. *American Psychologist*, *52*(4), 366–380.

Baltes, P. B., & Baltes, M. M. (1990). Psychological perspectives on successful aging: the mode of selective optimization with compensation. In P. B. Baltes & M. M. Baltes (Eds.), *Successful Aging: Perspectives from the Behavioral Sciences* (pp. 1–34). New York: Cambridge University Press.

Baltes, P. B., & Lindenberger, U. (1997). Emergence of a powerful connection between sensory and cognitive functions across the adult life span: a new window to the study of cognitive aging? *Psychology and Aging*, *12*(1), 12–21.

Barber, S. J. (2017). An examination of age-based stereotype threat about cognitive decline. *Perspectives on Psychological Science*, *12*(1), 62–90. doi:10.1177/1745691616656345

Baron, S. G., Gobbini, M. I., Engell, A. D., & Todorov, A. (2011). Amygdala and dorsomedial prefrontal cortex responses to appearance-based and behavior-based person impressions. *Social Cognitive and Affective Neuroscience*, *6*(5), 572–581. doi:10.1093/scan/nsq086

Baron-Cohen, S., Jolliffe, T., Mortimore, C., & Robertson, M. (1997). Another advanced test of theory of mind: evidence from very high functioning adults with autism or Asperger syndrome. *Journal of Child Psychology and Psychiatry and Allied Disciplines*, *38*(7), 813–822. doi:10.1111/j.1469-7610.1997.tb01599.x

Baron-Cohen, S., Wheelwright, S., Hill, J., Raste, Y., & Plumb, I. (2001). The "Reading the Mind in the Eyes" test revised version: a study with normal adults, and adults with Asperger syndrome or high-functioning autism. *Journal of Child Psychology and Psychiatry and Allied Disciplines*, *42*(2), 241–251. doi:10.1017/s0021963001006643

Basak, C., Voss, M. W., Erickson, K. I., Boot, W. R., & Kramer, A. F. (2011). Regional differences in brain volume predict the acquisition of skill in a complex real-time strategy videogame. *Brain and Cognition, 76*(3), 407–414.

Beadle, J. N., Sheehan, A. H., Dahlben, B., & Gutchess, A. H. (2015). Aging, empathy, and prosociality. *Journals of Gerontology. Series B, Psychological Sciences and Social Sciences, 70*(2), 213–222. doi:10.1093/geronb/gbt091

Beadle, J. N., Yoon, C., & Gutchess, A. H. (2012). Age-related neural differences in affiliation and isolation. *Cognitive, Affective, and Behavioral Neuroscience, 12,* 269–279.

Bechara, A., Damasio, A. R., Damasio, H., & Anderson, S. W. (1994). Insensitivity to future consequences following damage to human prefrontal cortex. *Cognition, 50*(1–3), 7–15.

Beckes, L., Coan, J. A., & Hasselmo, K. (2013). Familiarity promotes the blurring of self and other in the neural representation of threat. *Social Cognitive and Affective Neuroscience, 8*(6), 670–677. doi:10.1093/scan/nss046

Bejanin, A., Schonhaut, D. R., La Joie, R., Kramer, J. H., Baker, S. L., Sosa, N., . . . Rabinovici, G. D. (2017). Tau pathology and neurodegeneration contribute to cognitive impairment in Alzheimer's disease. *Brain, 140*(12), 3286–3300. doi:10.1093/brain/awx243

Benedict, C., Brooks, S. J., Kullberg, J., Nordenskjöld, R., Burgos, J., Le Grevès, M., . . . Ahlström, H. (2013). Association between physical activity and brain health in older adults. *Neurobiology of Aging, 34*(1), 83–90.

Bennett, D. A., Wilson, R. S., Schneider, J. A., Evans, D. A., Mendes de Leon, C. F., Arnold, S. E., . . . Bienias, J. L. (2003). Education modifies the relation of AD pathology to level of cognitive function in older persons. *Neurology, 60*(12), 1909–1915.

Bennett, I. J., & Rypma, B. (2013). Advances in functional neuroanatomy: a review of combined DTI and fMRI studies in healthy younger and older adults. *Neuroscience and Biobehavioral Reviews, 37*(7), 1201–1210. doi:10.1016/j.neubiorev.2013.04.008

Bergerbest, D., Gabrieli, J., Whitfield-Gabrieli, S., Kim, H., Stebbins, G., Bennett, D., & Fleischman, D. (2009). Age-associated reduction of asymmetry in prefrontal function and preservation of conceptual repetition priming. *NeuroImage, 45*(1), 237–246.

Berry, A. S., Shah, V. D., Baker, S. L., Vogel, J. W., O'Neil, J. P., Janabi, M., . . . Jagust, W. J. (2016). Aging affects dopaminergic neural mechanisms of cognitive flexibility. *Journal of Neuroscience, 36*(50), 12559–12569. doi:10.1523/jneurosci.0626-16.2016

Berryhill, M. E., & Jones, K. T. (2012). tDCS selectively improves working memory in older adults with more education. *Neuroscience Letters, 521*(2), 148–151. doi:10.1016/j.neulet.2012.05.074

Bialystok, E., Craik, F. I. M., & Luk, G. (2012). Bilingualism: consequences for mind and brain. *Trends in Cognitive Sciences, 16*(4), 240–250.

Boduroglu, A., Yoon, C., Luo, T., & Park, D. C. (2006). Age-related stereotypes: a comparison of American and Chinese cultures. *Gerontology, 52*(5), 324–333. doi:10.1159/000094614

Boggio, P. S., Campanha, C., Valasek, C. A., Fecteau, S., Pascual-Leone, A., & Fregni, F. (2010). Modulation of decision-making in a gambling task in older adults with transcranial direct current stimulation. *European Journal of Neuroscience, 31*(3), 593–597. doi:10.1111/j.1460-9568.2010.07080.x

Boggio, P. S., Ferrucci, R., Mameli, F., Martins, D., Martins, O., Vergari, M., ... Priori, A. (2012). Prolonged visual memory enhancement after direct current stimulation in Alzheimer's disease. *Brain Stimulation, 5*(3), 223–230. doi:10.1016/j.brs.2011.06.006

Bollinger, J., Rubens, M. T., Masangkay, E., Kalkstein, J., & Gazzaley, A. (2011). An expectation-based memory deficit in aging. *Neuropsychologia, 49*(6), 1466–1475.

Bookheimer, S., & Burggren, A. (2009). *APOE*-4 genotype and neurophysiological vulnerability to Alzheimer's and cognitive aging. *Annual Review of Clinical Psychology, 5,* 343–362. doi:10.1146/annurev.clinpsy.032408.153625

Boshyan, J., Zebrowitz, L. A., Franklin, R. G., McCormick, C. M., & Carre, J. M. (2014). Age similarities in recognizing threat from faces and diagnostic cues. *Journals of Gerontology. Series B, Psychological Sciences and Social Sciences, 69*(5), 710–718. doi:10.1093/geronb/gbt054

Bowen, H. J., Kark, S. M., & Kensinger, E. A. (2017). NEVER forget: negative emotional valence enhances recapitulation. *Psychonomic Bulletin and Review.* doi:10.3758/s13423-017-1313-9

Braak, H., & Braak, E. (1991). Neuropathological stageing of Alzheimer-related changes. *Acta Neuropathologica, 82*(4), 239–259.

Brassen, S., Gamer, M., Peters, J., Gluth, S., & Buchel, C. (2012). Don't look back in anger! Responsiveness to missed chances in successful and nonsuccessful aging. *Science, 336*(6081), 612–614. doi:10.1126/science.1217516

Braver, T. S., Krug, M. K., Chiew, K. S., Kool, W., Westbrook, J. A., Clement, N. J., ... MOMCIA Group. (2014). Mechanisms of motivation–cognition interaction: challenges and opportunities. *Cognitive, Affective, and Behavioral Neuroscience, 14*(2), 443–472. doi:10.3758/s13415-014-0300-0

Braver, T. S., Paxton, J. L., Locke, H. S., & Barch, D. M. (2009). Flexible neural mechanisms of cognitive control within human prefrontal cortex. *Proceedings of the National Academy of Sciences of the United States of America, 106*(18), 7351–7356. doi:10.1073/pnas.0808187106

Brehmer, Y., Rieckmann, A., Bellander, M., Westerberg, H., Fischer, H., & Bäckman, L. (2011). Neural correlates of training-related working-memory gains in old age. *NeuroImage, 58*(4), 1110–1120.

Brookmeyer, R., Evans, D. A., Hebert, L., Langa, K. M., Heeringa, S. G., Plassman, B. L., & Kukull, W. A. (2011). National estimates of the prevalence of Alzheimer's disease in the United States. *Alzheimer's Disease and Dementia, 7*(1), 61–73.

Buckner, R. L. (2004). Memory and executive function in aging and AD: multiple factors that cause decline and reserve factors that compensate. *Neuron, 44*(1), 195–208.

Buckner, R. L., Andrews-Hanna, J. R., & Schacter, D. L. (2008). The brain's default network: anatomy, function, and relevance to disease. *Annals of the New York Academy of Sciences, 1124*, 1–38.

Buckner, R. L., Sepulcre, J., Talukdar, T., Krienen, F. M., Liu, H., Hedden, T., . . . Johnson, K. A. (2009). Cortical hubs revealed by intrinsic functional connectivity: mapping, assessment of stability, and relation to Alzheimer's disease. *Journal of Neuroscience, 29*(6), 1860–1873. doi:10.1523/jneurosci.5062-08.2009

Buckner, R. L., Snyder, A. Z., Shannon, B. J., LaRossa, G., Sachs, R., Fotenos, A. F., . . . Mintun, M. A. (2005). Molecular, structural, and functional characterization of Alzheimer's disease: evidence for a relationship between default activity, amyloid, and memory. *Journal of Neuroscience, 25*(34), 7709–7717. doi:10.1523/jneurosci.2177-05.2005

Bucur, B., Madden, D. J., Spaniol, J., Provenzale, J. M., Cabeza, R., White, L. E., & Huettel, S. A. (2008). Age-related slowing of memory retrieval: contributions of perceptual speed and cerebral white matter integrity. *Neurobiology of Aging, 29*(7), 1070–1079.

Budson, A. E., & O'Connor, M. K. (2017). *Seven Steps to Managing Your Memory.* New York: Oxford University Press.

Burzynska, A. Z., Wong, C. N., Voss, M. W., Cooke, G. E., Gothe, N. P., Fanning, J., . . . Kramer, A. F. (2015). Physical activity is linked to greater moment-to-moment variability in spontaneous brain activity in older adults. *PLoS One, 10*(8), e0134819.

Cabeza, R. (2002). Hemispheric asymmetry reduction in older adults: the HAROLD model. *Psychology and Aging, 17*(1), 85–100.

Cabeza, R., Anderson, N. D., Locantore, J. K., & McIntosh, A. R. (2002). Aging gracefully: compensatory brain activity in high-performing older adults. *NeuroImage, 17*(3), 1394–1402. doi:10.1006/nimg.2002.1280

Cabeza, R., & Dennis, N. A. (2013). Frontal lobes and aging: deterioration and compensation. In D. T. Stuss & R. T. Knight (Eds.), *Principles of Frontal Lobe Function* (2nd edn, pp. 628–652). New York: Oxford University Press.

Cabeza, R., Grady, C. L., Nyberg, L., McIntosh, A. R., Tulving, E., Kapur, S., ... Craik, F. I. M. (1997). Age-related differences in neural activity during memory encoding and retrieval: a positron emission tomography study. *Journal of Neuroscience, 17*(1), 391–400.

Cacioppo, J. T., Berntson, G. G., Bechara, A., Tranel, D., & Hawkley, L. C. (2011). Could an aging brain contribute to subjective well-being? The value added by a social neuroscience perspective. In A. Todorov, S. T. Fiske, & D. A. Prentice (Eds.), *Social Neuroscience: Toward Understanding the Underpinnings of the Social Mind* (pp. 249–262). Oxford Series in Social Cognition and Social Neuroscience. Oxford University Press.

Cacioppo, J. T., Hawkley, L. C., Kalil, A., Hughes, M. E., Waite, L., & Thisted, R. A. (2008). Happiness and the invisible threads of social connection; the Chicago Health, Aging, and Social Relations Study. In M. Eid & R. J. Larsen (Eds.), *The Science of Subjective Well-Being* (pp. 195–219). New York: Guilford Press.

Cacioppo, J. T., Hawkley, L. C., & Thisted, R. A. (2010). Perceived social isolation makes me sad: 5-year cross-lagged analyses of loneliness and depressive symptomatology in the Chicago Health, Aging, and Social Relations Study. *Psychology and Aging, 25*(2), 453–463.

Cacioppo, J. T., Hughes, M. E., Waite, L. J., Hawkley, L. C., & Thisted, R. A. (2006). Loneliness as a specific risk factor for depressive symptoms: cross-sectional and longitudinal analyses. *Psychology and Aging, 21*(1), 140–151.

Campbell, K. L., Grady, C. L., Ng, C., & Hasher, L. (2012). Age differences in the frontoparietal cognitive control network: implications for distractibility. *Neuropsychologia, 50*(9), 2212–2223.

Campbell, K. L., Grigg, O., Saverino, C., Churchill, N., & Grady, C. L. (2013). Age differences in the intrinsic functional connectivity of default network subsystems. *Frontiers in Aging Neuroscience, 5*, Article 73. doi:10.3389/fnagi.2013.00073

Cappell, K. A., Gmeindl, L., & Reuter-Lorenz, P. A. (2010). Age differences in prefrontal recruitment during verbal working memory maintenance depend on memory load. *Cortex, 46*(4), 462–473. doi:10.1016/j.cortex.2009.11.009

Carmichael, O., Schwarz, C., Drucker, D., Fletcher, E., Harvey, D., Beckett, L., ... DeCarli, C. (2010). Longitudinal changes in white matter disease and cognition in the first year of the Alzheimer disease neuroimaging initiative. *Archives of Neurology, 67*(11), 1370–1378. doi:10.1001/archneurol.2010.284

Carne, R. P., Vogrin, S., Litewka, L., & Cook, M. J. (2006). Cerebral cortex: an MRI-based study of volume and variance with age and sex. *Journal of Clinical Neuroscience, 13*(1), 60–72.

Carp, J., Gmeindl, L., & Reuter-Lorenz, P. A. (2010). Age differences in the neural representation of working memory revealed by multi-voxel pattern analysis. *Frontiers in Human Neuroscience, 4.*

Carp, J., Park, J., Hebrank, A., Park, D. C., & Polk, T. A. (2011). Age-related neural dedifferentiation in the motor system. *PLoS One, 6*(12), e29411. doi:10.1371/journal.pone.0029411

Carp, J., Park, J., Polk, T. A., & Park, D. C. (2011). Age differences in neural distinctiveness revealed by multi-voxel pattern analysis. *NeuroImage, 56*(2), 736–743.

Carstensen, L. L., Isaacowitz, D. M., & Charles, S. T. (1999). Taking time seriously – a theory of socioemotional selectivity. *American Psychologist, 54*(3), 165–181.

Cassidy, B. S., & Gutchess, A. H. (2012a). Social relevance enhances memory for impressions in older adults. *Memory, 20*(4), 332–345.
  (2012b). Structural variation within the amygdala and ventromedial prefrontal cortex predicts memory for impressions in older adults. *Frontiers in Psychology, 3*, Article 319. doi:10.3389/fpsyg.2012.00319
  (2015). Influences of appearance-behavior congruity on memory and social judgments. *Memory, 23*, 1039–1055.

Cassidy, B. S., Hedden, T., Yoon, C., & Gutchess, A. H. (2014). Age differences in medial prefrontal activity for subsequent memory of truth value. *Frontiers in Psychology, 5*, Article 87. doi:10.3389/fpsyg.2014.00087

Cassidy, B. S., Leshikar, E. D., Shih, J. Y., Aizenman, A., & Gutchess, A. H. (2013). Valence-based age differences in medial prefrontal activity during impression formation. *Social Neuroscience, 8*(5), 462–473. doi:10.1080/17470919.2013.832373

Cassidy, B. S., Shih, J. Y., & Gutchess, A. H. (2012). Age-related changes to the neural correlates of social evaluation. *Social Neuroscience, 7*(6), 552–564. doi:10.1080/17470919.2012.674057

Castelli, I., Baglio, F., Blasi, V., Alberoni, M., Falini, A., Liverta-Sempio, O., . . . Marchetti, A. (2010). Effects of aging on mindreading ability through the eyes: an fMRI study. *Neuropsychologia, 48*(9), 2586–2594.

Castle, E., Eisenberger, N. I., Seeman, T. E., Moons, W. G., Boggero, I. A., Grinblatt, M. S., & Taylor, S. E. (2012). Neural and behavioral bases of age differences in perceptions of trust. *Proceedings of the National*

Academy of Sciences of the United States of America, 109(51), 20848–20852. doi:10.1073/pnas.1218518109

Celone, K. A., Calhoun, V. D., Dickerson, B. C., Atri, A., Chua, E. F., Miller, S. L., ... Sperling, R. A. (2006). Alterations in memory networks in mild cognitive impairment and Alzheimer's disease: an independent component analysis. *Journal of Neuroscience, 26*(40), 10222–10231. doi:10.1523/jneurosci.2250-06.2006

Chalfonte, B. L., & Johnson, M. K. (1996). Feature memory and binding in young and older adults. *Memory & Cognition, 24*(4), 403–416.

Chan, M. Y., Alhazmi, F. H., Park, D. C., Savalia, N. K., & Wig, G. S. (2017). Resting-state network topology differentiates task signals across the adult life span. *Journal of Neuroscience, 37*(10), 2734–2745. doi:10.1523/jneurosci.2406-16.2017

Chan, M. Y., Park, D. C., Savalia, N. K., Petersen, S. E., & Wig, G. S. (2014). Decreased segregation of brain systems across the healthy adult life span. *Proceedings of the National Academy of Sciences of the United States of America, 111*(46), E4997–E5006.

Chapman, S. B., Aslan, S., Spence, J. S., Hart, J. J., Bartz, E. K., Didehbani, N., ... DeFina, L. F. (2015). Neural mechanisms of brain plasticity with complex cognitive training in healthy seniors. *Cerebral Cortex, 25*(2), 396–405.

Charles, S. T., Mather, M., & Carstensen, L. L. (2003). Aging and emotional memory: the forgettable nature of negative images for older adults. *Journal of Experimental Psychology: General, 132*(2), 310–324. doi:10.1037/0096-3445.132.2.310

Charlton, R. A., Barrick, T. R., Markus, H. S., & Morris, R. G. (2009). Theory of mind associations with other cognitive functions and brain imaging in normal aging. *Psychology and Aging, 24*(2), 338–348. doi:10.1037/a0015225

Chee, M. W., Chen, K. H., Zheng, H., Chan, K. P., Isaac, V., Sim, S. K., ... Ng, T. P. (2009). Cognitive function and brain structure correlations in healthy elderly East Asians. *NeuroImage, 46*(1), 257–269.

Chee, M. W., Goh, J. O., Venkatraman, V., Tan, J. C., Gutchess, A. H., Sutton, B., ... Park, D. C. (2006). Age-related changes in object processing and contextual binding revealed using fMR adaptation. *Journal of Cognitive Neuroscience, 18*(4), 495–507. doi:10.1162/jocn.2006.18.4.495

Chee, M. W., Zheng, H., Goh, J. O., Park, D. C., & Sutton, B. P. (2011). Brain structure in young and old East Asians and Westerners: comparisons of structural volume and cortical thickness. *Journal of Cognitive Neuroscience, 23*, 1065–1079.

Chen, Y. C., Chen, C. C., Decety, J., & Cheng, Y. W. (2014). Aging is
    associated with changes in the neural circuits underlying empathy.
    Neurobiology of Aging, *35*(4), 827–836. doi:10.1016/j.
    neurobiolaging.2013.10.080

Chhatwal, J. P., & Sperling, R. A. (2012). Functional MRI of mnemonic
    networks across the spectrum of normal aging, mild cognitive
    impairment, and Alzheimer's disease. *Journal of Alzheimer's Disease*,
    31(s3), S155–S167.

Chowdhury, R., Guitart-Masip, M., Bunzeck, N., Dolan, R. J., & Düzel, E.
    (2012). Dopamine modulates episodic memory persistence in old age.
    Journal of Neuroscience, *32*(41), 14193–14204.

Chowdhury, R., Guitart-Masip, M., Lambert, C., Dayan, P., Huys, Q., Düzel, E.,
    & Dolan, R. J. (2013). Dopamine restores reward prediction errors in old
    age. *Nature Neuroscience*, *16*(5), 648–653.

Chung, H. K., Tymula, A., & Glimcher, P. (2017). The reduction of
    ventrolateral prefrontal cortex gray matter volume correlates with loss
    of economic rationality in aging. *Journal of Neuroscience*, *37*(49),
    12068–12077. doi:10.1523/jneurosci.1171-17.2017

Clewett, D., Bachman, S., & Mather, M. (2014). Age-related reduced
    prefrontal-amygdala structural connectivity is associated with lower
    trait anxiety. *Neuropsychology*, *28*(4), 631–642.

Colcombe, S. J., Erickson, K. I., Scalf, P. E., Kim, J. S., Prakash, R.,
    McAuley, E., ... Kramer, A. F. (2006). Aerobic exercise training
    increases brain volume in aging humans. *Journals of Gerontology.
    Series A, Biological Sciences and Medical Sciences*, *61*(11), 1166–1170.

Colcombe, S. J., Kramer, A. F., Erickson, K. I., & Scalf, P. (2005). The
    implications of cortical recruitment and brain morphology for
    individual differences in inhibitory function in aging humans.
    Psychology and Aging, *20*(3), 363–375.

Colcombe, S. J., Kramer, A. F., Erickson, K. I., Scalf, P., McAuley, E.,
    Cohen, N. J., ... Elavsky, S. (2004). Cardiovascular fitness, cortical
    plasticity, and aging. *Proceedings of the National Academy of Sciences
    of the United States of America*, *101*(9), 3316–3321.

Colton, G., Leshikar, E. D., & Gutchess, A. H. (2013). Age differences in
    neural response to stereotype threat and resiliency for self-referenced
    information. *Frontiers in Human Neuroscience*, *7*, 537. doi:10.3389/
    fnhum.2013.00537

Combs, H. L., Folley, B. S., Berry, D. T., Segerstrom, S. C., Han, D. Y.,
    Anderson-Mooney, A. J., ... van Horne, C. (2015). Cognition and
    depression following deep brain stimulation of the subthalamic nucleus
    and globus pallidus pars internus in Parkinson's disease: a meta-analysis.
    Neuropsychology Review, *25*(4), 439–454. doi:10.1007/s11065-015-9302-0

Costa, P. T., & McCrae, R. R. (1987). Neuroticism, somatic complaints, and disease: is the bark worse than the bite? *Journal of Personality*, *55*(2), 299–316.

Cotelli, M., Manenti, R., Brambilla, M., Petesi, M., Rosini, S., Ferrari, C., . . . Miniussi, C. (2014). Anodal tDCS during face–name associations memory training in Alzheimer's patients. *Frontiers in Aging Neuroscience*, *6*, Article 38. doi:10.3389/fnagi.2014.00038

Coupe, P., Catheline, G., Lanuza, E., & Manjon, J. V. (2017). Towards a unified analysis of brain maturation and aging across the entire life span: a MRI analysis. *Human Brain Mapping*, *38*(11), 5501–5518. doi:10.1002/hbm.23743

Cox, K. M., Aizenstein, H. J., & Fiez, J. A. (2008). Striatal outcome processing in healthy aging. *Cognitive, Affective, and Behavioral Neuroscience*, *8*(3), 304–317.

Craik, F. I. M., & Byrd, M. (1982). Aging and cognitive deficits: the role of attentional resources. In F. I. M. Craik & S. E. Trehub (Eds.), *Aging and Cognitive Processes* (pp. 191–211). New York: Plenum Press.

Craik, F. I. M., & Jennings, J. M. (1992). Human memory. In F. I. M. Craik & T. A. Salthouse (Eds.), *The Handbook of Aging and Cognition* (pp. 51–110). Hillsdale, NJ: Lawrence Erlbaum Associates, Inc.

Craik, F. I. M., & Lockhart, R. S. (1972). Levels of processing: a framework for memory research. *Journal of Verbal Learning and Verbal Behavior*, *11*(6), 671–684.

Craik, F. I. M., Moroz, T. M., Moscovitch, M., Stuss, D. T., Winocur, G., Tulving, E., & Kapur, S. (1999). In search of the self: a positron emission tomography study. *Psychological Science*, *10*(1), 26–34.

Craik, F. I. M., & Rabinowitz, J. C. (1984). Age differences in the acquisition and use of verbal information: a tutorial review. In H. Bouma & D. G. Bouwhuis (Eds.), *Attention and Performance X: Control of Language Processes* (pp. 471–499). Hillsdale, NJ: Erlbaum.

Craik, F. I. M., & Salthouse, T. A. (2007). *The Handbook of Aging and Cognition* (3rd edn). New York: Psychology Press.

Cronin-Golomb, A., Gilmore, G. C., Neargarder, S., Morrison, S. R., & Laudate, T. M. (2007). Enhanced stimulus strength improves visual cognition in aging and Alzheimer's disease. *Cortex*, *43*(7), 952–966.

Csernansky, J. G., Hamstra, J., Wang, L., McKeel, D., Price, J. L., Gado, M., & Morris, J. C. (2004). Correlations between antemortem hippocampal volume and postmortem neuropathology in AD subjects. *Alzheimer Disease and Associated Disorders*, *18*(4), 190–195.

Cutchin, M. P. (2003). The process of mediated aging-in-place: a theoretically and empirically based model. *Social Science and Medicine*, *57*(6), 1077–1090.

Daffner, K. R., Haring, A. E., Alperin, B. R., Zhuravleva, T. Y., Mott, K. K., & Holcomb, P. J. (2013). The impact of visual acuity on age-related differences in neural markers of early visual processing. *NeuroImage*, *67*, 127–136.

Dahlin, E., Nyberg, L., Bäckman, L., & Neely, A. S. (2008). Plasticity of executive functioning in young and older adults: immediate training gains, transfer, and long-term maintenance. *Psychology and Aging*, *23*(4), 720–730.

Damoiseaux, J. S., Beckmann, C. F., Arigita, E. J., Barkhof, F., Scheltens, P., Stam, C. J., ... Rombouts, S. A. (2008). Reduced resting-state brain activity in the "default network" in normal aging. *Cerebral Cortex*, *18*(8), 1856–1864. doi:10.1093/cercor/bhm207

Daselaar, S. M., Fleck, M. S., Dobbins, I. G., Madden, D. J., & Cabeza, R. (2006). Effects of healthy aging on hippocampal and rhinal memory functions: an event-related fMRI study. *Cerebral Cortex, 16*, 1771–1782.

Daselaar, S. M., Veitman, D. J., Rombouts, S. A., Raaijmakers, J. G., & Jonker, C. (2003). Neuroanatomical corelates of episodic encoding and retrieval in young and elderly subjects. *Brain, 126*, 43–56.

(2005). Aging affects both perceptual and lexical/semantic components of word stem priming: an event-related fMRI study. *Neurobiology of Learning and Memory, 83*(3), 251–262.

Davis, S. W., Dennis, N. A., Buchler, N. G., White, L. E., Madden, D. J., & Cabeza, R. (2009). Assessing the effects of age on long white matter tracts using diffusion tensor tractography. *NeuroImage, 46*(2), 530–541.

Davis, S. W., Dennis, N. A., Daselaar, S. M., Fleck, M. S., & Cabeza, R. (2008). Que PASA? The posterior–anterior shift in aging. *Cerebral Cortex, 18*(5), 1201–1209.

Davis, S. W., Kragel, J. E., Madden, D. J., & Cabeza, R. (2012). The architecture of cross-hemispheric communication in the aging brain: linking behavior to functional and structural connectivity. *Cerebral Cortex, 22*(1), 232–242.

Davis, T. M., & Jerger, J. (2014). The effect of middle age on the late positive component of the auditory event-related potential. *Journal of the American Academy of Audiology, 25*(2), 199–209.

Davis, T. M., Jerger, J., & Martin, J. (2013). Electrophysiological evidence of augmented interaural asymmetry in middle-aged listeners. *Journal of the American Academy of Audiology, 24*(3), 159–173.

Deary, I. J., & Batty, G. D. (2007). Cognitive epidemiology. *Journal of Epidemiology and Community Health, 61*(5), 378–384. doi:10.1136/jech.2005.039206

Deary, I. J., Pattie, A., & Starr, J. M. (2013). The stability of intelligence from age 11 to age 90 years: the Lothian Birth Cohort of 1921. *Psychological Science, 24*(12), 2361–2368. doi:10.1177/0956797613486487

Deary, I. J., Yang, J., Davies, G., Harris, S. E., Tenesa, A., Liewald, D., . . . Visscher, P. M. (2012). Genetic contributions to stability and change in intelligence from childhood to old age. *Nature, 482*(7384), 212–215. Retrieved from www.nature.com/nature/journal/v482/n7384/abs/nature10781.html – supplementary-information

De Marco, M., Meneghello, F., Duzzi, D., Rigon, J., Pilosio, C., & Venneri, A. (2015). Cognitive stimulation of the default-mode network modulates functional connectivity in healthy aging. *Brain Research Bulletin, 121*, 26–41. doi:10.1016/j.brainresbull.2015.12.001

Denburg, N. L., Cole, C. A., Hernandez, M., Yamada, T. H., Tranel, D., Bechara, A., & Wallace, R. B. (2007). The orbitofrontal cortex, real-world decision making, and normal aging. *Annals of the New York Academy of Sciences, 1121*, 480–498. doi:10.1196/annals.1401.031

Dennis, N. A., Bowman, C. R., & Peterson, K. M. (2014). Age-related differences in the neural correlates mediating false recollection. *Neurobiology of Aging, 35*(2), 395–407.

Dennis, N. A., & Cabeza, R. (2011). Age-related dedifferentiation of learning systems: an fMRI study of implicit and explicit learning. *Neurobiology of Aging, 32*(12), 2318. e17–2318. e30.

Dennis, N. A., Hayes, S. M., Prince, S. E., Madden, D. J., Huettel, S. A., & Cabeza, R. (2008). Effects of aging on the neural correlates of successful item and source memory encoding. *Journal of Experimental Psychology: Learning, Memory, and Cognition, 34*(4), 791–808.

Dennis, N. A., Kim, H., & Cabeza, R. (2007). Effects of aging on true and false memory formation: an fMRI study. *Neuropsychologia, 45*(14), 3157–3166. doi:10.1016/j.neuropsychologia.2007.07.003

(2008). Age-related differences in brain activity during true and false memory retrieval. *Journal of Cognitive Neuroscience, 20*(8), 1390–1402.

Dennis, N. A., & Turney, I. C. (2018). The influence of perceptual similarity and individual differences on false memories in aging. *Neurobiology of Aging, 62*, 221–230. doi:10.1016/j.neurobiolaging.2017.10.020

Derksen, B. J., Duff, M. C., Weldon, K., Zhang, J., Zamba, K. D., Tranel, D., & Denburg, N. L. (2015). Older adults catch up to younger adults on a learning and memory task that involves collaborative social interaction. *Memory, 23*(4), 612–624. doi:10.1080/09658211.2014.915974

De Souza, L. C., Chupin, M., Lamari, F., Jardel, C., Leclercq, D., Colliot, O., . . . Sarazin, M. (2012). CSF tau markers are correlated with hippocampal volume in Alzheimer's disease. *Neurobiology of Aging*, *33*(7), 1253–1257.

D'Esposito, M., Zarahn, E., Aguirre, G. K., & Rypma, B. (1999). The effect of normal aging on the coupling of neural activity to the BOLD hemodynamic response. *NeuroImage*, *10*(1), 6–14. doi:10.1006/ nimg.1999.0444

Deuschl, G., Schade-Brittinger, C., Krack, P., Volkmann, J., Schafer, H., Botzel, K., . . . German Parkinson Study Group, Neurostimulation Section. (2006). A randomized trial of deep-brain stimulation for Parkinson's disease. *New England Journal of Medicine*, *355*(9), 896–908. doi:10.1056/NEJMoa060281

Dickerson, B. C., Salat, D. H., Greve, D. N., Chua, E. F., Rand-Giovannetti, E., Rentz, D. M., . . . Sperling, R. A. (2005). Increased hippocampal activation in mild cognitive impairment compared to normal aging and AD. *Neurology*, *65*(3), 404–411. doi:10.1212/01. wnl.0000171450.97464.49

Dickerson, B. C., & Sperling, R. A. (2008). Functional abnormalities of the medial temporal lobe memory system in mild cognitive impairment and Alzheimer's disease: insights from functional MRI studies. *Neuropsychologia*, *46*(6), 1624–1635. doi:10.1016/j. neuropsychologia.2007.11.030

DiGirolamo, G. J., Kramer, A. F., Barad, V., Cepeda, N. J., Weissman, D. H., Milham, M. P., . . . Webb, A. (2001). General and task-specific frontal lobe recruitment in older adults during executive processes: a fMRI investigation of task-switching. *NeuroReport*, *12*(9), 2065–2071.

Döhnel, K., Sommer, M., Ibach, B., Rothmayr, C., Meinhardt, J., & Hajak, G. (2008). Neural correlates of emotional working memory in patients with mild cognitive impairment. *Neuropsychologia*, *46*(1), 37–48.

Dolcos, S., Katsumi, Y., & Dixon, R. A. (2014). The role of arousal in the spontaneous regulation of emotions in healthy aging: a fMRI investigation. *Frontiers in Psychology*, *5*, Article 681. doi:10.3389/ fpsyg.2014.00681

Donohue, M. C., Sperling, R. A., Petersen, R., Sun, C. K., Weiner, M. W., & Aisen, P. S. (2017). Association between elevated brain amyloid and subsequent cognitive decline among cognitively normal persons. *Journal of the American Medical Association*, *317*(22), 2305–2316. doi:10.1001/jama.2017.6669

Donovan, N. J., Okereke, O. I., Vannini, P., Amariglio, R. E., Rentz, D. M., Marshall, G. A., . . . Sperling, R. A. (2016). Association of higher cortical amyloid burden with loneliness in cognitively normal older adults. *JAMA Psychiatry*, *73*(12), 1230–1237. doi:10.1001/ jamapsychiatry.2016.2657

Drzezga, A., Becker, J. A., Van Dijk, K. R. A., Sreenivasan, A., Talukdar, T., Sullivan, C., … Greve, D. (2011). Neuronal dysfunction and disconnection of cortical hubs in non-demented subjects with elevated amyloid burden. *Brain*, *134*(6), 1635–1646.

Duarte, A., Graham, K. S., & Henson, R. N. (2010). Age-related changes in neural activity associated with familiarity, recollection and false recognition. *Neurobiology of Aging*, *31*(10), 1814–1830.

Duarte, A., Henson, R. N., & Graham, K. S. (2008). The effects of aging on the neural correlates of subjective and objective recollection. *Cerebral Cortex*, *18*(9), 2169–2180.

Duarte, A., Ranganath, C., Trujillo, C., & Knight, R. T. (2006). Intact recollection memory in high-performing older adults: ERP and behavioral evidence. *Journal of Cognitive Neuroscience*, *18*(1), 33–47.

Dulas, M. R., & Duarte, A. (2012). The effects of aging on material-independent and material-dependent neural correlates of source memory retrieval. *Cerebral Cortex*, *22*(1), 37–50.

(2013). The influence of directed attention at encoding on source memory retrieval in the young and old: an ERP study. *Brain Research*, *1500*, 55–71.

(2014). Aging affects the interaction between attentional control and source memory: an fMRI study. *Journal of Cognitive Neuroscience*, *26*(12), 2653–2669.

Dulas, M. R., Newsome, R. N., & Duarte, A. (2011). The effects of aging on ERP correlates of source memory retrieval for self-referential information. *Brain Research*, *1377*, 84–100. doi:10.1016/j. brainres.2010.12.087

Duval, C., Piolino, P., Bejanin, A., Eustache, F., & Desgranges, B. (2011). Age effects on different components of theory of mind. *Consciousness and Cognition*, *20*(3), 627–642. doi:10.1016/j.concog.2010.10.025

Earles, J. L., Smith, A. D., & Park, D. C. (1994). Age differences in the effects of facilitating and distracting context on recall. *Aging & Cognition*, *1*(2), 141–151.

Ebner, N. C., Chen, H., Porges, E., Lin, T., Fischer, H., Feifel, D., & Cohen, R. A. (2016). Oxytocin's effect on resting-state functional connectivity varies by age and sex. *Psychoneuroendocrinology*, *69*, 50–59. doi:10.1016/j.psyneuen.2016.03.013

Ebner, N. C., Gluth, S., Johnson, M. R., Raye, C. L., Mitchell, K. J., & Johnson, M. K. (2011). Medial prefrontal cortex activity when thinking about others depends on their age. *NeuroCase*, *17*(3), 260–269. doi:10.1080/13554794.2010.536953

Ebner, N. C., Johnson, M. K., & Fischer, H. (2012). Neural mechanisms of reading facial emotions in young and older adults. *Frontiers in Psychology*, *3*, Article 223. doi:10.3389/fpsyg.2012.00223

Ebner, N. C., Johnson, M. R., Rieckmann, A., Durbin, K. A., Johnson, M. K., & Fischer, H. (2013). Processing own-age versus other-age faces: neuro-behavioral correlates and effects of emotion. *NeuroImage, 78,* 363–371. doi:10.1016/j.neuroimage.2013.04.029

Ebner, N. C., Maura, G. M., Macdonald, K., Westberg, L., & Fischer, H. (2013). Oxytocin and socioemotional aging: current knowledge and future trends. *Frontiers in Human Neuroscience, 7,* Article 487. doi:10.3389/fnhum.2013.00487

Eich, T. S., Parker, D., Liu, D., Oh, H., Razlighi, Q., Gazes, Y., ... Stern, Y. (2016). Functional brain and age-related changes associated with congruency in task switching. *Neuropsychologia, 91,* 211–221. doi:10.1016/j.neuropsychologia.2016.08.009

Engell, A. D., Haxby, J. V., & Todorov, A. (2007). Implicit trustworthiness decisions: automatic coding of face properties in the human amygdala. *Journal of Cognitive Neuroscience, 19*(9), 1508–1519. doi:10.1162/jocn.2007.19.9.1508

Engert, V., Buss, C., Khalili-Mahani, N., Wadiwalla, M., Dedovic, K., & Pruessner, J. C. (2010). Investigating the association between early life parental care and stress responsivity in adulthood. *Developmental Neuropsychology, 35*(5), 570–581.

Erickson, K. I., Banducci, S. E., Weinstein, A. M., MacDonald, A. W., Ferrell, R. E., Halder, I., ... Manuck, S. B. (2013). The brain-derived neurotrophic factor Val66Met polymorphism moderates an effect of physical activity on working memory performance. *Psychological Science, 24*(9),1770–1779. doi:10.1177/0956797613480367

Erickson, K. I., Colcombe, S. J., Elavsky, S., McAuley, E., Korol, D. L., Scalf, P. E., & Kramer, A. F. (2007). Interactive effects of fitness and hormone treatment on brain health in postmenopausal women. *Neurobiology of Aging, 28*(2), 179–185.

Erickson, K. I., Colcombe, S. J., Wadhwa, R., Bherer, L., Peterson, M. S., Scalf, P. E., ... Kramer, A. F. (2007). Training-induced functional activation changes in dual-task processing: an fMRI study. *Cerebral Cortex, 17*(1), 192–204.

Erickson, K. I., Gildengers, A. G., & Butters, M. A. (2013). Physical activity and brain plasticity in late adulthood. *Dialogues in Clinical Neuroscience, 15*(1), 99–108.

Erickson, K. I., Voss, M. W., Prakash, R. S., Basak, C., Szabo, A., Chaddock, L., ... White, S. M. (2011). Exercise training increases size of hippocampus and improves memory. *Proceedings of the National Academy of Sciences of the United States of America, 108*(7), 3017–3022.

Ethier-Majcher, C., Joubert, S., & Gosselin, F. (2013). Reverse correlating trustworthy faces in young and older adults. *Frontiers in Psychology*, *4*. doi:10.3389/fpsyg.2013.00592

Fairfield, B., Mammarella, N., Di Domenico, A., & Palumbo, R. (2015). Running with emotion: when affective content hampers working memory performance. *International Journal of Psychology*, *50*(2), 161–164.

Feigin, A., Ghilardi, M. F., Huang, C., Ma, Y., Carbon, M., Guttman, M., ... Eidelberg, D. (2006). Preclinical Huntington's disease: compensatory brain responses during learning. *Annals of Neurology*, *59*(1), 53–59.

Felice, D., O'Leary, O. F., Cryan, J. F., Dinan, T. G., Gardier, A. M., Sánchez, C., & David, D. J. (2015). When ageing meets the blues: are current antidepressants effective in depressed aged patients? *Neuroscience and Biobehavioral Reviews*, *55*, 478–497.

Ferreira, L. K., & Busatto, G. F. (2013). Resting-state functional connectivity in normal brain aging. *Neuroscience and Biobehavioral Reviews*, *37*(3), 384–400. doi:10.1016/j.neubiorev.2013.01.017

Fertonani, A., Brambilla, M., Cotelli, M., & Miniussi, C. (2014). The timing of cognitive plasticity in physiological aging: a tDCS study of naming. *Frontiers in Aging Neuroscience*, *6*, Article 131. doi:10.3389/fnagi.2014.00131

Feyers, D., Collette, F., D'Argembeau, A., Majerus, S., & Salmon, E. (2010). Neural networks involved in self-judgement in young and elderly adults. *NeuroImage*, *53*, 341–347.

Filippi, M., van den Heuvel, M. P., Fornito, A., He, Y., Hulshoff Pol, H. E., Agosta, F., ... Rocca, M. A. (2013). Assessment of system dysfunction in the brain through MRI-based connectomics. *Lancet Neurology*, *12*(12), 1189–1199. doi:10.1016/S1474-4422(13)70144-3

Fischer, H., Nyberg, L., & Backman, L. (2010). Age-related differences in brain regions supporting successful encoding of emotional faces. *Cortex*, *46*(4), 490–497. doi:10.1016/j.cortex.2009.05.011

Fischer, H., Sandblom, J., Gavazzeni, J., Fransson, P., Wright, C. I., & Backman, L. (2005). Age-differential patterns of brain activation during perception of angry faces. *Neuroscience Letters*, *386*(2), 99–104. doi:10.1016/j.neulet.2005.06.002

Fiske, S. T. (2017). Prejudices in cultural contexts: shared stereotypes (gender, age) versus variable stereotypes (race, ethnicity, religion). *Perspectives on Psychological Science*, *12*(5), 791–799. doi:10.1177/1745691617708204

Fjell, A. M., McEvoy, L., Holland, D., Dale, A. M., Walhovd, K. B.; Alzheimer's Disease Neuroimaging Initiative. (2014). What is normal in normal aging? Effects of aging, amyloid and Alzheimer's disease on the cerebral cortex and the hippocampus. *Progress in Neurobiology*, *117*, 20–40.

Fjell, A. M., Westlye, L. T., Grydeland, H., Amlien, I., Espeseth, T., Reinvang, I., . . . Alzheimer Disease Neuroimaging Initiative. (2014). Accelerating cortical thinning: unique to dementia or universal in aging? *Cerebral Cortex*, *24*(4), 919–934. doi:10.1093/cercor/bhs379

Floel, A., Suttorp, W., Kohl, O., Kurten, J., Lohmann, H., Breitenstein, C., & Knecht, S. (2012). Non-invasive brain stimulation improves object-location learning in the elderly. *Neurobiology of Aging*, *33*(8), 1682–1689. doi:10.1016/j.neurobiolaging.2011.05.007

Ford, J. H., & Kensinger, E. A. (2014). The relation between structural and functional connectivity depends on age and on task goals. *Frontiers in Human Neuroscience*, *8*, Article 307. doi:10.3389/fnhum.2014.00307

(2017). Age-related reversals in neural recruitment across memory retrieval phases. *Journal of Neuroscience*, *37*(20), 5172–5182. doi:10.1523/jneurosci.0521-17.2017

Ford, J. H., Morris, J. A., & Kensinger, E. A. (2014). Neural recruitment and connectivity during emotional memory retrieval across the adult life span. *Neurobiology of Aging*, *35*(12), 2770–2784. doi:10.1016/j.neurobiolaging.2014.05.029

Freitas, C., Farzan, F., & Pascual-Leone, A. (2013). Assessing brain plasticity across the lifespan with transcranial magnetic stimulation: why, how, and what is the ultimate goal? *Frontiers in Neuroscience*, *7*, Article 42. doi:10.3389/fnins.2013.00042

Freund, A. M., & Isaacowitz, D. M. (2014). Aging and social perception: so far, more similarities than differences. *Psychology and Aging*, *29*(3), 451–453. doi:10.1037/a0037555

Friedman, D. (2012). Components of aging. In S. J. Luck & E. S. Kappenman (Eds.), *The Oxford Handbook of Event-Related Potential Components* (pp. 513–536). New York: Oxford University Press.

Friedman, D., de Chastelaine, M., Nessler, D., & Malcolm, B. (2010). Changes in familiarity and recollection across the lifespan: an ERP perspective. *Brain Research*, *1310*, 124–141.

Friedman, D., Ritter, W., & Snodgrass, J. G. (1996). ERPs during study as a function of subsequent direct and indirect memory testing in young and old adults. *Cognitive Brain Research*, *4*(1), 1–13.

Friedman, D., & Trott, C. (2000). An event-related potential study of encoding in young and older adults. *Neuropsychologia*, *38*(5), 542–557.

Gabrieli, J. D. E., Vaidya, C. J., Stone, M., Francis, W. S., Thompson-Schill, S. L., Fleischman, D. A., . . . Wilson, R. S. (1999). Convergent behavioral and neuropsychological evidence for a distinction between identification and production forms of repetition priming. *Journal of Experimental Psychology: General*, *128*(4), 479–498.

Gard, T., Taquet, M., Dixit, R., Hölzel, B. K., de Montjoye, Y.-A., Brach, N., ... Lazar, S. W. (2014). Fluid intelligence and brain functional organization in aging yoga and meditation practitioners. *Frontiers in Aging Neuroscience, 6*, 76.

Garrett, D. D., Kovacevic, N., McIntosh, A. R., & Grady, C. L. (2011). The importance of being variable. *Journal of Neuroscience, 31*(12), 4496–4503. doi:10.1523/JNEUROSCI.5641-10.2011

(2013). The modulation of BOLD variability between cognitive states varies by age and processing speed. *Cerebral Cortex, 23*(3), 684–693. doi:10.1093/cercor/bhs055

Garrett, D. D., Samanez-Larkin, G. R., MacDonald, S. W., Lindenberger, U., McIntosh, A. R., & Grady, C. L. (2013). Moment-to-moment brain signal variability: a next frontier in human brain mapping? *Neuroscience and Biobehavioral Reviews, 37*(4), 610–624. doi:10.1016/j. neubiorev.2013.02.015

Gazzaley, A., Clapp, W., Kelley, J., McEvoy, K., Knight, R. T., & D'Esposito, M. (2008). Age-related top-down suppression deficit in the early stages of cortical visual memory processing. *Proceedings of the National Academy of Sciences of the United States of America, 105*(35), 13122–13126. doi:10.1073/pnas.0806074105

Gazzaley, A., Cooney, J. W., Rissman, J., & D'Esposito, M. (2005). Top-down suppression deficit underlies working memory impairment in normal aging. *Nature Neuroscience, 8*, 1298–1300.

Ge, R., Fu, Y., Wang, D., Yao, L., & Long, Z. (2014). Age-related alterations of brain network underlying the retrieval of emotional autobiographical memories: an fMRI study using independent component analysis. *Frontiers in Human Neuroscience, 8*, Article 629. doi:10.3389/fnhum.2014.00629

Getzmann, S., Falkenstein, M., & Gajewski, P. D. (2015). Neuro-behavioral correlates of post-deviance distraction in middle-aged and old adults. *Journal of Psychophysiology, 28*(3), 178–186.

Getzmann, S., Gajewski, P. D., & Falkenstein, M. (2013). Does age increase auditory distraction? Electrophysiological correlates of high and low performance in seniors. *Neurobiology of Aging, 34*(8), 1952–1962.

Ghosh, S., & Lippa, C. F. (2015). Clinical subtypes of frontotemporal dementia. *American Journal of Alzheimer's Disease and Other Dementias, 30*(7), 653–661. doi:10.1177/1533317513494442

Gianaros, P. J., Manuck, S. B., Sheu, L. K., Kuan, D. C., Votruba-Drzal, E., Craig, A. E., & Hariri, A. R. (2011). Parental education predicts corticostriatal functionality in adulthood. *Cerebral Cortex, 21*(4), 896–910. doi:10.1093/cercor/bhq160

Gigandet, X., Hagmann, P., Kurant, M., Cammoun, L., Meuli, R., et al. (2008). Estimating the confidence level of white matter connections obtained with MRI tractography. *PLoS One*, *3*(12), e4006. doi:10.1371/journal.pone.0004006.

Giovanello, K. S., Kensinger, E. A., Wong, A. T., & Schacter, D. L. (2010). Age-related neural changes during memory conjunction errors. *Journal of Cognitive Neuroscience*, *22*(7), 1348–1361.

Giovanello, K. S., & Schacter, D. L. (2012). Reduced specificity of hippocampal and posterior ventrolateral prefrontal activity during relational retrieval in normal aging. *Journal of Cognitive Neuroscience*, *24*(1), 159–170.

Glisky, E. L., & Marquine, M. J. (2009). Semantic and self-referential processing of positive and negative trait adjectives in older adults. *Memory*, *17*(2), 144–157. doi:10.1080/09658210802077405

Goh, J. O., Beason-Held, L. L., An, Y., Kraut, M. A., & Resnick, S. M. (2013). Frontal function and executive processing in older adults: process and region specific age-related longitudinal functional changes. *NeuroImage*, *69*, 43–50. doi:10.1016/j.neuroimage.2012.12.026

Goh, J. O., Chee, M. W., Tan, J. C., Venkatraman, V., Hebrank, A., Leshikar, E. D., . . . Park, D. C. (2007). Age and culture modulate object processing and object-scene binding in the ventral visual area. *Cognitive, Affective, & Behavioral Neuroscience*, *7*(1), 44–52.

Goh, J. O., Hebrank, A. C., Sutton, B. P., Chee, M. W., Sim, S. K., & Park, D. C. (2013). Culture-related differences in default network activity during visuo-spatial judgments. *Social Cognitive and Affective Neuroscience*, *8*(2), 134–142. doi:10.1093/scan/nsr077

Goh, J. O., Su, Y. S., Tang, Y. J., McCarrey, A. C., Tereshchenko, A., Elkins, W., & Resnick, S. M. (2016). Frontal, striatal, and medial temporal sensitivity to value distinguishes risk-taking from risk-aversive older adults during decision making. *Journal of Neuroscience*, *36*(49), 12498–12509. doi:10.1523/jneurosci.1386-16.2016

Goh, J. O., Suzuki, A., & Park, D. C. (2010). Reduced neural selectivity increases fMRI adaptation with age during face discrimination. *NeuroImage*, *51*(1), 336–344.

Gold, B. T., Johnson, N. F., & Powell, D. K. (2013). Lifelong bilingualism contributes to cognitive reserve against white matter integrity declines in aging. *Neuropsychologia*, *51*(13), 2841–2846.

Gold, B. T., Kim, C., Johnson, N. F., Kryscio, R. J., & Smith, C. D. (2013). Lifelong bilingualism maintains neural efficiency for cognitive control in aging. *Journal of Neuroscience*, *33*(2), 387–396.

Gold, B. T., Powell, D. K., Xuan, L., Jicha, G. A., & Smith, C. D. (2010). Age-related slowing of task switching is associated with decreased integrity of frontoparietal white matter. *Neurobiology of Aging*, *31*(3), 512–522.

Gorbach, T., Pudas, S., Lundquist, A., Oradd, G., Josefsson, M., Salami, A., ... Nyberg, L. (2017). Longitudinal association between hippocampus atrophy and episodic-memory decline. *Neurobiology of Aging*, *51*, 167–176. doi:10.1016/j.neurobiolaging.2016.12.002

Gordon, B. A., Zacks, J. M., Blazey, T., Benzinger, T. L. S., Morris, J. C., Fagan, A. M., ... Balota, D. A. (2015). Task-evoked fMRI changes in attention networks are associated with preclinical Alzheimer's disease biomarkers. *Neurobiology of Aging*, *36*(5), 1771–1779.

Gow, A. J., Johnson, W., Pattie, A., Brett, C. E., Roberts, B., Starr, J. M., & Deary, I. J. (2011). Stability and change in intelligence from age 11 to ages 70, 79, and 87: the Lothian Birth Cohorts of 1921 and 1936. *Psychology and Aging*, *26*(1), 232–240.

Grady, C. L., Bernstein, L. J., Beig, S., & Siegenthaler, A. L. (2002). The effects of encoding task on age-related differences in the functional neuroanatomy of face memory. *Psychology and Aging*, *17*(1), 7–23.

Grady, C. L., & Garrett, D. D. (2017). Brain signal variability is modulated as a function of internal and external demand in younger and older adults. *NeuroImage*, *169*, 510–523. doi:10.1016/j.neuroimage.2017.12.031

Grady, C. L., Grigg, O., & Ng, C. (2012). Age differences in default and reward networks during processing of personally relevant information. *Neuropsychologia*, *50*(7), 1682–1697. doi:10.1016/j.neuropsychologia.2012.03.024

Grady, C. L., Luk, G., Craik, F. I. M., & Bialystok, E. (2015). Brain network activity in monolingual and bilingual older adults. *Neuropsychologia*, *66*, 170–181.

Grady, C. L., McIntosh, A. R., Horwitz, B., Maisog, J. M., Ungerleider, L. G., Mentis, M. J., ... Haxby, J. V. (1995). Age-related reductions in human recognition memory due to impaired encoding. *Science*, *269*(5221), 218–221.

Grady, C. L., McIntosh, A. R., Rajah, M. N., Beig, S., & Craik, F. (1999). The effects of age on the neural correlates of episodic encoding. *Cerebral Cortex*, *9*(8), 805–814.

Grady, C. L., Protzner, A. B., Kovacevic, N., Strother, S. C., Afshin-Pour, B., Wojtowicz, M., ... McIntosh, A. R. (2010). A multivariate analysis of age-related differences in default mode and task-positive networks across multiple cognitive domains. *Cerebral Cortex*, *20*(6), 1432–1447. doi:10.1093/cercor/bhp207

Grady, C. L., Sarraf, S., Saverino, C., & Campbell, K. (2016). Age differences in the functional interactions among the default, frontoparietal control, and dorsal attention networks. *Neurobiology of Aging*, *41*, 159–172. doi:10.1016/j.neurobiolaging.2016.02.020

Grady, C. L., Springer, M. V., Hongwanishkul, D., McIntosh, A. R., & Winocur, G. (2006). Age-related changes in brain activity across the adult lifespan. *Journal of Cognitive Neuroscience*, *18*(2), 227–241.

Graham, K. S., Barense, M. D., & Lee, A. C. (2010). Going beyond LTM in the MTL: a synthesis of neuropsychological and neuroimaging findings on the role of the medial temporal lobe in memory and perception. *Neuropsychologia*, *48*(4), 831–853. doi:10.1016/j.neuropsychologia.2010.01.001

Grant, A., Dennis, N. A., & Li, P. (2014). Cognitive control, cognitive reserve, and memory in the aging bilingual brain. *Frontiers in Psychology*, *5*, Article 1401. doi:10.3389/fpsyg.2014.01401

Greenwood, P. M. (2007). Functional plasticity in cognitive aging: review and hypothesis. *Neuropsychology*, *21*(6), 657–673. doi:10.1037/0894-4105.21.6.657

Grill-Spector, K., Henson, R., & Martin, A. (2006). Repetition and the brain: neural models of stimulus-specific effects. *Trends in Cognitive Sciences*, *10*(1), 14–23. doi:10.1016/j.tics.2005.11.006

Gross, J. J., Carstensen, L. L., Pasupathi, M., Tsai, J., Skorpen, C. G., & Hsu, A. Y. (1997). Emotion and aging: experience, expression, and control. *Psychology of Aging*, *12*(4), 590–599.

Grossman, M., Cooke, A., DeVita, C., Alsop, D., Detre, J., Chen, W., & Gee, J. (2002). Age-related changes in working memory during sentence comprehension: an fMRI study. *NeuroImage*, *15*(2), 302–317.

Grossman, M., Cooke, A., DeVita, C., Chen, W., Moore, P., Detre, J., … Gee, J. (2002). Sentence processing strategies in healthy seniors with poor comprehension: an fMRI study. *Brain and Language*, *80*(3), 296–313.

Grundy, J. G., Anderson, J. A. E., & Bialystok, E. (2017). Neural correlates of cognitive processing in monolinguals and bilinguals. *Annals of the New York Academy of Sciences*, *1396*(1), 183–201. doi:10.1111/nyas.13333

Gunning-Dixon, F. M., Brickman, A. M., Cheng, J. C., & Alexopoulos, G. S. (2009). Aging of cerebral white matter: a review of MRI findings. *International Journal of Geriatric Psychiatry*, *24*(2), 109–117. doi:10.1002/gps.2087

Gunning-Dixon, F. M., Gur, R. C., Perkins, A. C., Schroeder, L., Turner, T., Turetsky, B. I., … Gur, R. E. (2003). Age-related differences in brain activation during emotional face processing. *Neurobiology of Aging*, *24*(2), 285–295.

Gur, R. C., Gunning-Dixon, F. M., Turetsky, B. I., Bilker, W. B., & Gur, R. E. (2002). Brain region and sex differences in age association with brain volume: a quantitative MRI study of healthy young adults. *American Journal of Geriatric Psychiatry, 10*(1), 72–80.

Gutchess, A. H. (2014). Plasticity of the aging brain: new directions in cognitive neuroscience. *Science, 346*(6209), 579–582. doi:10.1126/science.1254604

Gutchess, A. H., Hebrank, A., Sutton, B. P., Leshikar, E., Chee, M. W., Tan, J. C., . . . Park, D. C. (2007). Contextual interference in recognition memory with age. *NeuroImage, 35*(3), 1338–1347. doi:S1053-8119(07) 00090-0 [pii] 10.1016/j.neuroimage.2007.01.043

Gutchess, A. H., Ieuji, Y., & Federmeier, K. D. (2007). Event-related potentials reveal age differences in the encoding and recognition of scenes. *Journal of Cognitive Neuroscience, 19*(7), 1089–1103. doi:10.1162/jocn.2007.19.7.1089

Gutchess, A. H., Kensinger, E. A., & Schacter, D. L. (2007). Aging, self-referencing, and medial prefrontal cortex. *Social Neuroscience, 2*(2), 117–133.

   (2010). Functional neuroimaging of self-referential encoding with age. *Neuropsychologia, 48*, 211–219.

Gutchess, A. H., Kensinger, E. A., Yoon, C., & Schacter, D. L. (2007). Ageing and the self-reference effect in memory. *Memory, 15*(8), 822–837. doi:783624081 [pii] 10.1080/09658210701701394

Gutchess, A. H., & Park, D. (2009). Effects of ageing on associative memory for related and unrelated pictures. *European Journal of Cognitive Psychology, 21*(2/3), 235–254.

Gutchess, A. H., & Park, D. C. (2006). fMRI environment can impair memory performance in young and elderly adults. *Brain Research, 1099*(1), 133–140. doi:S0006-8993(06)01303-5 [pii] 10.1016/j. brainres.2006.04.102

Gutchess, A. H., & Schacter, D. L. (2012). The neural correlates of gist-based true and false recognition. *NeuroImage, 59*(4), 3418–3426.

Gutchess, A. H., Sokal, R., Coleman, J. A., Gotthilf, G., Grewal, L., & Rosa, N. (2015). Age differences in self-referencing: evidence for common and distinct encoding strategies. *Brain Research, 1612*, 118–127. doi:10.1016/j.brainres.2014.08.033

Gutchess, A. H., Welsh, R. C., Hedden, T., Bangert, A., Minear, M., Liu, L. L., & Park, D. C. (2005). Aging and the neural correlates of successful picture encoding: frontal activations compensate for decreased medial-temporal activity. *Journal of Cognitive Neuroscience, 17*(1), 84–96.

Hackman, D. A., Farah, M. J., & Meaney, M. J. (2010). Socioeconomic status and the brain: mechanistic insights from human and animal research. *Nature Reviews Neuroscience, 11*(9), 651–659. doi:10.1038/nrn2897

Hakun, J. G., Zhu, Z., Johnson, N. F., & Gold, B. T. (2015). Evidence for reduced efficiency and successful compensation in older adults during task switching. *Cortex, 64*, 352–362.

Halberstadt, J., Ruffman, T., Murray, J., Taumoepeau, M., & Ryan, M. (2011). Emotion perception explains age-related differences in the perception of social gaffes. *Psychology and Aging, 26*(1), 133–136. doi:10.1037/a0021366

Halfmann, K., Hedgcock, W., Bechara, A., & Denburg, N. L. (2014). Functional neuroimaging of the Iowa Gambling Task in older adults. *Neuropsychology, 28*(6), 870–880. doi:10.1037/neu0000120

Halfmann, K., Hedgcock, W., Kable, J., & Denburg, N. L. (2015). Individual differences in the neural signature of subjective value among older adults. *Social Cognitive and Affective Neuroscience, 11*(7), 1111–1120. doi:10.1093/scan/nsv078

Hamami, A., Serbun, S. J., & Gutchess, A. H. (2011). Self-referential processing and memory specificity with age. *Psychology and Aging, 26*, 636–646.

Hardwick, R. M., & Celnik, P. A. (2014). Cerebellar direct current stimulation enhances motor learning in older adults. *Neurobiology of Aging, 35*(10), 2217–2221. doi:10.1016/j.neurobiolaging.2014.03.030

Harle, K. M., & Sanfey, A. G. (2012). Social economic decision-making across the life span: an fMRI investigation. *Neuropsychologia, 50*(7), 1416–1424. doi:10.1016/j.neuropsychologia.2012.02.026

Harris, C. B., Keil, P. G., Sutton, J., Barnier, A. J., & McIlwain, D. J. F. (2011). We remember, we forget: collaborative remembering in older couples. *Discourse Processes, 48*(4), 267–303. doi:10.1080/0163853x.2010.541854

Harty, S., Robertson, I. H., Miniussi, C., Sheehy, O. C., Devine, C. A., McCreery, S., & O'Connell, R. G. (2014). Transcranial direct current stimulation over right dorsolateral prefrontal cortex enhances error awareness in older age. *Journal of Neuroscience, 34*(10), 3646–3652. doi:10.1523/JNEUROSCI.5308-13.2014

Hasher, L., & Zacks, R. T. (1988). Working memory, comprehension, and aging: a review and a new view. In G. H. Bower (Ed.), *The Psychology of Learning and Motivation: Advances in Research and Theory, 22* (vol. XXII, pp. 193–225). San Diego, CA: Academic Press.

Hay, J. F., & Jacoby, L. L. (1999). Separating habit and recollection in young and older adults: effects of elaborative processing and distinctiveness. *Psychology and Aging, 14*(1), 122–134.

He, Y., Ebner, N. C., & Johnson, M. K. (2011). What predicts the own-age bias in face recognition memory? *Social Cognition, 29*(1), 97–109.

Head, D., Buckner, R. L., Shimony, J. S., Williams, L. E., Akbudak, E., Conturo, T. E., ... Snyder, A. Z. (2004). Differential vulnerability of anterior white matter in nondemented aging with minimal acceleration in dementia of the Alzheimer type: evidence from diffusion tensor imaging. *Cerebral Cortex*, *14*(4), 410–423.

Heatherton, T. F., Krendl, A. C., Macrae, C. N., & Kelley, W. M. (2007). A social brain sciences approach to understanding self. In C. Sedikides & S. Spencer (Eds.), *The Self* (pp. 3–20). New York: Psychology Press.

Heatherton, T. F., Wyland, C. L., Macrae, C. N., Demos, K. E., Denny, B. T., & Kelley, W. M. (2006). Medial prefrontal activity differentiates self from close others. *Social Cognitive and Affective Neuroscience*, *1*(1), 18–25.

Hedden, T., & Gabrieli, J. D. E. (2004). Insights into the ageing mind: a view from cognitive neuroscience. *Nature Reviews Neuroscience*, *5*(2), 87–96. doi:10.1038/nrn1323

Hedden, T., Mormino, E. C., Amariglio, R. E., Younger, A. P., Schultz, A. P., Becker, J. A., ... Rentz, D. M. (2012). Cognitive profile of amyloid burden and white matter hyperintensities in cognitively normal older adults. *Journal of Neuroscience*, *32*(46), 16233–16242.

Hedden, T., Schultz, A. P., Rieckmann, A., Mormino, E. C., Johnson, K. A., Sperling, R. A., & Buckner, R. L. (2014). Multiple brain markers are linked to age-related variation in cognition. *Cerebral Cortex*, *26*(4), 1388–1400.

Hedden, T., Van Dijk, K. R. A., Becker, J. A., Mehta, A., Sperling, R. A., Johnson, K. A., & Buckner, R. L. (2009). Disruption of functional connectivity in clinically normal older adults harboring amyloid burden. *Journal of Neuroscience*, *29*(40), 12686–12694.

Hedden, T., & Yoon, C. (2006). Individual differences in executive processing predict susceptibility to interference in verbal working memory. *Neuropsychology*, *20*(5), 511.

Heneka, M. T., Carson, M. J., El Khoury, J., Landreth, G. E., Brosseron, F., Feinstein, D. L., ... Ransohoff, R. M. (2015). Neuroinflammation in Alzheimer's disease. *Lancet Neurology*, *14*(4), 388–405.

Henkel, L. A., & Rajaram, S. (2011). Collaborative remembering in older adults: age-invariant outcomes in the context of episodic recall deficits. *Psychology and Aging*, *26*(3), 532–545. doi:10.1037/a0023106

Henry, J. D., Phillips, L. H., Ruffman, T., & Bailey, P. E. (2013). A meta-analytic review of age differences in theory of mind. *Psychology and Aging*, *28*(3), 826–839. doi:10.1037/a0030677

Henry, J. D., Phillips, L. H., & Von Hippel, C. (2014). A meta-analytic review of theory of mind difficulties in behavioural-variant frontotemporal dementia. *Neuropsychologia*, *56*, 53–62.

Herrera, A. Y., & Mather, M. (2015). Actions and interactions of estradiol and glucocorticoids in cognition and the brain: implications for aging women. *Neuroscience & Biobehavioral Reviews*, *55*, 36–52.

Herrmann, L. L., Le Masurier, M., & Ebmeier, K. P. (2008). White matter hyperintensities in late life depression: a systematic review. *Journal of Neurology, Neurosurgery, and Psychiatry*, *79*(6), 619–624. doi:10.1136/jnnp.2007.124651

Herrup, K., Carrillo, M. C., Schenk, D., Cacace, A., Desanti, S., Fremeau, R., ... Budd, S. (2013). Beyond amyloid: getting real about nonamyloid targets in Alzheimer's disease. *Alzheimers & Dementia*, *9*(4), 452–458.e1. doi:10.1016/j.jalz.2013.01.017

Hertzog, C., Kramer, A. F., Wilson, R. S., & Lindenberger, U. (2008). Enrichment effects on adult cognitive development: can the functional capacity of older adults be preserved and enhanced? *Psychological Science in the Public Interest*, *9*(1), 1–65.

Herz, D. M., Eickhoff, S. B., Løkkegaard, A., & Siebner, H. R. (2014). Functional neuroimaging of motor control in Parkinson's disease: a meta-analysis. *Human Brain Mapping*, *35*(7), 3227–3237.

Hess, T. M. (2014). Selective engagement of cognitive resources: motivational influences on older adults' cognitive functioning. *Perspectives on Psychological Science*, *9*(4), 388–407. doi:10.1177/1745691614527465

Hess, T. M., Auman, C., Colcombe, S. J., & Rahhal, T. (2003). The impact of stereotype threat on age differences in memory performance. *Journals of Gerontology. Series B, Psychological Sciences and Social Sciences*, *58*(1), 3–11.

Hess, T. M., Bolstad, C. A., Woodburn, S. M., & Auman, C. (1999). Trait diagnosticity versus behavioral consistency as determinants of impression change in adulthood. *Psychology and Aging*, *14*(1), 77–89.

Hess, T. M., & Pullen, S. M. (1994). Adult age-differences in impression change processes. *Psychology and Aging*, *9*(2), 237–250.

Hess, T. M., & Tate, C. S. (1991). Adult age-differences in explanations and memory for behavioral information. *Psychology and Aging*, *6*(1), 86–92.

Heuninckx, S., Wenderoth, N., & Swinnen, S. P. (2008). Systems neuroplasticity in the aging brain: recruiting additional neural resources for successful motor performance in elderly persons. *Journal of Neuroscience*, *28*(1), 91–99.

Hidalgo, V., Almela, M., Villada, C., & Salvador, A. (2014). Acute stress impairs recall after interference in older people, but not in young people. *Hormones and Behavior*, *65*(3), 264–272.

Hsu, W. Y., Ku, Y., Zanto, T. P., & Gazzaley, A. (2015). Effects of noninvasive brain stimulation on cognitive function in healthy aging and Alzheimer's disease: a systematic review and meta-analysis. *Neurobiology of Aging, 36*(8), 2348–2359. doi:10.1016/j. neurobiolaging.2015.04.016

Huettel, S. A., Singerman, J. D., & McCarthy, G. (2001). The effects of aging upon the hemodynamic response measured by functional MRI. *NeuroImage, 13*(1), 161–175. doi:10.1006/nimg.2000.0675

Huijbers, W., Mormino, E. C., Wigman, S. E., Ward, A. M., Vannini, P., McLaren, D. G., ... Johnson, K. A. (2014). Amyloid deposition is linked to aberrant entorhinal activity among cognitively normal older adults. *Journal of Neuroscience, 34*(15), 5200–5210.

Iidaka, T., Okada, T., Murata, T., Omori, M., Kosaka, H., Sadato, N., & Yonekura, Y. (2002). Age-related differences in the medial temporal lobe responses to emotional faces as revealed by fMRI. *Hippocampus, 12*(3), 352–362.

Isaacowitz, D. M., Wadlinger, H. A., Goren, D., & Wilson, H. R. (2006a). Is there an age-related positivity effect in visual attention? A comparison of two methodologies. *Emotion, 6*(3), 511–516. doi:10.1037/1528-3542.6.3.511

(2006b). Selective preference in visual fixation away from negative images in old age? An eye-tracking study. *Psychology and Aging, 21*(2), 221.

Jackson, J., Balota, D. A., & Head, D. (2011). Exploring the relationship between personality and regional brain volume in healthy aging. *Neurobiology of Aging, 32*(12), 2162–2171. doi:10.1016/j. neurobiolaging.2009.12.009

Jagust, W. (2009). Amyloid + activation = Alzheimer's? *Neuron, 63*(2), 141–143.

Jimura, K., & Braver, T. S. (2010). Age-related shifts in brain activity dynamics during task switching. *Cerebral Cortex, 20*(6), 1420–1431.

Johnson, K. A., Fox, N. C., Sperling, R. A., & Klunk, W. E. (2012). Brain imaging in Alzheimer disease. *Cold Spring Harbor Perspectives in Medicine, 2*(4), a006213.

Johnson, M. K., Kim, J. K., & Risse, G. (1985). Do alcoholic Korsakoff's syndrome patients acquire affective reactions? *Journal of Experimental Psychology: Learning, Memory, and Cognition, 11*(1), 22–36.

Johnson, M. K., Mitchell, K. J., Raye, C. L., & Greene, E. J. (2004). An age-related deficit in prefrontal cortical function associated with refreshing information. *Psychological Science, 15*(2), 127–132.

Karama, S., Bastin, M., Murray, C., Royle, N., Penke, L., Munoz Maniega, S., ... Lewis, J. (2014). Childhood cognitive ability accounts for associations between cognitive ability and brain cortical thickness in old age. *Molecular Psychiatry, 19*(5), 555–559.

Karlsson, S., Nyberg, L., Karlsson, P., Fischer, H., Thilers, P., Macdonald, S., … Backman, L. (2009). Modulation of striatal dopamine D1 binding by cognitive processing. *NeuroImage, 48*(2), 398–404. doi:10.1016/j.neuroimage.2009.06.030

Kehoe, E. G., Toomey, J. M., Balsters, J. H., & Bokde, A. L. (2013). Healthy aging is associated with increased neural processing of positive valence but attenuated processing of emotional arousal: an fMRI study. *Neurobiology of Aging, 34*(3), 809–821. doi:10.1016/j. neurobiolaging.2012.07.006

Keightley, M. L., Chiew, K. S., Winocur, G., & Grady, C. L. (2007). Age-related differences in brain activity underlying identification of emotional expressions in faces. *Social Cognitive and Affective Neuroscience, 2*(4), 292–302. doi:10.1093/scan/nsm024

Kelley, W. M., Macrae, C. N., Wyland, C. L., Caglar, S., Inati, S., & Heatherton, T. F. (2002). Finding the self? An event-related fMRI study. *Journal of Cognitive Neuroscience, 14*(5), 785–794.

Kemp, J., Després, O., Sellal, F., & Dufour, A. (2012). Theory of mind in normal ageing and neurodegenerative pathologies. *Ageing Research Reviews, 11*(2), 199–219.

Kennedy, K. M., & Raz, N. (2005). Age, sex and regional brain volumes predict perceptual-motor skill acquisition. *Cortex, 41*(4), 560–569.

  (2009). Aging white matter and cognition: differential effects of regional variations in diffusion properties on memory, executive functions, and speed. *Neuropsychologia, 47*(3), 916–927.

Kennedy, K. M., Reese, E. D., Horn, M. M., Sizemore, A. N., Unni, A. K., Meerbrey, M. E., … Rodrigue, K. M. (2015). *BDNF* val66met polymorphism affects aging of multiple types of memory. *Brain Research, 1612*, 104–117.

Kennedy, K. M., Rodrigue, K. M., Bischof, G. N., Hebrank, A. C., Reuter-Lorenz, P. A., & Park, D. C. (2015). Age trajectories of functional activation under conditions of low and high processing demands: an adult lifespan fMRI study of the aging brain. *NeuroImage, 104*, 21–34.

Kennedy, K. M., Rodrigue, K. M., Devous, M. D., Sr., Hebrank, A. C., Bischof, G. N., & Park, D. C. (2012). Effects of beta-amyloid accumulation on neural function during encoding across the adult lifespan. *NeuroImage, 62*(1), 1–8. doi:10.1016/j. neuroimage.2012.03.077

Kennedy, Q., Mather, M., & Carstensen, L. L. (2004). The role of motivation in the age-related positivity effect in autobiographical memory. *Psychological Science, 15*(3), 208–214.

Kensinger, E. A., & Gutchess, A. H. (2017). Cognitive aging in a social and affective context: advances over the past 50 years. *Journals of*

Gerontology. Series B, Psychological Sciences and Social Sciences,
72(1), 61–70. doi:10.1093/geronb/gbw056

Kensinger, E. A., & Leclerc, C. M. (2009). Age-related changes in the neural mechanisms supporting emotion processing and emotional memory. *European Journal of Cognitive Psychology, 21*(2–3), 192–215. doi:10.1080/09541440801937116

Kensinger, E. A., & Schacter, D. L. (2008). Neural processes supporting young and older adults' emotional memories. *Journal of Cognitive Neuroscience, 20*(7), 1161–1173.

Kirchhoff, B. A., Anderson, B. A., Barch, D. M., & Jacoby, L. L. (2012). Cognitive and neural effects of semantic encoding strategy training in older adults. *Cerebral Cortex, 22*(4), 788–799.

Kirchhoff, B. A., Anderson, B. A., Smith, S. E., Barch, D. M., & Jacoby, L. L. (2012). Cognitive training-related changes in hippocampal activity associated with recollection in older adults. *NeuroImage, 62*(3), 1956–1964.

Kirchhoff, B. A., Gordon, B. A., & Head, D. (2014). Prefrontal gray matter volume mediates age effects on memory strategies. *NeuroImage, 90*, 326–334.

Kisley, M. A., Wood, S., & Burrows, C. L. (2007). Looking at the sunny side of life: age-related change in an event-related potential measure of the negativity bias. *Psychological Science, 18*(9), 838–843. doi:10.1111/ j.1467-9280.2007.01988.x

Knowlton, B. J., Mangels, J. A., & Squire, L. R. (1996). A neostriatal habit learning system in humans. *Science, 273*(5280), 1399–1402.

Koutstaal, W., & Schacter, D. L. (1997). Gist-based false recognition of pictures in older and younger adults. *Journal of Memory and Language, 37*(4), 555–583.

Krendl, A. C. (in press). Reduced cognitive capacity impairs the malleability of older adults' negative attitudes to stigmatized individuals. *Experimental Aging Research.*

Krendl, A. C., Heatherton, T. F., & Kensinger, E. A. (2009). Aging minds and twisting attitudes: an fMRI investigation of age differences in inhibiting prejudice. *Psychology and Aging, 24*(3), 530–541.

Krendl, A. C., Richeson, J. A., Kelley, W. M., & Heatherton, T. F. (2008). The negative consequences of threat – a functional magnetic resonance imaging investigation of the neural mechanisms underlying women's underperformance in math. *Psychological Science, 19*(2), 168–175. doi:10.1111/j.1467-9280.2008.02063.x

Krendl, A. C., Rule, N. O., & Ambady, N. (2014). Does aging impair first impression accuracy? Differentiating emotion recognition from complex social inferences. *Psychology and Aging, 29*(3), 482–490. doi:10.1037/a0037146

Kubarych, T. S., Prom-Wormley, E. C., Franz, C. E., Panizzon, M. S., Dale, A. M., Fischl, B., . . . Hauger, R. L. (2012). A multivariate twin study of hippocampal volume, self-esteem and well-being in middle-aged men. *Genes, Brain, and Behavior, 11*(5), 539–544.

Kurkela, K. A., & Dennis, N. A. (2016). Event-related fMRI studies of false memory: an activation likelihood estimation meta-analysis. *Neuropsychologia, 81*, 149–167. doi:10.1016/j.neuropsychologia.2015. 12.006

Kurth, F., Luders, E., Wu, B., & Black, D. S. (2014). Brain gray matter changes associated with mindfulness meditation in older adults: an exploratory pilot study using voxel-based morphometry. *Neuro–Open Journal, 1*(1), 23–26.

Kwon, D., Maillet, D., Pasvanis, S., Ankudowich, E., Grady, C. L., & Rajah, M. N. (2015). Context memory decline in middle-aged adults is related to changes in prefrontal cortex function. *Cerebral Cortex, 26*(6), 2440–2460.

La Joie, R., Bejanin, A., Fagan, A. M., Ayakta, N., Baker, S. L., Bourakova, V., . . . Rabinovici, G. D. (2017). Associations between [(18)F]AV1451 tau PET and CSF measures of tau pathology in a clinical sample. *Neurology, 90*(4), e282–e290. doi:10.1212/wnl.0000000000004860

Lamar, M., Charlton, R. A., Ajilore, O., Zhang, A., Yang, S., Barrick, T. R., . . . Kumar, A. (2013). Prefrontal vulnerabilities and whole brain connectivity in aging and depression. *Neuropsychologia, 51*(8), 1463–1470.

Lan, C.-C., Tsai, S.-J., Huang, C.-C., Wang, Y.-H., Chen, T.-R., Yeh, H.-L., . . . Yang, A. C. (2015). Functional connectivity density mapping of depressive symptoms and loneliness in non-demented elderly male. *Frontiers in Aging Neuroscience, 7*.

Lang, P. J., Bradley, M. M., & Cuthbert, B. N. (1997). *International Affective Picture System (IAPS): Technical Manual and Affective Ratings*. NIMH Center for the Study of Emotion and Attention, Gainsville, pp. 39–58.

Langenecker, S. A., Nielson, K. A., & Rao, S. M. (2004). fMRI of healthy older adults during Stroop interference. *NeuroImage, 21*(1), 192–200.

Langenecker, S. A., Zubieta, J.-K., Young, E. A., Akil, H., & Nielson, K. A. (2007). A task to manipulate attentional load, set-shifting, and inhibitory control: convergent validity and test–retest reliability of the Parametric Go/No-Go Test. *Journal of Clinical and Experimental Neuropsychology, 29*(8), 842–853.

Langeslag, S. J., & Van Strien, J. W. (2008). Age differences in the emotional modulation of ERP old/new effects. *International Journal of Psychophysiology, 70*(2), 105–114.

(2009). Aging and emotional memory: the co-occurrence of
    neurophysiological and behavioral positivity effects. *Emotion*, *9*(3),
    369–377. doi:10.1037/a0015356

Lantrip, C., & Huang, J. H. (2017). Cognitive control of emotion in older
    adults: a review. *Clinical Psychiatry (Wilmington)*, *3*(1). doi:10.21767/
    2471-9854.100040

Lazar, S. W., Kerr, C. E., Wasserman, R. H., Gray, J. R., Greve, D. N.,
    Treadway, M. T., . . . Benson, H. (2005). Meditation experience is
    associated with increased cortical thickness. *NeuroReport*, *16*(17),
    1893–1897.

Lebowitz, B. D., Pearson, J. L., Schneider, L. S., Reynolds, C. F.,
    Alexopoulos, G. S., Bruce, M. L., . . . Morrison, M. F. (1997). Diagnosis
    and treatment of depression in late life: consensus statement update.
    Journal of the American Medical Association, *278*(14), 1186–1190.

Leclerc, C. M., & Kensinger, E. A. (2008). Age-related differences in medial
    prefrontal activation in response to emotional images. *Cognitive,
    Affective, and Behavioral Neuroscience*, *8*(2), 153–164.

    (2010). Age-related valence-based reversal in recruitment of medial
    prefrontal cortex on a visual search task. *Social Neuroscience*, *5*(5–6),
    560–576. doi:10.1080/17470910903512296

    (2011). Neural processing of emotional pictures and words: a comparison
    of young and older adults. *Developmental Neuropsychology*, *36*(4),
    519–538. doi:10.1080/87565641.2010.549864

Le Couteur, D. G., Hunter, S., & Brayne, C. (2016). Solanezumab and the
    amyloid hypothesis for Alzheimer's disease. *British Medical Journal*,
    355, i6771. doi:10.1136/bmj.i6771

Lee, A. C., Buckley, M. J., Gaffan, D., Emery, T., Hodges, J. R., & Graham,
    K. S. (2006). Differentiating the roles of the hippocampus and
    perirhinal cortex in processes beyond long-term declarative memory: a
    double dissociation in dementia. *Journal of Neuroscience*, *26*(19),
    5198–5203. doi:10.1523/jneurosci.3157-05.2006

Lee, T. M., Leung, A. W., Fox, P. T., Gao, J. H., & Chan, C. C. (2008). Age-
    related differences in neural activities during risk taking as revealed by
    functional MRI. *Social Cognitive and Affective Neuroscience*, *3*(1),
    7–15. doi:10.1093/scan/nsm033

Lemaire, P. (2016). *Cognitive Aging: The Role of Strategies*. New York:
    Routledge/Taylor & Francis Group.

Leshikar, E. D., Cassidy, B. S., & Gutchess, A. H. (2015). Similarity to the
    self influences cortical recruitment during impression formation.
    Cognitive, Affective, and Behavioral Neuroscience, *16*(2), 302–314.
    doi:10.3758/s13415-015-0390-3

Leshikar, E. D., & Duarte, A. (2014). Medial prefrontal cortex supports
    source memory for self-referenced materials in young and older adults.

Cognitive, Affective, and Behavioral Neuroscience, 14(1), 236–252. doi:10.3758/s13415-013-0198-y

Leshikar, E. D., & Gutchess, A. H. (2015). Similarity to the self affects memory for impressions of others. *Journal of Applied Research in Memory and Cognition, 4*(1), 20–28. doi:10.1016/j.jarmac.2014.10.002

Leshikar, E. D., Gutchess, A. H., Hebrank, A. C., Sutton, B. P., & Park, D. C. (2010). The impact of increased relational encoding demands on frontal and hippocampal function in older adults. *Cortex, 46*(4), 507–521. doi:10.1016/j.cortex.2009.07.011

Leshikar, E. D., Park, J. M., & Gutchess, A. H. (2015). Similarity to the self affects memory for impressions of others in younger and older adults. *Journals of Gerontololgy. Series B, Psychological Sciences and Social Sciences, 70*(5), 737–742. doi:10.1093/geronb/gbt132

Levine, B., Svoboda, E., Hay, J. F., Winocur, G., & Moscovitch, M. (2002). Aging and autobiographical memory: dissociating episodic from semantic retrieval. *Psychology and Aging, 17*(4), 677–689.

Levy, B. R. (2003). Mind matters: cognitive and physical effects of aging self-stereotypes. *Journals of Gerontology. Series B,Psychological Sciences and Social Sciences, 58*(4), P203-P211.

Li, J., Morcom, A. M., & Rugg, M. D. (2004). The effects of age on the neural correlates of successful episodic retrieval: an ERP study. *Cognitive, Affective, and Behavioral Neuroscience, 4*(3), 279–293.

Li, R., Ma, Z., Yu, J., He, Y., & Li, J. (2014). Altered local activity and functional connectivity of the anterior cingulate cortex in elderly individuals with subthreshold depression. *Psychiatry Research: Neuroimaging, 222*(1), 29–36.

Li, S. C., Lindenberger, U., & Sikstrom, S. (2001). Aging cognition: from neuromodulation to representation. *Trends in Cognitive Sciences, 5*(11), 479–486.

Li, S. C., Papenberg, G., Nagel, I. E., Preuschhof, C., Schroder, J., Nietfeld, W., … Backman, L. (2013). Aging magnifies the effects of dopamine transporter and D_2 receptor genes on backward serial memory. *Neurobiology of Aging, 34*(1), 358.e1–358.e10. doi:10.1016/j.neurobiolaging.2012.08.001

Lieberman, M. D. (2007). Social cognitive neuroscience: a review of core processes. *Annual Review of Psychology, 58*, 259–289. doi:10.1146/annurev.psych.58.110405.085654

Light, L. L. (1992). The organization of memory in old age. In F. I. M. Craik & T. A. Salthouse (Eds.), *The Handbook of Aging and Cognition* (pp. 111–165). Hillsdale, NJ: Lawrence Erlbaum Associates, Inc.

Light, L. L., & Singh, A. (1987). Implicit and explicit memory in young and older adults. *Journal of Experimental Psychology: Learning, Memory, and Cognition*, *13*(4), 531–541.

Lim, Y. Y., Villemagne, V. L., Pietrzak, R. H., Ames, D., Ellis, K. A., Harrington, K., ... Rowe, C. C. (2015). *APOE* ε4 moderates amyloid-related memory decline in preclinical Alzheimer's disease. *Neurobiology of Aging*, *36*(3), 1239–1244.

Limbert, M. J., Coleman, J. A., & Gutchess, A. H. (2018). Effects of aging on general and specific memory for impressions. *Collabra: Psychology*, *4*(1), 17. DOI: http://doi.org/10.1525/collabra.109.

Lin, F. R., Ferrucci, L., An, Y., Goh, J. O., Doshi, J., Metter, E. J., ... Resnick, S. M. (2014). Association of hearing impairment with brain volume changes in older adults. *NeuroImage*, *90*, 84–92.

Lindenberger, U., & Baltes, P. B. (1994). Sensory functioning and intelligence in old age: a strong connection. *Psychology and Aging*, *9*(3), 339–355.

Lisman, J., Grace, A. A., & Duzel, E. (2011). A neoHebbian framework for episodic memory: role of dopamine-dependent late LTP. *Trends in Neurosciences*, *34*(10), 536–547.

Logan, J. M., Sanders, A. L., Snyder, A. Z., Morris, J. C., & Buckner, R. L. (2002). Under-recruitment and nonselective recruitment: dissociable neural mechanisms associated with aging. *Neuron*, *33*(5), 827–840.

Luck, S. J. (2014). *An Introduction to the Event-Related Potential Technique* (2nd edn). Cambridge, MA: MIT Press.

Luck, S. J., & Kappenman, E. S. (2012). *Oxford Handbook of Event-Related Potential Components*. Oxford University Press.

Luders, E., & Cherbuin, N. (2016). Searching for the philosopher's stone: promising links between meditation and brain preservation. *Annals of the New York Academy of Sciences*, *1373*(1), 38–44. doi:10.1111/nyas.13082

Luk, G., Bialystok, E., Craik, F. I. M., & Grady, C. L. (2011). Lifelong bilingualism maintains white matter integrity in older adults. *Journal of Neuroscience*, *31*(46), 16808–16813.

Lustig, C., & Buckner, R. L. (2004). Preserved neural correlates of priming in old age and dementia. *Neuron*, *42*(5), 865–875.

Lustig, C., Snyder, A. Z., Bhakta, M., O'Brien, K. C., McAvoy, M., Raichle, M. E., ... Buckner, R. L. (2003). Functional deactivations: change with age and dementia of the Alzheimer type. *Proceedings of the National Academy of Sciences of the United States of America*, *100*(24), 14504–14509. doi:10.1073/pnas.2235925100

Maass, A., Lockhart, S. N., Harrison, T. M., Bell, R. K., Mellinger, T., Swinnerton, K., ... Jagust, W. J. (2018). Entorhinal tau pathology,

episodic memory decline and neurodegeneration in aging.
Journal of Neuroscience, 38(3), 530–543. doi:10.1523/jneurosci.2028-17.2017

Machulda, M. M., Jones, D. T., Vemuri, P., McDade, E., Avula, R., Przybelski, S. A., ... Jack, C. R. (2011). Effect of *APOE* ε4 status on intrinsic network connectivity in cognitively normal elderly subjects. *Archives of Neurology, 68*(9), 1131–1136.

Macrae, C. N., Moran, J. M., Heatherton, T. F., Banfield, J. F., & Kelley, W. M. (2004). Medial prefrontal activity predicts memory for self. *Cerebral Cortex, 14*(6), 647–654. doi:10.1093/cercor/bhh025

Madan, C. R. (2015). Creating 3D visualizations of MRI data: a brief guide. *F1000Res, 4*, 466. doi:10.12688/f1000research.6838.1

Madden, D. J., Costello, M. C., Dennis, N. A., Davis, S. W., Shepler, A. M., Spaniol, J., ... Cabeza, R. (2010). Adult age differences in functional connectivity during executive control. *NeuroImage, 52*(2), 643–657.

Madden, D. J., Parks, E. L., Davis, S. W., Diaz, M. T., Potter, G. G., Chou, Y., ... Cabeza, R. (2014). Age mediation of frontoparietal activation during visual feature search. *NeuroImage, 102*, 262–274.

Madden, D. J., Spaniol, J., Whiting, W. L., Bucur, B., Provenzale, J. M., Cabeza, R., ... Huettel, S. A. (2007). Adult age differences in the functional neuroanatomy of visual attention: a combined fMRI and DTI study. *Neurobiology of Aging, 28*(3), 459–476.

Madden, D. J., Turkington, T. G., Provenzale, J. M., Hawk, T. C., Hoffman, J. M., & Coleman, R. E. (1997). Selective and divided visual attention: age-related changes in regional cerebral blood flow measured by H2 (15)O PET. *Human Brain Mapping, 5*(6), 389–409. doi:10.1002/(SICI) 1097-0193(1997)5:6<389::AID-HBM1>3.0.CO;2-#

Madden, D. J., Whiting, W. L., Cabeza, R., & Huettel, S. A. (2004). Age-related preservation of top-down attentional guidance during visual search. *Psychology and Aging, 19*(2), 304–309.

Madden, D. J., Whiting, W. L., Huettel, S. A., White, L. E., MacFall, J. R., & Provenzale, J. M. (2004). Diffusion tensor imaging of adult age differences in cerebral white matter: relation to response time. *NeuroImage, 21*(3), 1174–1181. doi:10.1016/j.neuroimage.2003.11.004

Maguire, E. A., & Frith, C. D. (2003). Aging affects the engagement of the hippocampus during autobiographical memory retrieval. *Brain, 126*(7), 1511–1523.

Maillet, D., & Rajah, M. N. (2013). Association between prefrontal activity and volume change in prefrontal and medial temporal lobes in aging and dementia: a review. *Ageing Research Reviews, 12*(2), 479–489. doi:10.1016/j.arr.2012.11.001

(2014). Age-related differences in brain activity in the subsequent memory paradigm: a meta-analysis. *Neuroscience & Biobehavioral Reviews, 45*, 246–257.

Manan, H. A., Franz, E. A., Yusoff, A. N., & Mukari, S. Z.-M. S. (2015). The effects of aging on the brain activation pattern during a speech perception task: an fMRI study. *Aging Clinical and Experimental Research, 27*(1), 27–36.

Manenti, R., Brambilla, M., Petesi, M., Ferrari, C., & Cotelli, M. (2013). Enhancing verbal episodic memory in older and young subjects after non-invasive brain stimulation. *Frontiers in Aging Neuroscience, 5*, Article 49. doi:10.3389/fnagi.2013.00049

Manenti, R., Cotelli, M., & Miniussi, C. (2011). Successful physiological aging and episodic memory: a brain stimulation study. *Behavioural Brain Research, 216*(1), 153–158. doi:10.1016/j.bbr.2010.07.027

Manenti, R., Sandrini, M., Gobbi, E., Cobelli, C., Brambilla, M., Binetti, G., & Cotelli, M. (2017). Strengthening of existing episodic memories through non-invasive stimulation of prefrontal cortex in older adults with subjective memory complaints. *Frontiers in Aging Neuroscience, 9*, Article 401. doi:10.3389/fnagi.2017.00401

Manza, P., Zhang, S., Li, C. S. R., & Leung, H. C. (2015). Resting-state functional connectivity of the striatum in early-stage Parkinson's disease: cognitive decline and motor symptomatology. *Human Brain Mapping, 37*(2), 648–662.

Mark, R. E., & Rugg, M. D. (1998). Age effects on brain activity associated with episodic memory retrieval. *Brain, 121*, 861–873.

Marsolais, Y., Perlbarg, V., Benali, H., & Joanette, Y. (2014). Age-related changes in functional network connectivity associated with high levels of verbal fluency performance. *Cortex, 58*, 123–138.

Martin, S., Al Khleifat, A., & Al-Chalabi, A. (2017). What causes amyotrophic lateral sclerosis? *F1000Res, 6*, 371. doi:10.12688/f1000research.10476.1

Martinelli, P., Sperduti, M., Devauchelle, A.-D., Kalenzaga, S., Gallarda, T., Lion, S., ... Meder, J. F. (2013). Age-related changes in the functional network underlying specific and general autobiographical memory retrieval: a pivotal role for the anterior cingulate cortex. *PLoS One, 8*(12), e82385.

Martins, B., Ponzio, A., Velasco, R., Kaplan, J., & Mather, M. (2015). Dedifferentiation of emotion regulation strategies in the aging brain. *Social Cognitive and Affective Neuroscience, 10*(6), 840–847. doi:10.1093/scan/nsu129

Mata, R., Josef, A. K., Samanez-Larkin, G. R., & Hertwig, R. (2011). Age differences in risky choice: a meta-analysis. *Annals of the New York Academy of Sciences, 1235*, 18–29. doi:10.1111/j.1749-6632.2011.06200.x

Mather, M. (2012). The emotion paradox in the aging brain. *Annals of the New York Academy of Sciences, 1251,* 33–49. doi:10.1111/j.1749-6632.2012.06471.x

(2016). The affective neuroscience of aging. *Annual Review of Psychology, 67,* 213–238. doi:10.1146/annurev-psych-122414-033540

Mather, M., Canli, T., English, T., Whitfield, S., Wais, P., Ochsner, K., . . . Carstensen, L. L. (2004). Amygdala responses to emotionally valenced stimuli in older and younger adults. *Psychological Science, 15*(4), 259–263.

Mather, M., & Carstensen, L. L. (2003). Aging and attentional biases for emotional faces. *Psychological Science, 14*(5), 409–415.

(2005). Aging and motivated cognition: the positivity effect in attention and memory. *Trends in Cognitive Sciences, 9*(10), 496–502. doi:10.1016/j.tics.2005.08.005

Mather, M., Gorlick, M. A., & Lighthall, N. R. (2009). To brake or accelerate when the light turns yellow? Stress reduces older adults' risk taking in a driving game. *Psychological Science, 20*(2), 174–176.

Mather, M., & Knight, M. (2005). Goal-directed memory: the role of cognitive control in older adults' emotional memory. *Psychology and Aging, 20*(4), 554–570.

Mather, M., Mazar, N., Gorlick, M. A., Lighthall, N. R., Burgeno, J., Schoeke, A., & Ariely, D. (2012). Risk preferences and aging: the "certainty effect" in older adults' decision making. *Psychology and Aging, 27*(4), 801–816. doi:10.1037/a0030174

Mattay, V. S., Fera, F., Tessitore, A., Hariri, A. R., Das, S., Callicott, J. H., & Weinberger, D. R. (2002). Neurophysiological correlates of age-related changes in human motor function. *Neurology, 58*(4), 630–635.

Matzen, L. E., & Benjamin, A. S. (2013). Older and wiser: older adults' episodic word memory benefits from sentence study contexts. *Psychology and Aging, 28*(3), 754–767. doi:10.1037/a0032945

Maylor, E. A., Moulson, J. M., Muncer, A. M., & Taylor, L. A. (2002). Does performance on theory of mind tasks decline in old age? *British Journal of Psychology, 93,* 465–485. doi:10.1348/000712602761381358

McCarrey, A. C., Henry, J. D., von Hippel, W., Weidemann, G., Sachdev, P. S., Wohl, M. J., & Williams, M. (2012). Age differences in neural activity during slot machine gambling: an fMRI study. *PLoS One, 7*(11), e49787. doi:10.1371/journal.pone.0049787

McDonough, I. M. (2017). Beta-amyloid and cortical thickness reveal racial disparities in preclinical Alzheimer's disease. *NeuroImage: Clinical, 16,* 659–667. doi:10.1016/j.nicl.2017.09.014

McDonough, I. M., Cervantes, S. N., Gray, S. J., & Gallo, D. A. (2014). Memory's aging echo: age-related decline in neural reactivation of perceptual details during recollection. *NeuroImage, 98,* 346–358.

McDonough, I. M., Wong, J. T., & Gallo, D. A. (2013). Age-related differences in prefrontal cortex activity during retrieval monitoring: testing the compensation and dysfunction accounts. *Cerebral Cortex*, *23*(5), 1049–1060.

McEwen, B. S. (2006). Protective and damaging effects of stress mediators: central role of the brain. *Dialogues in Clinical Neuroscience*, *8*(4), 367–381.

Meinzer, M., Lindenberg, R., Antonenko, D., Flaisch, T., & Floel, A. (2013). Anodal transcranial direct current stimulation temporarily reverses age-associated cognitive decline and functional brain activity changes. *Journal of Neuroscience*, *33*(30), 12470–12478. doi:10.1523/JNEUROSCI.5743-12.2013

Mikels, J. A., Larkin, G. R., Reuter-Lorenz, P. A., & Carstensen, L. L. (2005). Divergent trajectories in the aging mind: changes in working memory for affective versus visual information with age. *Psychology and Aging*, *20*, 542–553.

Milham, M. P., Erickson, K. I., Banich, M. T., Kramer, A. F., Webb, A., Wszalek, T., & Cohen, N. J. (2002). Attentional control in the aging brain: insights from an fMRI study of the Stroop Task. *Brain and Cognition*, *49*(3), 277–296. doi:10.1006/brcg.2001.1501

Mishra, J., de Villers-Sidani, E., Merzenich, M., & Gazzaley, A. (2014). Adaptive training diminishes distractibility in aging across species. *Neuron*, *84*(5), 1091–1103.

Mishra, J., Rolle, C., & Gazzaley, A. (2015). Neural plasticity underlying visual perceptual learning in aging. *Brain Research*, *1612*, 140–151.

Mitchell, J. P. (2008). Contributions of functional neuroimaging to the study of social cognition. *Current Directions in Psychological Science*, *17*(2), 142–146. doi:10.1111/j.1467-8721.2008.00564.x

Mitchell, J. P., Macrae, C. N., & Banaji, M. R. (2004). Encoding-specific effects of social cognition on the neural correlates of subsequent memory. *Journal of Neuroscience*, *24*(21), 4912–4917.

Mitchell, K. J., Ankudowich, E., Durbin, K. A., Greene, E. J., & Johnson, M. K. (2013). Age-related differences in agenda-driven monitoring of format and task information. *Neuropsychologia*, *51*(12), 2427–2441.

Mitchell, K. J., & Johnson, M. K. (2009). Source monitoring 15 years later: what have we learned from fMRI about the neural mechanisms of source memory? *Psychological Bulletin*, *135*(4), 638–677.

Mitchell, K. J., Johnson, M. K., Raye, C. L., & D'Esposito, M. (2000). fMRI evidence of age-related hippocampal dysfunction in feature binding in working memory. *Cognitive Brain Research*, *10*, 197–206.

Mitchell, K. J., Raye, C. L., Ebner, N. C., Tubridy, S. M., Frankel, H., & Johnson, M. K. (2009). Age-group differences in medial cortex activity associated with thinking about self-relevant agendas. *Psychology and Aging, 24*(2), 438–449.

Miyake, A., Friedman, N., Emerson, M., Witzki, A., & Howerter, A. (2000). The unity and diversity of executive functions and their contributions to complex "frontal lobe" tasks: a latent variable analysis. *Cognitive Psychology, 41*, 49–100.

Montague, P. R., Berns, G. S., Cohen, J. D., McClure, S. M., Pagnoni, G., Dhamala, M., . . . Fisher, R. E. (2002). Hyperscanning: simultaneous fMRI during linked social interactions. *NeuroImage, 16*(4), 1159–1164.

Moran, J. M. (2013). Lifespan development: the effects of typical aging on theory of mind. *Behavioural Brain Research, 237*, 32–40. doi:10.1016/j.bbr.2012.09.020

Moran, J. M., Jolly, E., & Mitchell, J. P. (2012). Social-cognitive deficits in normal aging. *Journal of Neuroscience, 32*(16), 5553–5561.

Morcom, A. M., Li, J., & Rugg, M. D. (2007). Age effects on the neural correlates of episodic retrieval: increased cortical recruitment with matched performance. *Cerebral Cortex, 17*(11), 2491–2506.

Moriguchi, Y., Negreira, A., Weierich, M., Dautoff, R., Dickerson, B. C., Wright, C. I., & Barrett, L. F. (2011). Differential hemodynamic response in affective circuitry with aging: an fMRI study of novelty, valence, and arousal. *Journal of Cognitive Neuroscience, 23*(5), 1027–1041. doi:10.1162/jocn.2010.21527

Mormino, E. C., Betensky, R. A., Hedden, T., Schultz, A. P., Ward, A., Huijbers, W., . . . Alzheimer's Disease Neuroimaging Initiative. (2014). Amyloid and *APOE* ε4 interact to influence short-term decline in preclinical Alzheimer disease. *Neurology, 82*(20), 1760–1767.

Mowszowski, L., Hermens, D. F., Diamond, K., Norrie, L., Hickie, I. B., Lewis, S. J. G., & Naismith, S. L. (2012). Reduced mismatch negativity in mild cognitive impairment: associations with neuropsychological performance. *Journal of Alzheimer's Disease, 30*(1), 209–219.

Mueller, J. H., Wonderlich, S., & Dugan, K. (1986). Self-referent processing of age-specific material. *Psychology and Aging, 1*(4), 293–299. doi:10.1037/0882-7974.1.4.293

Mufson, E. J., Mahady, L., Waters, D., Counts, S. E., Perez, S. E., DeKosky, S. T., . . . Binder, L. I. (2015). Hippocampal plasticity during the progression of Alzheimer's disease. *Neuroscience, 309*, 51–67.

Murphy, K., & Garavan, H. (2004). Artifactual fMRI group and condition differences driven by performance confounds. *NeuroImage, 21*(1), 219–228.

Murphy, N. A., & Isaacowitz, D. M. (2008). Preferences for emotional information in older and younger adults: a meta-analysis of memory and attention tasks. *Psychology and Aging, 23*, 263–286.

Murty, V. P., Ritchey, M., Adcock, R. A., & LaBar, K. S. (2010). fMRI studies of successful emotional memory encoding: a quantitative meta-analysis. *Neuropsychologia, 48*(12), 3459–3469. doi:10.1016/j.neuropsychologia.2010.07.030

Nakamura, T., Ghilardi, M., Mentis, M., Dhawan, V., Fukuda, M., Hacking, A., ... Eidelberg, D. (2001). Functional networks in motor sequence learning: abnormal topographies in Parkinson's disease. *Human Brain Mapping, 12*(1), 42–60.

Nashiro, K., Sakaki, M., Braskie, M. N., & Mather, M. (2017). Resting-state networks associated with cognitive processing show more age-related decline than those associated with emotional processing. *Neurobiology of Aging, 54*, 152–162. doi:10.1016/j.neurobiolaging.2017.03.003

Nashiro, K., Sakaki, M., & Mather, M. (2012). Age differences in brain activity during emotion processing: reflections of age-related decline or increased emotion regulation? *Gerontology, 58*(2), 156–163. doi:10.1159/000328465

Naveh-Benjamin, M. (2000). Adult age differences in memory performance: tests of an associative deficit hypothesis. *Journal of Experimental Psychology: Learning, Memory, and Cognition, 26*(5), 1170–1187. https://doi.org/10.1037//0278-7393.26.5.1170

Nessler, D., Friedman, D., Johnson, R., Jr., & Bersick, M. (2007). Does repetition engender the same retrieval processes in young and older adults? *NeuroReport, 18*(17), 1837–1840.

Nevalainen, T., Kananen, L., Marttila, S., Jylhä, M., Hervonen, A., Hurme, M., & Jylhävä, J. (2015). Transcriptomic and epigenetic analyses reveal a gender difference in aging-associated inflammation: the Vitality 90+ Study. *Age, 37*(4), 1–13.

Newsome, R. N., Duarte, A., & Barense, M. D. (2012). Reducing perceptual interference improves visual discrimination in mild cognitive impairment: implications for a model of perirhinal cortex function. *Hippocampus, 22*(10), 1990–1999.

Newsome, R. N., Dulas, M. R., & Duarte, A. (2012). The effects of aging on emotion-induced modulations of source retrieval ERPs: evidence for valence biases. *Neuropsychologia, 50*(14), 3370–3384. doi:10.1016/j.neuropsychologia.2012.09.024

Ng, K. K., Lo, J. C., Lim, J. K. W., Chee, M. W. L., & Zhou, J. (2016). Reduced functional segregation between the default mode network and the executive control network in healthy older adults: a longitudinal study. *NeuroImage, 133*, 321–330. doi:10.1016/j.neuroimage.2016.03.029

Nielsen, L., & Mather, M. (2011). Emerging perspectives in social neuroscience and neuroeconomics of aging. *Social Cognitive and Affective Neuroscience, 6*(2), 149–164. doi:10.1093/scan/nsr019

Nielson, K. A., Langenecker, S. A., & Garavan, H. (2002). Differences in the functional neuroanatomy of inhibitory control across the adult life span. *Psychology and Aging, 17*(1), 56–71.

Norman, K. A., Polyn, S. M., Detre, G. J., & Haxby, J. V. (2006). Beyond mind-reading: multi-voxel pattern analysis of fMRI data. *Trends in Cognitive Science, 10*(9), 424–430. doi:10.1016/j.tics.2006.07.005

North, M. S., & Fiske, S. T. (2012). An inconvenienced youth? Ageism and its potential intergenerational roots. *Psychological Bulletin, 138*(5), 982–997. doi:10.1037/a0027843

Northoff, G., Heinzel, A., de Greck, M., Bermpohl, F., Dobrowolny, H., & Panksepp, J. (2006). Self-referential processing in our brain – a meta-analysis of imaging studies of the self. *NeuroImage, 31*(1), 440–457.

Nosheny, R. L., Insel, P. S., Truran, D., Schuff, N., Jack, C. R., Aisen, P. S., ... Alzheimer's Disease Neuroimaging Initiative. (2015). Variables associated with hippocampal atrophy rate in normal aging and mild cognitive impairment. *Neurobiology of Aging, 36*(1), 273–282.

Novak, M. J. U., Seunarine, K. K., Gibbard, C. R., McColgan, P., Draganski, B., Friston, K., ... Tabrizi, S. J. (2015). Basal ganglia-cortical structural connectivity in Huntington's disease. *Human Brain Mapping, 36*(5), 1728–1740.

Nyberg, L., Sandblom, J., Jones, S., Neely, A. S., Petersson, K. M., Ingvar, M., & Backman, L. (2003). Neural correlates of training-related memory improvement in adulthood and aging. *Proceedings of the National Academy of Sciences of the United States of America, 100*(23), 13728–13733. doi:10.1073/pnas.1735487100

Oberlin, L. E., Verstynen, T. D., Burzynska, A. Z., Voss, M. W., Prakash, R. S., Chaddock-Heyman, L., ... Erickson, K. I. (2016). White matter microstructure mediates the relationship between cardiorespiratory fitness and spatial working memory in older adults. *NeuroImage, 131*, 91–101. doi:10.1016/j.neuroimage.2015.09.053

O'Brien, J. L., O'Keefe, K. M., LaViolette, P. S., DeLuca, A. N., Blacker, D., Dickerson, B. C., & Sperling, R. A. (2010). Longitudinal fMRI in elderly reveals loss of hippocampal activation with clinical decline. *Neurology, 74*(24), 1969–1976. doi:10.1212/WNL.0b013e3181e3966e

Ochsner, K. N., & Gross, J. J. (2005). The cognitive control of emotion. *Trends in Cognitive Science, 9*(5), 242–249. doi:10.1016/j.tics.2005.03.010

Oh, H., & Jagust, W. J. (2013). Frontotemporal network connectivity during memory encoding is increased with aging and disrupted by beta-amyloid. *Journal of Neuroscience, 33*(47), 18425–18437.

Oishi, K., & Lyketsos, C. G. (2014). Alzheimer's disease and the fornix. *Frontiers in Aging Neuroscience, 6*.

Olsen, R. K., Pangelinan, M. M., Bogulski, C., Chakravarty, M. M., Luk, G., Grady, C. L., & Bialystok, E. (2015). The effect of lifelong bilingualism on regional grey and white matter volume. *Brain Research, 1612*, 128–139.

Opitz, P. C., Lee, I. A., Gross, J. J., & Urry, H. L. (2014). Fluid cognitive ability is a resource for successful emotion regulation in older and younger adults. *Frontiers in Psychology, 5*, Article 609. doi:10.3389/ fpsyg.2014.00609

Opitz, P. C., Rauch, L. C., Terry, D. P., & Urry, H. L. (2012). Prefrontal mediation of age differences in cognitive reappraisal. *Neurobiology of Aging, 33*(4), 645–655. doi:10.1016/j.neurobiolaging.2010.06.004

Pagnoni, G., & Cekic, M. (2007). Age effects on gray matter volume and attentional performance in Zen meditation. *Neurobiology of Aging, 28*(10), 1623–1627.

Paige, L. E., Cassidy, B. S., Schacter, D. L., & Gutchess, A. H. (2016). Age differences in hippocampal activation during gist-based false recognition. *Neurobiology of Aging, 46*, 76–83. doi:10.1016/j. neurobiolaging.2016.06.014

Park, D. C., Lautenschlager, G., Hedden, T., Davidson, N. S., Smith, A. D., & Smith, P. K. (2002). Models of visuospatial and verbal memory across the adult life span. *Psychology and Aging, 17*(2), 299–320.

Park, D. C., Polk, T. A., Park, R., Minear, M., Savage, A., & Smith, M. R. (2004). Aging reduces neural specialization in ventral visual cortex. *Proceedings of the National Academy of Sciences of the United States of America, 101*(35), 13091–13095.

Park, D. C., & Reuter-Lorenz, P. A. (2009). The adaptive brain: aging and neurocognitive scaffolding. *Annual Review of Psychology, 60*, 173–196.

Park, D. C., & Schwarz, N. (2000). *Cognitive Aging: A Primer*. Philadelphia: Psychology Press.

Park, D. C., Smith, A. D., Lautenschlager, G., Earles, J. L., Frieske, D., Zwahr, M., & Gaines, C. L. (1996). Mediators of long-term memory performance across the life span. *Psychology and Aging, 11*(4), 621–637.

Park, J., Carp, J., Kennedy, K. M., Rodrigue, K. M., Bischof, G. N., Huang, C.-M., . . . Park, D. C. (2012). Neural broadening or neural attenuation? Investigating age-related dedifferentiation in the face network in a large lifespan sample. *Journal of Neuroscience, 32*(6), 2154–2158.

Park, J. M., Cassidy, B. S., & Gutchess, A. H. (2017). Memory for trait inferences with age. Unpublished manuscript.

Park, S., Han, Y., Kim, B., & Dunkle, R. E. (2015). Aging in place of vulnerable older adults: person–environment fit perspective. *Journal of Applied Gerontology, 36*(11), 1327–1350. doi:10.1177/ 0733464815617286

Paxton, J. L., Barch, D. M., Racine, C. A., & Braver, T. S. (2008). Cognitive control, goal maintenance, and prefrontal function in healthy aging. *Cerebral Cortex*, *18*(5), 1010–1028.

Peelle, J. E., Troiani, V., Grossman, M., & Wingfield, A. (2011). Hearing loss in older adults affects neural systems supporting speech comprehension. *Journal of Neuroscience*, *31*(35), 12638–12643.

Penner, M. R., Roth, T. L., Barnes, C., & Sweatt, D. (2010). An epigenetic hypothesis of aging-related cognitive dysfunction. *Frontiers in Aging Neuroscience*, *2*, Article 9.

Perani, D., & Abutalebi, J. (2015). Bilingualism, dementia, cognitive and neural reserve. *Current Opinion in Neurology*, *28*(6), 618–625.

Pereira, A. C., Huddleston, D. E., Brickman, A. M., Sosunov, A. A., Hen, R., McKhann, G. M., … Small, S. A. (2007). An *in vivo* correlate of exercise-induced neurogenesis in the adult dentate gyrus. *Proceedings of the National Academy of Sciences of the United States of America*, *104*(13), 5638–5643.

Perfect, T. J., & Maylor, E. A. (2000). *Models of Cognitive Aging.* New York: Oxford University Press.

Perrotin, A., Mormino, E. C., Madison, C. M., Hayenga, A. O., & Jagust, W. J. (2012). Subjective cognition and amyloid deposition imaging: a Pittsburgh compound B positron emission tomography study in normal elderly individuals. *Archives of Neurology*, *69*(2), 223–229.

Persson, J., Lustig, C., Nelson, J. K., & Reuter-Lorenz, P. A. (2007). Age differences in deactivation: a link to cognitive control? *Journal of Cognitive Neuroscience*, *19*(6), 1021–1032.

Persson, J., Pudas, S., Lind, J., Kauppi, K., Nilsson, L.-G., & Nyberg, L. (2011). Longitudinal structure–function correlates in elderly reveal MTL dysfunction with cognitive decline. *Cerebral Cortex*, *22*(10), 2297–1304.

Phillips, L. H., Bull, R., Allen, R., Insch, P., Burr, K., & Ogg, W. (2011). Lifespan aging and belief reasoning: influences of executive function and social cue decoding. *Cognition*, *120*(2), 236–247. doi:10.1016/j.cognition.2011.05.003

Phillips, L. H., Henry, J. D., Hosie, J. A., & Milne, A. B. (2006). Age, anger regulation and well-being. *Aging and Mental Health*, *10*(3), 250–256.

Phillips, L. H., MacLean, R. D. J., & Allen, R. (2002). Age and the understanding of emotions: neuropsychological and sociocognitive perspectives. *Journals of Gerontology. Series B, Psychological Sciences and Social Sciences*, *57*(6), P526–P530.

Poldrack, R. A. (2006). Can cognitive processes be inferred from neuroimaging data? *Trends in Cognitive Sciences, 10*(2), 59–63. doi:10.1016/j.tics.2005.12.004

Poletti, M., Enrici, I., & Adenzato, M. (2012). Cognitive and affective theory of mind in neurodegenerative diseases: neuropsychological, neuroanatomical and neurochemical levels. *Neuroscience & Biobehavioral Reviews*, *36*(9), 2147–2164.

Poletti, M., Enrici, I., Bonuccelli, U., & Adenzato, M. (2011). Theory of mind in Parkinson's disease. *Behavioural Brain Research*, *219*(2), 342–350.

Power, J. D., Barnes, K. A., Snyder, A. Z., Schlaggar, B. L., & Petersen, S. E. (2012). Spurious but systematic correlations in functional connectivity MRI networks arise from subject motion. *NeuroImage*, *59*(3), 2142–2154. doi:10.1016/j.neuroimage.2011.10.018

Prakash, R. S., De Leon, A. A., Patterson, B., Schirda, B. L., & Janssen, A. L. (2014). Mindfulness and the aging brain: a proposed paradigm shift. *Frontiers in Aging Neuroscience*, *6*.

Prenderville, J. A., Kennedy, P. J., Dinan, T. G., & Cryan, J. F. (2015). Adding fuel to the fire: the impact of stress on the ageing brain. *Trends in Neurosciences*, *38*(1), 13–25.

Pruessner, J. C., Baldwin, M. W., Dedovic, K., Renwick, R., Mahani, N. K., Lord, C., ... Lupien, S. (2005). Self-esteem, locus of control, hippocampal volume, and cortisol regulation in young and old adulthood. *NeuroImage*, *28*(4), 815–826.

Pruessner, M., Pruessner, J. C., Hellhammer, D. H., Pike, G. B., & Lupien, S. J. (2007). The associations among hippocampal volume, cortisol reactivity, and memory performance in healthy young men. *Psychiatry Research: Neuroimaging*, *155*(1), 1–10.

Pudas, S., Persson, J., Nilsson, L. G., & Nyberg, L. (2014). Midlife memory ability accounts for brain activity differences in healthy aging. *Neurobiology of Aging*, *35*(11), 2495–2503. doi:10.1016/j.neurobiolaging.2014.05.022

Pulopulos, M. M., Almela, M., Hidalgo, V., Villada, C., Puig-Perez, S., & Salvador, A. (2013). Acute stress does not impair long-term memory retrieval in older people. *Neurobiology of Learning and Memory*, *104*, 16–24.

Qin, P., & Northoff, G. (2011). How is our self related to midline regions and the default-mode network? *NeuroImage*, *57*(3), 1221–1233. doi:10.1016/j.neuroimage.2011.05.028

Rankin, K. P., Salazar, A., Gorno-Tempini, M. L., Sollberger, M., Wilson, S. M., Pavlic, D., ... Miller, B. L. (2009). Detecting sarcasm from paralinguistic cues: anatomic and cognitive correlates in neurodegenerative disease. *NeuroImage*, *47*(4), 2005–2015.

Raye, C. L., Mitchell, K. J., Reeder, J. A., Greene, E. J., & Johnson, M. K. (2008). Refreshing one of several active representations: behavioral and functional magnetic resonance imaging differences between young and older adults. *Journal of Cognitive Neuroscience*, *20*(5), 852–862.

Raz, N. (2000). Aging of the brain and its impact on cognitive performance: integration of structural and functional findings. In F. I. M. Craik & T. A. Salthouse (Eds.), *The Handbook of Aging and Cognition*, (2nd edn, pp. 1–90). Mahwah, NJ: Lawrence Erlbaum Associates, Inc.

Raz, N., Ghisletta, P., Rodrigue, K. M., Kennedy, K. M., & Lindenberger, U. (2010). Trajectories of brain aging in middle-aged and older adults: regional and individual differences. *NeuroImage*, *51*(2), 501–511. doi:10.1016/j.neuroimage.2010.03.020

Raz, N., Lindenberger, U., Rodrigue, K. M., Kennedy, K. M., Head, D., Williamson, A., . . . Acker, J. D. (2005). Regional brain changes in aging healthy adults: general trends, individual differences and modifiers. *Cerebral Cortex*, *15*(11), 1676–1689.

Reed, A. E., Chan, L., & Mikels, J. A. (2014). Meta-analysis of the age-related positivity effect: age differences in preferences for positive over negative information. *Psychology and Aging*, *29*(1), 1–15. doi:10.1037/a0035194

Reuter-Lorenz, P. A., & Cappell, K. A. (2008). Neurocognitive aging and the compensation hypothesis. *Current Directions in Psychological Science*, *17*(3), 177–182. doi:10.1111/j.1467-8721.2008.00570.x

Reuter-Lorenz, P. A., Jonides, J., Smith, E. E., Hartley, A., Miller, A., Marshuetz, C., & Koeppe, R. A. (2000). Age differences in the frontal lateralization of verbal and spatial working memory revealed by PET. *Journal of Cognitive Neuroscience*, *12*(1), 174–187.

Reuter-Lorenz, P. A., Marshuetz, C., Jonides, J., Smith, E. E., Hartley, A., & Koeppe, R. (2001). Neurocognitive ageing of storage and executive processes. *European Journal of Cognitive Psychology*, *13*(1–2), 257–278.

Reuter-Lorenz, P. A., & Park, D. C. (2014). How does it STAC up? Revisiting the scaffolding theory of aging and cognition. *Neuropsychology Review*, *24*(3), 355–370. doi:10.1007/s11065-014-9270-9

Rhodes, M. G., & Anastasi, J. S. (2012). The own-age bias in face recognition: a meta-analytic and theoretical review. *Psychological Bulletin*, *138*(1), 146–174. doi:10.1037/a0025750

Riecker, A., Gröschel, K., Ackermann, H., Steinbrink, C., Witte, O., & Kastrup, A. (2006). Functional significance of age-related differences in motor activation patterns. *NeuroImage*, *32*(3), 1345–1354.

Rieckmann, A., Fischer, H., & Bäckman, L. (2010). Activation in striatum and medial temporal lobe during sequence learning in younger and older adults: relations to performance. *NeuroImage*, *50*(3), 1303–1312.

Ritchey, M., Bessette-Symons, B., Hayes, S. M., & Cabeza, R. (2011). Emotion processing in the aging brain is modulated by semantic elaboration. *Neuropsychologia, 49*(4), 640–650. doi:10.1016/j. neuropsychologia.2010.09.009

Ritchey, M., LaBar, K. S., & Cabeza, R. (2011). Level of processing modulates the neural correlates of emotional memory formation. *Journal of Cognitive Neuroscience, 23*(4), 757–771. doi:10.1162/jocn.2010.21487

Ritchie, S. J., Dickie, D. A., Cox, S. R., Valdes Hernandez, M. D. C., Sibbett, R., Pattie, A., . . . Deary, I. J. (2017). Brain structural differences between 73- and 92-year-olds matched for childhood intelligence, social background, and intracranial volume. *Neurobiology of Aging, 62*, 146–158. doi:10.1016/j.neurobiolaging.2017.10.005

Roalf, D. R., Pruis, T. A., Stevens, A. A., & Janowsky, J. S. (2011). More is less: emotion induced prefrontal cortex activity habituates in aging. *Neurobiology of Aging, 32*(9), 1634–1650. doi:10.1016/j. neurobiolaging.2009.10.007

Rodrigue, K. M., & Raz, N. (2004). Shrinkage of the entorhinal cortex over five years predicts memory performance in healthy adults. *Journal of Neuroscience, 24*(4), 956–963. doi:10.1523/JNEUROSCI.4166-03.2004

Rogers, T. B., Kuiper, N. A., & Kirker, W. S. (1977). Self-reference and the encoding of personal information. *Journal of Personality and Social Psychology, 35*(9), 677–688.

Rosa, N. M., & Gutchess, A. H. (2011). Source memory for actions in young and older adults: self vs. close or unknown others. *Psychology and Aging, 26*, 625–630. doi:10.1037/a0022827

(2013). False memory in aging resulting from self-referential processing. *Journals of Gerontology. Series B, Psychological Sciences and Social Sciences, 68B*(6), 882–892. doi:10.1093/geronb/gbt018

Rosano, C., Venkatraman, V. K., Guralnik, J., Newman, A. B., Glynn, N. W., Launer, L., . . . Pahor, M. (2010). Psychomotor speed and functional brain MRI 2 years after completing a physical activity treatment. *Journals of Gerontology. Series A, Biological Sciences and Medical Sciences, 65*(6), 639–647.

Rosenbaum, R. S., Furey, M. L., Horwitz, B., & Grady, C. L. (2010). Altered connectivity among emotion-related brain regions during short-term memory in Alzheimer's disease. *Neurobiology of Aging, 31*(5), 780–786.

Ross, L. A., McCoy, D., Coslett, H. B., Olson, I. R., & Wolk, D. A. (2011). Improved proper name recall in aging after electrical stimulation of the anterior temporal lobes. *Frontiers in Aging Neuroscience, 3*, Article 16. doi:10.3389/fnagi.2011.00016

Ross, M., Grossmann, I., & Schryer, E. (2014). Contrary to psychological and popular opinion, there is no compelling evidence that older adults are disproportionately victimized by consumer fraud. *Perspectives on Psychological Science, 9*(4), 427–442. doi:10.1177/1745691614535935

Rossi, S., Miniussi, C., Pasqualetti, P., Babiloni, C., Rossini, P. M., & Cappa, S. F. (2004). Age-related functional changes of prefrontal cortex in long-term memory: a repetitive transcranial magnetic stimulation study. *Journal of Neuroscience, 24*(36), 7939–7944. doi:10.1523/jneurosci.0703-04.2004

Ruby, P., Fabienne, C., D'Argembeau, A., Peters, F., Degueldre, C., Balteau, E., & Salmon, E. (2009). Perspective taking to assess self-personality: what's modified in Alzheimer's disease. *Neurobiology of Aging, 30*, 1637–1651. doi:10.1016.2007.12.014

Ruffman, T., Henry, J. D., Livingstone, V., & Phillips, L. H. (2008). A meta-analytic review of emotion recognition and aging: implications for neuropsychological models of aging. *Neuroscience and Biobehavioral Reviews, 32*(4), 863–881. doi:10.1016/j.neubiorev.2008.01.001

Ruffman, T., Murray, J., Halberstadt, J., & Vater, T. (2012). Age-related differences in deception. *Psychology and Aging, 27*(3), 543–549. doi:10.1037/a0023380

Russell, J. A. (1980). A circumplex model of affect. *Journal of Personality and Social Psychology, 39*(6), 1161–1178. doi:10.1037/h0077714

Rypma, B., & D'Esposito, M. (2001). Age-related changes in brain–behaviour relationships: evidence from event-related functional MRI studies. *European Journal of Cognitive Psychology, 13*(1–2), 235–256.

Sakaki, M., Nga, L., & Mather, M. (2013). Amygdala functional connectivity with medial prefrontal cortex at rest predicts the positivity effect in older adults' memory. *Journal of Cognitive Neuroscience, 25*(8), 1206–1224. doi:10.1162/jocn_a_00392

Sala-Llonch, R., Bartrés-Faz, D., & Junqué, C. (2015). Reorganization of brain networks in aging: a review of functional connectivity studies. *Frontiers in Psychology, 6.*

Salami, A., Rieckmann, A., Fischer, H., & Bäckman, L. (2014). A multivariate analysis of age-related differences in functional networks supporting conflict resolution. *NeuroImage, 86*, 150–163.

Salat, D. H., Buckner, R. L., Snyder, A. Z., Greve, D. N., Desikan, R. S. R., Busa, E., ... Fischl, B. (2004). Thinning of the cerebral cortex in aging. *Cerebral Cortex, 14*(7), 721–730.

Salat, D. H., Tuch, D. S., Hevelone, N. D., Fischl, B., Corkin, S., Rosas, H. D., & Dale, A. M. (2005). Age-related changes in prefrontal white matter measured by diffusion tensor imaging. *Annals of the New York Academy of Science, 1064*, 37–49. doi:10.1196/annals.1340.009

Salthouse, T. A. (1996). The processing-speed theory of adult age differences in cognition. *Psychological Review, 103*(3), 403–428.

(2017). Shared and unique influences on age-related cognitive change. *Neuropsychology*, *31*(1), 11–19. doi:10.1037/neu0000330

Salthouse, T. A., & Babcock, R. L. (1991). Decomposing adult age-differences in working memory. *Developmental Psychology*, *27*(5), 763–776.

Samanez-Larkin, G. R., Gibbs, S. E. B., Khanna, K., Nielsen, L., Carstensen, L. L., & Knutson, B. (2007). Anticipation of monetary gain but not loss in healthy older adults. *Nature Neuroscience*, *10*(6), 787–791. doi:10.1038/nn1894

Samanez-Larkin, G. R., & Knutson, B. (2015). Decision making in the ageing brain: changes in affective and motivational circuits. *Nature Reviews Neuroscience*, *16*(5), 278–289. doi:10.1038/nrn3917

Samanez-Larkin, G. R., Kuhnen, C. M., Yoo, D. J., & Knutson, B. (2010). Variability in nucleus accumbens activity mediates age-related suboptimal financial risk taking. *Journal of Neuroscience*, *30*(4), 1426–1434. doi:10.1523/JNEUROSCI.4902-09.2010

Samanez-Larkin, G. R., Levens, S. M., Perry, L. M., Dougherty, R. F., & Knutson, B. (2012). Frontostriatal white matter integrity mediates adult age differences in probabilistic reward learning. *Journal of Neuroscience*, *32*(15), 5333–5337. doi:10.1523/JNEUROSCI.5756-11.2012

Samanez-Larkin, G. R., Mata, R., Radu, P. T., Ballard, I. C., Carstensen, L. L., & McClure, S. M. (2011). Age differences in striatal delay sensitivity during intertemporal choice in healthy adults. *Frontiers in Neuroscience*, *5*, Article 126. doi:10.3389/fnins.2011.00126

Samanez-Larkin, G. R., Worthy, D. A., Mata, R., McClure, S. M., & Knutson, B. (2014). Adult age differences in frontostriatal representation of prediction error but not reward outcome. *Cognitive, Affective, and Behavioral Neuroscience*, *14*(2), 672–682. doi:10.3758/s13415-014-0297-4

Sander, M. C., Werkle-Bergner, M., & Lindenberger, U. (2012). Amplitude modulations and inter-trial phase stability of alpha-oscillations differentially reflect working memory constraints across the lifespan. *NeuroImage*, *59*(1), 646–654.

Schacter, D. L., Addis, D. R., & Buckner, R. L. (2007). Remembering the past to imagine the future: the prospective brain. *Nature Reviews Neuroscience*, *8*(9), 657–661. doi:10.1038/nrn2213

Schacter, D. L., Guerin, S. A., & St. Jacques, P. L. (2011). Memory distortion: an adaptive perspective. *Trends in Cognitive Sciences*, *15*, 467–474.

Schacter, D. L., & Slotnick, S. D. (2004). The cognitive neuroscience of memory distortion. *Neuron*, *44*(1), 149–160.

Schaefer, J. D., Caspi, A., Belsky, D. W., Harrington, H., Houts, R., Israel, S., . . . Moffitt, T. E. (2016). Early-Life intelligence predicts midlife biological age. *Journals of Gerontology. Series B, Psychological Sciences and Social Sciences, 12*(6), 968–977. doi:10.1093/geronb/gbv035

Schiller, D., Freeman, J. B., Mitchell, J. P., Uleman, J. S., & Phelps, E. A. (2009). A neural mechanism of first impressions. *Nature Neuroscience, 12*, 508–514.

Schmitz, T. W., Cheng, F. H., & De Rosa, E. (2010). Failing to ignore: paradoxical neural effects of perceptual load on early attentional selection in normal aging. *Journal of Neuroscience, 30*(44), 14750–14758.

Schneider-Garces, N. J., Gordon, B. A., Brumback-Peltz, C. R., Shin, E., Lee, Y., Sutton, B. P., . . . Fabiani, M. (2010). Span, CRUNCH, and beyond: working memory capacity and the aging brain. *Journal of Cognitive Neuroscience, 22*(4), 655–669.

Schröder, J., & Pantel, J. (2016). Neuroimaging of hippocampal atrophy in early recognition of Alzheimer's disease – a critical appraisal after two decades of research. *Psychiatry Research: Neuroimaging, 247*, 71–78.

Seaman, K. L., Leong, J. K., Wu, C. C., Knutson, B., & Samanez-Larkin, G. R. (2017). Individual differences in skewed financial risk-taking across the adult life span. *Cognitive, Affective, and Behavioral Neuroscience, 17*(6), 1232–1241. doi:10.3758/s13415-017-0545-5

Sebastian, A., Baldermann, C., Feige, B., Katzev, M., Scheller, E., Hellwig, B., . . . Klöppel, S. (2013). Differential effects of age on subcomponents of response inhibition. *Neurobiology of Aging, 34*(9), 2183–2193.

Seidler, R. D., Bernard, J. A., Burutolu, T. B., Fling, B. W., Gordon, M. T., Gwin, J. T., . . . Lipps, D. B. (2010). Motor control and aging: links to age-related brain structural, functional, and biochemical effects. *Neuroscience & Biobehavioral Reviews, 34*(5), 721–733.

Sexton, C. E., Mackay, C. E., & Ebmeier, K. P. (2013). A systematic review and meta-analysis of magnetic resonance imaging studies in late-life depression. *American Journal of Geriatric Psychiatry, 21*(2), 184–195.

Shafto, M. A., & Tyler, L. K. (2014). Language in the aging brain: the network dynamics of cognitive decline and preservation. *Science, 346*(6209), 583–587.

Shammi, P., & Stuss, D. T. (1999). Humour appreciation: a role of the right frontal lobe. *Brain, 122*, 657–666. doi:10.1093/brain/122.4.657

   (2003). The effects of normal aging on humor appreciation. *Journal of the International Neuropsychological Society, 9*(6), 855–863. doi:10.1017/s135561770396005x

Shany-Ur, T., Lin, N., Rosen, H. J., Sollberger, M., Miller, B. L., & Rankin, K. P. (2014). Self-awareness in neurodegenerative disease relies on neural structures mediating reward-driven attention. *Brain*, *137*(8), 2368–2381.

Shany-Ur, T., Poorzand, P., Grossman, S. N., Growdon, M. E., Jang, J. Y., Ketelle, R. S., ... Rankin, K. P. (2012). Comprehension of insincere communication in neurodegenerative disease: lies, sarcasm, and theory of mind. *Cortex*, *48*(10), 1329–1341.

Shany-Ur, T., & Rankin, K. P. (2011). Personality and social cognition in neurodegenerative disease. *Current Opinion in Neurology*, *24*(6), 550–555.

Smart, C. M., Segalowitz, S. J., Mulligan, B. P., & MacDonald, S. W. (2014). Attention capacity and self-report of subjective cognitive decline: a P3 ERP study. *Biological Psychology*, *103*, 144–151.

Smith, A. D., Park, D. C., Cherry, K., & Berkovsky, K. (1990). Age differences in memory for concrete and abstract pictures. *Journal of Gerontology*, *45*(5), P205–209.

Smith, E. E., & Jonides, J. (1998). Neuroimaging analyses of human working memory. *Proceedings of the National Academy of Sciences of the United States of America*, *95*(20), 12061–12068.

Spaniol, J., Bowen, H. J., Wegier, P., & Grady, C. (2015). Neural responses to monetary incentives in younger and older adults. *Brain Research*, *1612*, 70–82. doi:10.1016/j.brainres.2014.09.063

Spencer, W. D., & Raz, N. (1995). Differential effects of aging on memory for content and context: a meta-analysis. *Psychology and Aging*, *10*(4), 527–539. https://doi.org/10.1037//0882-7974.10.4.527

Sperling, R. A., Aisen, P. S., Beckett, L. A., Bennett, D. A., Craft, S., Fagan, A. M., ... Phelps, C. H. (2011). Toward defining the preclinical stages of Alzheimer's disease: recommendations from the National Institute on Aging–Alzheimer's Association workgroups on diagnostic guidelines for Alzheimer's disease. *Alzheimers & Dementia*, *7*(3), 280–292. doi:10.1016/j.jalz.2011.03.003

Sperling, R. A., Bates, J. F., Chua, E. F., Cocchiarella, A. J., Rentz, D. M., Rosen, B. R., ... Albert, M. S. (2003). fMRI studies of associative encoding in young and elderly controls and mild Alzheimer's disease. *Journal of Neurology, Neurosurgery, and Psychiatry*, *74*(1), 44–50.

Sperling, R. A., LaViolette, P. S., O'Keefe, K., O'Brien, J., Rentz, D. M., Pihlajamaki, M., ... Hedden, T. (2009). Amyloid deposition is associated with impaired default network function in older persons without dementia. *Neuron*, *63*(2), 178–188.

Spiegel, A. M., Sewal, A. S., & Rapp, P. R. (2014). Epigenetic contributions to cognitive aging: disentangling mindspan and lifespan. *Learning & Memory*, *21*(10), 569–574.

Spreng, R. N., Cassidy, B. N., Darboh, B. S., DuPre, E., Lockrow, A. W., Setton, R., & Turner, G. R. (2017). Financial exploitation is associated with structural and functional brain differences in healthy older adults. *Journals of Gerontology. Series A, Biological Sciences and Medical Sciences, 72*(10), 1365–1368. doi:10.1093/gerona/glx051

Spreng, R. N., & Schacter, D. L. (2012). Default network modulation and large-scale network interactivity in healthy young and old adults. *Cerebral Cortex, 22*(11), 2610–2621. doi:10.1093/cercor/bhr339

Spreng, R. N., Stevens, W. D., Viviano, J. D., & Schacter, D. L. (2016). Attenuated anticorrelation between the default and dorsal attention networks with aging: evidence from task and rest. *Neurobiology of Aging, 45*, 149–160. doi:10.1016/j.neurobiolaging.2016.05.020

Spreng, R. N., Wojtowicz, M., & Grady, C. L. (2010). Reliable differences in brain activity between young and old adults: a quantitative meta-analysis across multiple cognitive domains. *Neuroscience & Biobehavioral Reviews, 34*(8), 1178–1194.

Stanley, J. T., & Blanchard-Fields, F. (2008). Challenges older adults face in detecting deceit: the role of emotion recognition. *Psychology and Aging, 23*(1), 24–32. doi:10.1037/0882-7974.23.1.24

Stanley, J. T., Lohani, M., & Isaacowitz, D. M. (2014). Age-related differences in judgments of inappropriate behavior are related to humor style preferences. *Psychology and Aging, 29*(3), 528–541. doi:10.1037/a0036666

Stark, S. M., Yassa, M. A., Lacy, J. W., & Stark, C. E. L. (2013). A task to assess behavioral pattern separation (BPS) in humans: data from healthy aging and mild cognitive impairment. *Neuropsychologia, 51*(12), 2442–2449.

Stark, S. M., Yassa, M. A., & Stark, C. E. L. (2010). Individual differences in spatial pattern separation performance associated with healthy aging in humans. *Learning & Memory, 17*(6), 284–288.

Stebbins, G. T., Carrillo, M. C., Dorfman, J., Dirksen, C., Desmond, J. E., Turner, D. A., … Gabrieli, J. D. (2002). Aging effects on memory encoding in the frontal lobes. *Psychology and Aging, 17*(1), 44–55.

Steele, C. M., & Aronson, J. (1995). Stereotype threat and the intellectual test performance of African Americans. *Journal of Personality and Social Psychology, 69*(5), 797–811.

Stephens, J. A., & Berryhill, M. E. (2016). Older adults improve on everyday tasks after working memory training and neurostimulation. *Brain Stimulation, 9*(4), 553–559. doi:10.1016/j.brs.2016.04.001

Stern, Y. (2002). What is cognitive reserve? Theory and research application of the reserve concept. *Journal of the International Neuropsychological Society, 8*(3), 448–460.

(2009). Cognitive reserve. *Neuropsychologia, 47*(10), 2015–2028. doi:10.1016/j.neuropsychologia.2009.03.004

Stevens, W. D., Hasher, L., Chiew, K. S., & Grady, C. L. (2008). A neural mechanism underlying memory failure in older adults. *Journal of Neuroscience, 28*(48), 12820–12824.

St Jacques, P. L., Bessette-Symons, B., & Cabeza, R. (2009). Functional neuroimaging studies of aging and emotion: fronto-amygdalar differences during emotional perception and episodic memory. *Journal of the International Neuropsychology Society, 15*(6), 819–825. doi:10.1017/S1355617709990439

St Jacques, P. L., Dolcos, F., & Cabeza, R. (2009). Effects of aging on functional connectivity of the amygdala for subsequent memory of negative pictures: a network analysis of functional magnetic resonance imaging data. *Psychological Science, 20*(1), 74–84. doi:10.1111/j.1467-9280.2008.02258.x

(2010). Effects of aging on functional connectivity of the amygdala during negative evaluation: a network analysis of fMRI data. *Neurobiology of Aging, 31*(2), 315–327. doi:10.1016/j.neurobiolaging.2008.03.012

(2012). Age-related effects on the neural correlates of autobiographical memory retrieval. *Neurobiology of Aging, 33*(7), 1298–1310.

St-Laurent, M., Abdi, H., Bondad, A., & Buchsbaum, B. R. (2014). Memory reactivation in healthy aging: evidence of stimulus-specific dedifferentiation. *Journal of Neuroscience, 34*(12), 4175–4186. doi:10.1523/JNEUROSCI.3054-13.2014

St-Laurent, M., Abdi, H., Burianová, H., & Grady, C. L. (2011). Influence of aging on the neural correlates of autobiographical, episodic, and semantic memory retrieval. *Journal of Cognitive Neuroscience, 23*(12), 4150–4163.

Sturm, V. E., Yokoyama, J. S., Seeley, W. W., Kramer, J. H., Miller, B. L., & Rankin, K. P. (2013). Heightened emotional contagion in mild cognitive impairment and Alzheimer's disease is associated with temporal lobe degeneration. *Proceedings of the National Academy of Sciences of the United States of America, 110*(24), 9944–9949.

Sullivan, S., & Ruffman, T. (2004). Social understanding: how does it fare with advancing years? *British Journal of Psychology, 95*, 1–18. doi:10.1348/000712604322779424

Sutin, A. R., Beason-Held, L. L., Resnick, S. M., & Costa, P. T. (2009). Sex differences in resting-state neural correlates of openness to experience among older adults. *Cerebral Cortex, 19*(12), 2797–2802.

Suzuki, H., Gao, H., Bai, W., Evangelou, E., Glocker, B., O'Regan, D. P., . . . Matthews, P. M. (2017). Abnormal brain white matter microstructure is associated with both pre-hypertension and hypertension. *PLoS One, 12*(11), e0187600. doi:10.1371/journal.pone.0187600

Symons, C. S., & Johnson, B. T. (1997). The self-reference effect in memory: a meta-analysis. *Psychological Bulletin*, *121*(3), 371–394. doi:10.1037/0033-2909.121.3.371

Tessitore, A., Hariri, A. R., Fera, F., Smith, W. G., Das, S., Weinberger, D. R., & Mattay, V. S. (2005). Functional changes in the activity of brain regions underlying emotion processing in the elderly. *Psychiatry Research*, *139*(1), 9–18.

Todorov, A., & Engell, A. D. (2008). The role of the amygdala in implicit evaluation of emotionally neutral faces. *Social Cognitive and Affective Neuroscience*, *3*(4), 303–312. doi:10.1093/scan/nsn033

Todorov, A., & Olson, I. R. (2008). Robust learning of affective trait associations with faces when the hippocampus is damaged, but not when the amygdala and temporal pole are damaged. *Social Cognitive and Affective Neuroscience*, *3*, 195–203.

Tomasi, D., & Volkow, N. D. (2012). Aging and functional brain networks. *Molecular Psychiatry*, *17*(5), 471, 549–458. doi:10.1038/mp.2011.81

Trachtenberg, A. J., Filippini, N., & Mackay, C. E. (2012). The effects of *APOE-*ε4 on the BOLD response. *Neurobiology of Aging*, *33*(2), 323–334.

Trebbastoni, A., Pichiorri, F., D'Antonio, F., Campanelli, A., Onesti, E., Ceccanti, M., . . . Inghilleri, M. (2015). Altered cortical synaptic plasticity in response to 5-Hz repetitive transcranial magnetic stimulation as a new electrophysiological finding in amnestic mild cognitive impairment converting to Alzheimer's disease: results from a 4-year prospective cohort study. *Frontiers in Aging Neuroscience*, *7*, Article 253. doi:10.3389/fnagi.2015.00253

Trott, C. T., Friedman, D., Ritter, W., Fabiani, M., & Snodgrass, J. G. (1999). Episodic priming and memory for temporal source: event-related potentials reveal age-related differences in prefrontal functioning. *Psychology and Aging*, *14*(3), 390–413.

Tucker-Drob, E. M. (2011). Global and domain-specific changes in cognition throughout adulthood. *Developmental Psychology*, *47*(2), 331–343. doi:10.1037/a0021361

Tucker-Drob, E. M., Briley, D. A., Starr, J. M., & Deary, I. J. (2014). Structure and correlates of cognitive aging in a narrow age cohort. *Psychology and Aging*, *29*(2), 236–249. doi:10.1037/a0036187

Tulving, E. (2002). Episodic memory: from mind to brain. *Annual Review of Psychology*, *53*, 1–25.

Tulving, E., & Thomson, D. M. (1973). Encoding specificity and retrieval processes in episodic memory. *Psychological Review*, *80*(5), 352–373.

Tun, P. A., Wingfield, A., Rosen, M. J., & Blanchard, L. (1998). Response latencies for false memories: gist-based processes in normal aging. *Psychology and Aging*, *13*(2), 230–241.

Turner, G. R., & Spreng, R. N. (2012). Executive functions and neurocognitive aging: dissociable patterns of brain activity. *Neurobiology of Aging*, *33*(4), 826.e821–826.e813.

(2015). Prefrontal engagement and reduced default network suppression co-occur and are dynamically coupled in older adults: the default–executive coupling hypothesis of aging. *Journal of Cognitive Neuroscience*, *27*(12), 2462–2476.

Uekermann, J., Channon, S., & Daum, I. (2006). Humor processing, mentalizing, and executive function in normal aging. *Journal of the International Neuropsychological Society*, *12*(2), 184–191. doi:10.1017/s1355617706060280

Underwood, E. (2014). Starting young. *Science*, *346*(6209), 568–571.

Urry, H. L., & Gross, J. J. (2010). Emotion regulation in older age. *Current Directions in Psychological Science*, *19*(6), 352–357. doi:10.1177/0963721410388395

Vannini, P., Hedden, T., Becker, J. A., Sullivan, C., Putcha, D., Rentz, D., . . . Sperling, R. A. (2012). Age and amyloid-related alterations in default network habituation to stimulus repetition. *Neurobiology of Aging*, *33*(7), 1237–1252. doi:10.1016/j.neurobiolaging.2011.01.003

Velanova, K., Lustig, C., Jacoby, L. L., & Buckner, R. L. (2007). Evidence for frontally mediated controlled processing differences in older adults. *Cerebral Cortex*, *17*(5), 1033–1046. doi:10.1093/cercor/bhl013

Viard, A., Chételat, G., Lebreton, K., Desgranges, B., Landeau, B., de La Sayette, V., . . . Piolino, P. (2011). Mental time travel into the past and the future in healthy aged adults: an fMRI study. *Brain and Cognition*, *75*(1), 1–9.

Viard, A., Lebreton, K., Chételat, G., Desgranges, B., Landeau, B., Young, A., . . . Piolino, P. (2010). Patterns of hippocampal–neocortical interactions in the retrieval of episodic autobiographical memories across the entire life-span of aged adults. *Hippocampus*, *20*(1), 153–165.

Viard, A., Piolino, P., Desgranges, B., Chételat, G., Lebreton, K., Landeau, B., . . . Eustache, F. (2007). Hippocampal activation for autobiographical memories over the entire lifetime in healthy aged subjects: an fMRI study. *Cerebral Cortex*, *17*(10), 2453–2467.

Volkow, N. D., Gur, R. C., Wang, G.-J., Fowler, J. S., Moberg, P. J., Ding, Y.-S., . . . Logan, J. (1998). Association between decline in brain dopamine activity with age and cognitive and motor impairment in healthy individuals. *American Journal of Psychiatry*, *155*(3), 344–349.

Voss, M. W., Heo, S., Prakash, R. S., Erickson, K. I., Alves, H., Chaddock, L., . . . White, S. M. (2013). The influence of aerobic fitness on cerebral white matter integrity and cognitive function in older adults: results of a one-year exercise intervention. *Human Brain Mapping, 34*(11), 2972–2985.

Voss, M. W., Weng, T. B., Burzynska, A. Z., Wong, C. N., Cooke, G. E., Clark, R., . . . Kramer, A. F. (2016). Fitness, but not physical activity, is related to functional integrity of brain networks associated with aging. *NeuroImage, 131*, 113–125. doi:10.1016/j.neuroimage.2015.10.044

Voss, M. W., Wong, C. N., Baniqued, P. L., Burdette, J. H., Erickson, K. I., Prakash, R. S., . . . Kramer, A. F. (2013). Aging brain from a network science perspective: something to be positive about? *PLoS One, 8*(11), e78345. doi:10.1371/journal.pone.0078345

Waldinger, R. J., Kensinger, E. A., & Schulz, M. S. (2011). Neural activity, neural connectivity, and the processing of emotionally valenced information in older adults: links with life satisfaction. *Cognitive, Affective, and Behavioral Neuroscience, 11*(3), 426–436. doi:10.3758/s13415-011-0039-9

Wang, J. X., Rogers, L. M., Gross, E. Z., Ryals, A. J., Dokucu, M. E., Brandstatt, K. L., . . . Voss, J. L. (2014). Targeted enhancement of cortical-hippocampal brain networks and associative memory. *Science, 345*(6200), 1054–1057. doi:10.1126/science.1252900

Wang, L., Li, Y., Metzak, P., He, Y., & Woodward, T. S. (2010). Age-related changes in topological patterns of large-scale brain functional networks during memory encoding and recognition. *NeuroImage, 50*(3), 862–872.

Wang, T. H., Johnson, J. D., de Chastelaine, M., Donley, B. E., & Rugg, M. D. (2016). The effects of age on the neural correlates of recollection success, recollection-related cortical reinstatement, and post-retrieval monitoring. *Cerebral Cortex, 26*(4), 1698–1714.

Wang, X., Ren, P., Baran, T. M., Raizada, R. D. S., Mapstone, M., & Lin, F. (2017). Longitudinal functional brain mapping in supernormals. *Cerebral Cortex*, Nov 23, 1–11 [epub ahead of print]. doi:10.1093/cercor/bhx322

Ward, A. M., Mormino, E. C., Huijbers, W., Schultz, A. P., Hedden, T., & Sperling, R. A. (2015). Relationships between default-mode network connectivity, medial temporal lobe structure, and age-related memory deficits. *Neurobiology of Aging, 36*(1), 265–272.

Waring, J. D., Addis, D. R., & Kensinger, E. A. (2013). Effects of aging on neural connectivity underlying selective memory for emotional scenes. *Neurobiology of Aging, 34*(2), 451–467. doi:10.1016/j.neurobiolaging.2012.03.011

Wedig, M. M., Rauch, S. L., Albert, M. S., & Wright, C. I. (2005). Differential amygdala habituation to neutral faces in young and elderly adults. *Neuroscience Letters, 385*(2), 114–119. doi:10.1016/j.neulet.2005.05.039

Wegesin, D. J., Friedman, D., Varughese, N., & Stern, Y. (2002). Age-related changes in source memory retrieval: an ERP replication and extension. *Cognitive Brain Research, 13*(3), 323–338.

West, R. (1996). An application of prefrontal cortex function theory to cognitive aging. *Psychological Bulletin, 120*(2), 272–292.

West, R., & Moore, K. (2005). Adjustments of cognitive control in younger and older adults. *Cortex, 41*(4), 570–581.

West, R., & Travers, S. (2008). Differential effects of aging on processes underlying task switching. *Brain and Cognition, 68*(1), 67–80.

Westerberg, C., Mayes, A., Florczak, S. M., Chen, Y., Creery, J., Parrish, T., . . . Paller, K. A. (2013). Distinct medial temporal contributions to different forms of recognition in amnestic mild cognitive impairment and Alzheimer's disease. *Neuropsychologia, 51*(12), 2450–2461.

Wheeler, M. E., Petersen, S. E., & Buckner, R. L. (2000). Memory's echo: vivid remembering reactivates sensory-specific cortex. *Proceedings of the National Academy of Sciences of the United States of America, 97*(20), 11125–11129.

Wiese, H., Schweinberger, S. R., & Hansen, K. (2008). The age of the beholder: ERP evidence of an own-age bias in face memory. *Neuropsychologia, 46*(12), 2973–2985.

Wieser, M. J., Muhlberger, A., Kenntner-Mabiala, R., & Pauli, P. (2006). Is emotion processing affected by advancing age? An event-related brain potential study. *Brain Research, 1096*(1), 138–147. doi:10.1016/j.brainres.2006.04.028

Wild-Wall, N., Falkenstein, M., & Gajewski, P. D. (2012). Neural correlates of changes in a visual search task due to cognitive training in seniors. *Neural Plasticity*, Article ID 529057 (11 pp). doi:10.1155/2012/529057

Williams, L. M., Brown, K. J., Palmer, D., Liddell, B. J., Kemp, A. H., Olivieri, G., . . . Gordon, E. (2006). The mellow years?: neural basis of improving emotional stability over age. *Journal of Neuroscience, 26*(24), 6422–6430.

Wilson, R. S., & Bennett, D. A. (2017). How does psychosocial behavior contribute to cognitive health in old age? *Brain Science, 7*(6), 56. doi:10.3390/brainsci7060056

Wilson, R. S., Krueger, K. R., Arnold, S. E., Schneider, J. A., Kelly, J. F., Barnes, L. L., . . . Bennett, D. A. (2007). Loneliness and risk of Alzheimer disease. *Archives of General Psychiatry, 64*(2), 234–240. doi:10.1001/archpsyc.64.2.234

Winecoff, A., Labar, K. S., Madden, D. J., Cabeza, R., & Huettel, S. A. (2011). Cognitive and neural contributors to emotion regulation in aging. *Social Cognitive and Affective Neuroscience, 6*(2), 165–176. doi:10.1093/scan/nsq030

Wingfield, A., Amichetti, N. M., & Lash, A. (2015). Cognitive aging and hearing acuity: modeling spoken language comprehension. *Frontiers in Psychology*, 6, Article 684. doi:10.3389/fpsyg.2015.00684

Wingfield, A., & Grossman, M. (2006). Language and the aging brain: patterns of neural compensation revealed by functional brain imaging. *Journal of Neurophysiology*, 96(6), 2830–2839.

Wirth, M., Villeneuve, S., Haase, C. M., Madison, C. M., Oh, H., Landau, S. M., ... Jagust, W. J. (2013). Associations between Alzheimer disease biomarkers, neurodegeneration, and cognition in cognitively normal older people. *JAMA Neurology*, 70(12), 1512–1519.

Wolff, N., Wiese, H., & Schweinberger, S. R. (2012). Face recognition memory across the adult life span: event-related potential evidence from the own-age bias. *Psychology and Aging*, 27(4), 1066–1081. doi:10.1037/a0029112

Wood, S., & Kisley, M. A. (2006). The negativity bias is eliminated in older adults: age-related reduction in event-related brain potentials associated with evaluative categorization. *Psychology and Aging*, 21(4), 815–820. doi:10.1037/0882-7974.21.4.815

Wright, C. I., Dickerson, B. C., Feczko, E., Negeira, A., & Williams, D. (2007). A functional magnetic resonance imaging study of amygdala responses to human faces in aging and mild Alzheimer's disease. *Biological Psychiatry*, 62(12), 1388–1395.

Wright, C. I., Feczko, E., Dickerson, B. C., & Williams, D. (2007). Neuroanatomical correlates of personality in the elderly. *NeuroImage*, 35(1), 263–272.

Wright, C. I., Wedig, M. M., Williams, D., Rauch, S. L., & Albert, M. S. (2006). Novel fearful faces activate the amygdala in healthy young and elderly adults. *Neurobiology of Aging*, 27(2), 361–374. doi:10.1016/j.neurobiolaging.2005.01.014

Wu, T., & Hallett, M. (2005a). A functional MRI study of automatic movements in patients with Parkinson's disease. *Brain*, 128(10), 2250–2259.

(2005b). The influence of normal human ageing on automatic movements. *Journal of Physiology*, 562(2), 605–615.

Yassa, M. A., Lacy, J. W., Stark, S. M., Albert, M. S., Gallagher, M., & Stark, C. E. (2011). Pattern separation deficits associated with increased hippocampal CA3 and dentate gyrus activity in nondemented older adults. *Hippocampus*, 21(9), 968–979. doi:10.1002/hipo.20808

Yassa, M. A., Mattfeld, A. T., Stark, S. M., & Stark, C. E. L. (2011). Age-related memory deficits linked to circuit-specific disruptions in the hippocampus. *Proceedings of the National Academy of Sciences of the United States of America*, 108(21), 8873–8878.

Yassa, M. A., Muftuler, L. T., & Stark, C. E. L. (2010). Ultrahigh-resolution microstructural diffusion tensor imaging reveals perforant path degradation in aged humans *in vivo*. *Proceedings of the National Academy of Sciences of the United States of America, 107*(28), 12687–12691.

Yassa, M. A., & Stark, C. E. L. (2011). Pattern separation in the hippocampus. *Trends in Neurosciences, 34*(10), 515–525.

Yuan, P., & Raz, N. (2014). Prefrontal cortex and executive functions in healthy adults: a meta-analysis of structural neuroimaging studies. *Neuroscience & Biobehavioral Reviews, 42*, 180–192.

Zacks, R., & Hasher, L. (1997). Cognitive gerontology and attentional inhibition: a reply to Burke and McDowd. *Journals of Gerontology. Series B,Psychological Sciences and Social Sciences, 52*(6), P274–P283.

Zahn, R., Moll, J., Krueger, F., Huey, E. D., Garrido, G., & Grafman, J. (2007). Social concepts are represented in the superior anterior temporal cortex. *Proceedings of the National Academy of Sciences of the United States of America, 104*(15), 6430–6435. doi:0607061104 [pii] 10.1073/pnas.0607061104 [doi]

Zahodne, L. B., Schofield, P. W., Farrell, M. T., Stern, Y., & Manly, J. J. (2014). Bilingualism does not alter cognitive decline or dementia risk among Spanish-speaking immigrants. *Neuropsychology, 28*(2), 238–246.

Zamboni, G., de Jager, C. A., Drazich, E., Douaud, G., Jenkinson, M., Smith, A. D., . . . Wilcock, G. K. (2013). Structural and functional bases of visuospatial associative memory in older adults. *Neurobiology of Aging, 34*(3), 961–972.

Zanto, T. P., Sekuler, R., Dube, C., & Gazzaley, A. (2013). Age-related changes in expectation based modulation of motion detectability. *PLoS One, 8*(8).

Zebrowitz, L. A., & Franklin, R. G. (2014). The attractiveness halo effect and the babyface stereotype in older and younger adults: similarities, own-age accentuation, and older adult positivity effects. *Experimental Aging Research, 40*(3), 375–393. doi:10.1080/0361073x.2014.897151

Zebrowitz, L. A., Franklin, R. G., Boshyan, J., Luevano, V., Agrigoroaei, S., Milosavljevic, B., & Lachman, M. E. (2014). Older and younger adults' accuracy in discerning health and competence in older and younger faces. *Psychology and Aging, 29*(3), 454–468. doi:10.1037/a0036255

Zebrowitz, L. A., Franklin, R. G., Hillman, S., & Boc, H. (2013). Older and younger adults' first impressions from faces: similar in agreement but different in positivity. *Psychology and Aging, 28*(1), 202–212. doi:10.1037/a0030927

Zebrowitz, L. A., Ward, N., Boshyan, J., Gutchess, A., & Hadjikhani, N. (in press). Older adults' neural activation in the reward circuit is sensitive to face trustworthiness. *Cognitive, Affective, & Behavioral Neuroscience*, 18, 21–34. doi: 10.3758/s13415-017-0549-1.

Zhang, B., Lin, Y., Gao, Q., Zawisza, M., Kang, Q., & Chen, X. (2017). Effects of aging stereotype threat on working self-concepts: an event-related potentials approach. *Frontiers in Aging Neuroscience*, *9*, Article 223. doi:10.3389/fnagi.2017.00223

Zhu, D. C., Zacks, R. T., & Slade, J. M. (2010). Brain activation during interference resolution in young and older adults: an fMRI study. *NeuroImage*, *50*(2), 810–817.

Zhu, L., Walsh, D., & Hsu, M. (2012). Neuroeconomic measures of social decision-making across the lifespan. *Frontiers in Neuroscience*, *6*, Article 128. doi:10.3389/fnins.2012.00128

Zimerman, M., Heise, K. F., Gerloff, C., Cohen, L. G., & Hummel, F. C. (2014). Disrupting the ipsilateral motor cortex interferes with training of a complex motor task in older adults. *Cerebral Cortex*, *24*(4), 1030–1036. doi:10.1093/cercor/bhs385

Zimerman, M., & Hummel, F. C. (2010). Non-invasive brain stimulation: enhancing motor and cognitive functions in healthy old subjects. *Frontiers in Aging Neuroscience*, *2*, Article 149. doi:10.3389/fnagi.2010.00149

Zimerman, M., Nitsch, M., Giraux, P., Gerloff, C., Cohen, L. G., & Hummel, F. C. (2013). Neuroenhancement of the aging brain: restoring skill acquisition in old subjects. *Annals of Neurology*, *73*(1), 10–15. doi:10.1002/ana.23761twelve

Index